The Schools and the Cloister

MS Oxford, Jesus College, 94, fol. 5ᵛ, Nequam's *Gloss on the Psalter*, with what may well be autograph annotations

The Schools and the Cloister

The Life and Writings of Alexander Nequam
(1157–1217)

by
R. W. HUNT

Edited and revised by
MARGARET GIBSON

CLARENDON PRESS · OXFORD

1984

Oxford University Press, Walton Street, Oxford OX2 2DP

London New York Toronto
Delhi Bombay Calcutta Madras Karachi
Kuala Lumpur Singapore Hong Kong Tokyo
Nairobi Dar es Salaam Cape Town
Melbourne Auckland
and associated companies in
Beirut Berlin Ibadan Mexico City Nicosia

Oxford is a trade mark of Oxford University Press

Published in the United States by
Oxford University Press, New York

British Library Cataloguing in Publication Data
Hunt, R. W.
The schools and the cloister: the life and writings
of Alexander Nequam (1157-1217)
1. Nequam, Alexander   2. Philosophy, Medieval
3. Scholasticism
I. Title   II. Gibson, Margaret
189'.4   B765.N/
ISBN 0-19-822398-6

Library of Congress Cataloging in Publication Data
Hunt, Richard William, 1908-
The schools and the cloister.
Originally presented as the author's thesis
(doctoral—Oxford, 1936) under title: Alexander Nequam.
Bibliography: p.
Includes index.
1. Nequam, Alexander, 1157-1217. 2. Monks—England—
Biography. 3. Scholars—England—Biography.
I. Gibson, Margaret T. II. Title.
BX4705.N395H86 1984   189'.4   83-23204
ISBN 0-19-822398-6

Typeset by Joshua Associates, Oxford
Printed in Great Britain
at the University Press, Oxford

No man seweth a piece of new cloth on an old garment: else the new piece that filled it up taketh away from the old, and the rent is made worse.

Mark 2:21

PREFACE

RICHARD HUNT left the writing of his thesis until shortly before the maximum extension of time allowed by the Faculty Board ran out. 'Pray for me!', he wrote in a despairing moment. This will explain both presentation and substance. The thesis reads more like an outsize notice in the *Histoire littéraire* than a book. The facts, stated clearly and concisely, are set before the reader to make what he can of them. There is a lot to make: Nequam's critical self-awareness, shown in the verses quoted in Chapter I, adds a fascinating note to the topic of 'the discovery of the individual' in the twelfth century, to mention one of many examples. The long years of preparation before the hurried write-up partly account for Richard's encyclopaedic and minute knowledge of such varied themes in medieval history. Few scholars can have mastered so many diverse skills in a lifetime. He worked thoroughly, never satisfied with a statement until he had traced it to its source. It was typical that when he had to lecture on English constitutional history to students at Liverpool he felt obliged to look at the originals of the extracts in *Stubbs' Select Charters*. A manuscript became a living creature in his hands. Nequam led him to numerous sources. Polymath, secular master, teacher and preacher, then Austin Canon, Nequam lived through a period of elusive changes in each of his spheres of activity. Richard studied all of them in depth. In order to put Nequam's Psalter-commentary in its setting, he made an index of all known Psalter-commentaries of the twelfth and early thirteenth centuries, nearly all still in manuscript. The reference books and editions of texts which we have come to take for granted did not exist in the 1930s. Yet even today *Alexander Nequam* strikes its readers as a pioneering work, still fresh and meaty. It is probably the most consulted thesis of any from an Arts Faculty deposited in the Bodleian.

Why did Richard not publish it? A simple answer would be that he never had time. It was possible to write papers for learned journals and catalogues in the few hours of leisure snatched from a full-time job (and he wrote many); he would have needed a sabbatical term to update his thesis and bring out the significance of its substance in book form. Another reason is that he was always making discoveries and starting off on new lines of inquiry. The history of manuscripts took him from the medieval to later periods. He also helped others, putting his vast learning and memory at their disposal, correcting their mistakes and suggesting better ways of using their material. Richard's 'invisible exports' far exceeded his visible output. The advance of knowledge mattered more to him than recognition of his own contribution, which had little interest for him.

Margaret Gibson gallantly took over the author's copy of his thesis, stuffed with additions and notes on loose bits of paper. With devoted efficiency she has prepared it for publication. She checked all the references; she incorporated Richard's notes; she updated editions of texts referred to; she added bibliography to the footnotes; she chose the illustrations. The text remains as it was, except in rare cases where later research has made a statement misleading. Margaret keeps her enterprising self in the background, so that Richard speaks to us directly. All thanks to her for the long-awaited appearance of a monument to the scholarship of the 1930s and a memorial to the author.

BERYL SMALLEY

The editor is most grateful to the Trustees of the Jowett Fund for their assistance in the publication of the work of a late Fellow of Balliol.

CONTENTS

Illustrations   x

Sigla   x

Abbreviations   xi

    I. Alexander's life   1

   II. The Authenticity and Chronology of his Works   19

  III. The Grammarian   32

  IV. Alexander's Use and Knowledge of the Classics   43

   V. The Versifier and Stylist   54

  VI. The Scientist   67

 VII. The Preacher   84

VIII. The Commentator   95

  IX. The Theologian   111

   X. The Survival of Alexander's Works   118

APPENDICES

  A. Nequam's works
      i. Authentic writings   125
     ii. *Dubia et spuria*   147

  B. Nequam's sermons   150

INDEXES

Index of Manuscripts   155

General Index   159

ILLUSTRATIONS

MS Oxford, Jesus College, 94, fol. 5^v *frontispiece*

PLATE I. MS Cambridge, Gonville and Caius College,
385 (605), p. 7

PLATE II. MS Cambridge, University Library, Gg. 6. 42,
fol. 46

*between pages
146 and 147*

SIGLA

B MS Oxford, Bodleian Library, Bodley 550
C MS Oxford, Corpus Christi College, 45
G MS Cambridge, University Library, Gg. 6. 42
J MS Oxford, Jesus College, 94
M MS Oxford, Magdalen College, 149
P MS Paris, Bibliothèque Nationale, lat. 11867
R MS London, BL, Royal 7 F. I
W MS Oxford, Bodleian Library, Wood empt. 13

ABBREVIATIONS

NEQUAM'S WORKS

CAth.	Commentary on the Athanasian Creed
CCant.	Commentary on the Song of Songs
CMC	Commentary on Martianus Capella, *De Nuptiis*
CNP	*Corrogationes Noui Promethei*
CP	*Corrogationes Promethei*
CPV	*Corrogationes Promethei* versified
CProv.	Commentary on Proverbs
DCV	*De commendatione uini*
DNR	*De naturis rerum*
DNV	*De nominibus utensilium*
GP	Gloss on the Psalter
in Eccles.	Commentary on Ecclesiastes (= *DNR* iii-v)
LBV	*Laus beatissime uirginis*
LSD	*Laus sapientie diuine*
NA	*Nouus Auianus* (= *Fables*)
NE	*Nouus Esopus* (= *Fables*)
SA	*Sacerdos ad altare*
SD	*Suppletio defectuum*
SFA	*Solatium fidelis anime*
SMF	*Super mulerem fortem*
SS	*Speculum speculationum*

OTHER ABBREVIATIONS

AH	*Analecta Hymnica Medii Aevi*, edd. G. M. Dreves *et al.*, 55 vols., 1886–1922.
AHDLMA	*Archives d'Histoire doctrinale et littéraire du Moyen Âge.*
Bale	J. Bale, *Index Britanniae Scriptorum*, edd. R. L. Poole and M. Bateson, Oxford, 1902 (Anecdota Oxoniensa).
Bale (1548)	J. Bale, *Illustrium Maioris Britanniae Scriptorum ... Summarium*, Ipswich 1548.
Bale (1559)	Id. *Scriptorum Illustrium Maioris Brytannie ... Catalogus*, Basel, 1559.
BGPM	*Beiträge zur Geschichte der Philosophie des Mittelalters.*
BHL	*Bibliotheca Hagiographica Latina*, 2 vols. (Bollandists).
BL	British Library, London.
BN	Bibliothèque Nationale, Paris.

CBMLC	*Corpus of British Medieval Library Catalogues*, 1984– .
CCSL	*Corpus Christianorum, Series Latina*, 1954– .
CSEL	*Corpus Scriptorum Ecclesiasticorum Latinorum*, 1866– .
CUL	Cambridge University Library.
Doctrinale	Alexander of Villa Dei, *Doctrinale*, ed. D. Reichling, 1893.
EHR	*The English Historical Review.*
Emden, *BRUC*	A. B. Emden, *A Biographical Register of the University of Cambridge to 1500*, 1963.
Emden, *BRUO*	Id., *A Biographical Register of the University of Oxford to A.D. 1500*, 3 vols., 1957–9.
Esposito	M. Esposito, 'On some unpublished poems attributed to Alexander Neckam', *EHR* xxx (1915), 450–71.
Hain	L. Hain, *Repertorium Bibliographicum*, 2 vols., 1826–38.
Haskins	C. H. Haskins, *Studies in the History of Mediaeval Science*, 2nd edn., 1927.
Hauréau, *Notices*, i–vi	B. Hauréau, *Notices et extraits de quelques manuscrits latins de la Bibliothèque Nationale*, 6 vols., 1890–3.
Herbert, *Cat. Rom.*	H. L. D. Ward and J. A. Herbert, *Catalogue of Romances in the Department of Manuscripts in the British Museum*, 3 vols., 1883–1910.
Hervieux, i–v	L. Hervieux, *Les Fabulistes latins*, 5 vols., 1893–9.
JWCI	*Journal of the Warburg and Courtauld Institutes.*
Ker, *MLGB*	N. R. Ker, *Medieval Libraries of Great Britain*, 2nd edn., 1964.
Ker, *MMBL*	Id., *Medieval Manuscripts in British Libraries*, 4 vols. and index, 1969– .
Ker Essays	*Medieval Scribes, Manuscripts and Libraries: essays presented to N. R. Ker*, edd. M. B. Parkes and A. G. Watson, 1978.
Leland	J. Leland, *De rebus britannicis collectanea*, ed. T. Hearne, 1715; 2nd edn., 1774.
Manitius, i–iii	M. Manitius, *Geschichte der lateinischen Literatur des Mittelalters*, 3 vols., 1911–31.
MARS	*Mediaeval and Renaissance Studies.*
Metalogicon	John of Salisbury, *Metalogicon*, ed. C. C. J. Webb, 1929.
Meyer 1868	P. Meyer, review of Scheler (below) in *Revue critique d'histoire et de littérature* (7 Nov. 1868), 295–9.
Meyer 1896	Id., 'Notice sur les *Corrogationes Promethei* d'Alexandre Neckam', *Notices et extraits des*

	Manuscrits de la Bibliothèque Nationale, xxxv[2] (1896), 641–82.
MGH	*Monumenta Germaniae Historica.*
MPG	J.-P. Migne, *Patrologiae Graecae Cursus Completus*, 161 vols., 1857–66.
MPL	J.-P. Migne, *Patrologiae Latinae Cursus Completus*, 221 vols., 1844–64.
MS	*Mediaeval Studies.*
OHS	*Oxford Historical Society.*
PBA	*Proceedings of the British Academy.*
RS	Rolls Series, 99 vols., 1858–96.
SB Munich	*Sitzungsberichte der konigl. bayerischen Akademie der Wissenschaften*, phil.-hist. Klasse.
SB Vienna	*Sitzungsberichte der Österreichischen Akademie der Wissenschaften*, phil.-hist. Klasse.
SC	*A Summary Catalogue of Western Manuscripts in the Bodleian Library at Oxford*, 7 vols., 1895–1953; reprinted 1980.
Scheler	A. Scheler, 'Trois traités de lexicographie latine du XIIe et du XIIIe siècle', *Jahrbuch für romanische und englische Literatur*, vii (1866), 58–74, 155–73.
Schneyer, *Repertorium*	J.-B. Schneyer, *Repertorium der lateinischen Sermones des Mittelalters*, 5 vols., 1969–74.
Thomson, *St Albans*	R. M. Thomson, *Manuscripts from St Albans Abbey 1066–1235*, 2 vols., 1982.
Thorndike	L. Thorndike, *A History of Magic and Experimental Science*, 8 vols. 1923–58.
TRHS	*Transactions of the Royal Historical Society.*
Walther	H. Walther, *Initia Carminum ac versuum medii aevi posterioris Latinorum*, 1959.
Walther, 'Neckam'	Id., 'Zu den kleineren Gedichten des Alexander Neckam', *Mittellateinisches Jahrbuch*, ii (1965), 111–29.
Walther, *Sprichwörter*	Id., *Lateinische Sprichwörter und Sentenzen des Mittelalters*, 6 vols. 1963–7; additional vol. A–G, ed. P. G. Schmidt, 1982.
Watson, *Savile*	A. G. Watson, *The Manuscripts of Henry Savile of Banke*, 1969.
Wright	T. Wright, *Alexandri Neckam de naturis rerum libri duo with . . . De laudibus diuinae sapientiae* (RS), 1863.
ZdA	*Zeitschrift für deutsches Alterum.*

I
ALEXANDER'S LIFE

THE facts about Alexander's life can be told in a few words; and there is scarcely a passage in it where we can say that such and such a thing happened in such and such a year. We are told that he was born at St Albans in September 1157 on the same night as the future Richard I was born at Windsor; and that his mother fostered him and Richard. The source of this statement is unknown. It occurs in a Chronicle which ends at the year 1357 and which is headed in the manuscript 'Extracts from Trivet'.[1] This title is in the main correct. It is made up of extracts, but there are occasional words and phrases not from Trivet's *Annals*. This is one of them. Trivet simply says that Richard was born in September 1157.[2] Since the source of the addition remains unknown, we can only test its validity by the other information we have. One thing in it is certainly wrong. Richard was born at Oxford, not at Windsor.[3] But the rest may well be true. Richard later gave his nurse a pension, and from the records of the payments we know that her name was Hodierna. The year before he died Alexander wrote a *Supplement* to his poem the *Laus sapientie diuine*, and in it he put an elegy on his mother.[4] It contains but one fact—that her name was Hodierna. He also

---

[1] Mense Septembri natus est regi filius, Ricardus nomine, apud Windeshore. Eadem nocte natus est Alexander Necham apud sanctum Albanum, cuius mater fouit Ricardum ex mamilla dextra, sed Alexandrum fouit ex mamilla sua sinistra: MS London, College of Arms, Arundel 6, fol. 135ᵛ; cf. T. Tanner, *Bibliotheca Britannico-Hibernica* (London, 1748), p. 539, note d. The manuscript belonged to the Austin Friars at York: Ker, *MLGB*, pp. 218, 321, with references.

[2] Nicholas Trivet, *Annales*, ed. T. Hog (London, 1845), p. 43.

[3] R. W. Eyton, *Court, Household, and Itinerary of King Henry II* (London, 1878), p. 30, with references.

[4]
    Vix, Hodierna, tui dignantur adire locellum,
       quo mater felix et miseranda iaces.
    Illis mater eras dum uixisti, mihi uiuis,
       nec mihi defuncto mortua mater eris . . .
        SD i. 833-5 (**P**, fol. 221ᵛᵇ)

tells us that he was born at St Albans.[5] Therefore as far as he
is concerned the accuracy of this notice is borne out, and we
may accept 1157 as the year of his birth. The name of his
father nowhere appears. He was evidently very fond of
his mother. We suspect that she was a remarkable person.
Unfortunately her name, which is an odd one, tells us nothing
of her family.[6] Soon after coming to the throne Richard
gave her a pension of £7 a year blanche in Chippenham for
life. It is entered every year in the Pipe Roll in Richard's
reign, and was still being paid at the beginning of John's.[7]
It was a considerable sum of money. She had probably
recently died when Alexander wrote about her. In 1220 the
seven librates in Chippenham, 'which Hodierna nurse of our
uncle the king had', were granted to Willelmus Mercator, a
falconer; and in a later return of tenants-in-chief in Wiltshire
(1236) we find that Jacobus Hose holds the land which
belonged to Hodierna the nurse. It is said that her name
survives in Knoyle Hodierne.[8]

Alexander went to school at St Albans and there learned
the rudiments. Little information about this school has
survived.[9] It was already established early in the century, and
its second known master became abbot. It was in the town,
not in the monastery, though the abbot seems to have
appointed the master. A generation later Matthew Paris says
that there was no better school in England, and Alexander
himself says that it was the beginning of his fame.[10]

We now come to the most difficult chronological problem

[5] Hic locus sortis nostrae primordia nouit: *LSD* x. 319 (Wright, p. 503, corr.).

[6] The name Hodierna also occurs in *Curia Regis Rolls*, iii. 320, iv. 16, v. 106
(all different persons); it was also an aristocratic name—see e.g. the sister and
daughter of Baldwin II, king of Jerusalem. Its origin may be the collects for the
Innocents and Epiphany: 'Deus cuius hodierna die . . .'.

[7] *Pipe Roll 2 Richard I*, p. 118 (cf. Stubbs, *Roger of Hoveden* [RS, London,
1870], iii. p. xviii n. 2); *Pipe Roll 1 John*, pp. 168-9.

[8] *Rotuli litterarum clausarum*, ed. T. D. Hardy (London, 1833), i. 416b
(William Mercator); *Book of Fees*, i (Public Record Office, London, 1920), 586;
cf. a return made in 1242-3 (ibid. ii [1923], 739). For Knoyle Hodierne see
The Place-Names of Wiltshire (English Place-Name Soc. XVI, Cambridge, 1939),
p. 176.

[9] *Gesta Abbatum S. Albani*, ed. H. T. Riley (RS, London, 1867) i. 72-3,
196; cf. A. F. Leach, *The Schools of Medieval England* (London, 1915),
pp. 115-19.

[10] 'Nostrae laudis origo fuit': *LSD* x. 322 (Wright, p. 503); cf. *Gesta Abbatum*,
ed. cit. (n. 9), p. 196.

in his life. We know that he was master at Dunstable and at St Albans and a student and teacher at Paris. Which came first? The traditional date of his going to Paris is 1180, which rests on the unsupported testimony of Du Boulay.[11] Our only source of information is the account of Matthew Paris in the *Gesta Abbatum*. Matthew is recounting the election of Garinus as abbot in 1183. He says that Garinus and his brother Matthew had studied at Salerno and become monks at St Albans. Garinus became prior and then abbot at the death of Simon. Matthew soon after succeeded him as prior. They had a nephew also called Garinus. He was master at St Albans for several years and succeeded Alexander, called Nequam, in that position. He later transferred his attention to canon law, for which his uncles generously supplied him with books. This is how the text originally ran.[12] Paris later added in the bottom margin the story of the vow of the uncles and nephew with their two 'discipuli' and 'socii' Fabianus and Robertus de Salerno to become monks at St Albans. They all fulfilled their vow except the nephew Garinus, who ended his days in a house in St Albans near the nuns of Sopwell.[13] The other addition is in the side margin by the mention of Alexander.[14] It is framed and headed: 'Quiddam iocosum'. The funny story is that when Alexander had been at Dunstable a year, Abbot Garinus summoned him by a short and witty letter (for Alexander had asked instantly for the school at St Albans): 'Si bonus es uenias; si nequam, nequaquam.' To which Alexander replied in kind: 'Si uelis, ueniam; sin autem, tu autem.'[15] This is the sort of story which it is difficult for a modern reader to accept. But it is fortified by chronological references, and in itself contains nothing incredible. Further, we have an apparently independent

---

[11] C. E. du Boulay, *Historia Vniuersitatis Parisiensis* (Paris, 1665), ii. 427, 725; cf. Haskins, p. 360.

[12] *Gesta Abbatum*, ed. cit. (n. 9 above), i. 194-6.

[13] MS London, BL, Cotton Nero D. I, fol. 50ra: *Gesta Abbatum*, pp. 195-6 ('Iste Magister Garinus . . . de Sopwelle'). Fabianus is probably the subprior in 1214, d. 1223: *Gesta Abbatum*, i. 254.

[14] MS London, BL, Cotton Nero D. I, fol. 50rb: *Gesta Abbatum*, i. 196.

[15] 'Tu autem' are the first words of a liturgical formula for bringing a lesson to a close: see W. Meyer, 'Die Oxforder Gedichte des Primas: magister Hugo von Orleans 16-22', *Nachrichten v. d. Akademie· d. Wissenschaften in Göttingen*, Phil.-hist. Klasse (1907), 125-6.

witness to it in the catalogue of Henry of Kirkestede.[16]
His version is that Alexander sought to be admitted as
a monk and wrote to the abbot: 'Si uis, ueniam; sin autem, tu
autem.' The abbot replied: 'Si bonus es, uenias; si nequam,
nequaquam.' Indignant at this Alexander betook himself to
Cirencester. In comparison with the story of Matthew Paris it
is obvious that Henry gives a distorted version in which the
roles are reversed and the circumstances generalized to fit
the best-known facts about Alexander—that he was connected with St Albans, yet not a monk there, and that he
was a canon at Cirencester. Furthermore he is made to take
offence at the name Nequam. Now the great attraction of
the story as told by Matthew Paris is that it offers an explanation of the Nequam, by which name he was undoubtedly
known in his lifetime,[17] whereas all the other stories told
about him are based on it. In this story the 'si nequam,
nequaquam' has a point of its own in the play on words.

The chronological indications in this passage are presumably to be referred to the year in which Garinus became
abbot, namely 1183. If this interpretation is sound, Alexander
had been at Dunstable for a year after 1183, and then
earnestly besought Garinus for the school of St Albans,
which he obtained. He was not the only master in the twelfth
century to move from Dunstable to St Albans.[18] He would
then be 28 years old. This would allow time for a period of
study in Paris c.1175–82. How long he stayed at St Albans
we do not know. As we shall see, he was teaching in Oxford
not long after 1190. Conjecturally we may give here a rather
charming fragment of verse:

> Dulce Verolamium linquo recessurus—
> linquere uix dixerim cum sim reuersurus.
> Quis tamen recedens est reditus securus?
> Succubuit uictus undis etiam Palinurus.[19]

---

[16] *Catalogus* ad loc., ed. T. Tanner, *Bibliotheca Britannico-Hibernica* (London,
1748), p. xxvib: see the forthcoming edition by R. H. and M. A. Rouse (*CBMLC*
ii), in which Nequam = no. 4. For the identification of 'Boston of Bury' as Henry
of Kirkestede see R. H. Rouse, *'Bostonus Buriensis* and the author of the *Catalogus Scriptorum Ecclesiae'*, *Speculum*, xli (1966), 471–99.

[17] See p. 17 below.

[18] Cf. Abbot Geoffrey (1119–46): *Gesta Abbatum*, i. 73.

[19] P, fol. 215[vb].

Paris was at this time the goal of all students in the arts and theology. That Alexander could afford to go there on his own resources is not likely. Probably some ecclesiastic sent him. It may possibly have been the Abbey itself. He had made his name at St Albans. Promising young men were kept, or to use the technical term 'exhibited',[20] in the schools by patrons. Later in life Alexander himself sent a nephew there.[21] He gives an all too brief account of his studies in the *Laus sapientie diuine*.[22] He learned and taught the liberal arts, and then went on to study theology ('lectio sacra'). He went to lectures on canon and civil law and medicine. We know too little about the arrangement of courses in Paris in the twelfth century to be able to fill in the details. The first part conforms to the pattern which became fixed in the thirteenth century. A student in the faculty of arts, after becoming a master, was bound to teach for a certain period. He might then proceed to study in one of the higher faculties; but if he studied theology he would not have time to study law and medicine. The programme sketched by Alexander is that of a less sophisticated age.

In arts he was a member of the school on the Petit Pont ('Modici Pontis parua columna fui'),[23] which had been made famous by the logician Adam. Alexander mentions a mistaken reading of Thierry of Chartres in the *Sophistici Elenchi* before it came into the hands of Adam,[24] and refers to a logical doctrine held by another master of the school, Ethion, who is not otherwise known.[25] In the *Suppletio defectuum* there is a section on theology and the arts. Here after enumerating the ancient logicians he goes on to medieval writers:

> En Porretanus, Albricus, Petrus Alardi,
> Terricus monachus, Gualo sophista potens
> temporibus micuere suis quasi lumina terre
> et nostro fulgens tempore sidus Adam.

---

[20] See J. Boussard, 'Ralph Neville, évêque de Chichester et chancelier d'Angleterre (†1244)', *Revue historique*, clxxvi (1935), 222 n. 3.

[21] Quem tibi transmitto, doctor Radulfe, nepotem | suscipe; deuota sedulitate doce: P, fol. 238rb.

[22] *LSD* x (Wright, pp. 496–503).

[23] *LSD* x. 334 (p. 503).

[24] *CP* in Isaiah 3: 18, 'lunulas': Meyer 1896, p. 677.

[25] *DNR* ii. 173 (Wright, p. 307).

Inter Ledeos crocitaui coruus olores,
dii bene, nam coruus esse columba potest.[26]

The reference to Adam as 'the light of our times' is puzzling.
The *Ars disserendi* of Adam de Parvo Ponte was finished by
1132 and he taught John of Salisbury.[27] He probably died
about 1158. No work on logic by Alexander is known; but
there are traces of his logical 'croakings' in the *De naturis
rerum*.[28] His grammatical teaching is reflected in the *De
nominibus utensilium* and the *Corrogationes Promethei*. The
former is directly in the tradition of the school of Petit Pont.
He probably supported himself for a time by his teaching. He
is fierce against those who keep their knowledge to themselves; 'but far be it from me', he says, 'to reprove those
teachers in the liberal arts who keep poverty from their door
by the exercise of their task'.[29]

He also studied theology, canon law, medicine and civil
law. How far he progressed in all these it is hard to say.
Later, in the *Sacerdos ad altare* he was to make out a
programme for the study of them all. But there is nothing in
his works which suggests that he pursued his legal studies
very far. The importance of his medical studies and their
connection with his scientific interests we shall consider
later. *Ex professo* he became a theologian. There are two
allusions to the opinion of his master on passages of the
Bible.[30] But they have not been identified. There is no

---

[26] *SD* ii. 1575-80; **P**, fol. 230va. Thierry is mentioned again *CP*, loc. cit.
(n. 24 above), and in *CMP* i-ii (MS Oxford, Bodleian, Digby 221, fols. 49rb,
87vb). The second line is difficult. 'Terricus' never became a monk. There was a
monk and versifier Gualo of Caen (Manitius, iii. 943), probably not the 'Gualo
sophista' who has been identified with Cornificius: C. C. J. Webb (ed.), *Metalogicon* (Oxford, 1929), p. 8 app. See further (i) Walther 6665; (ii) Walther 10706;
(iii) verses on Thierry of Chartres, ed. A. Vernet, *Études médiévales* (Études
Augustiniennes, Paris, 1981), pp. 661-2 n. 5; (iv) MS Oxford, Bodleian, Laud
Misc. 112, fol. 303ra: '*Galo*. Sic sapias ne disipias, sapientia cara est | Sed quouis
caro carior esto tibi'. There are at least two people here.

[27] See L. Minio-Paluello, 'The *Ars Disserendi* of Adam of Balsham *Paruipontanus*', *MARS* iii (1954), 116-69.

[28] *DNR* ii. 173 (Wright, pp. 283-307).

[29] Absit ut doctores liberalium artium reprehendam, qui nonnumquam
exercitio laboris sui rei familiaris excludunt inopiam: *in Eccles.* iv. 5 (**C**,
fol. 148ra).

[30] Magister meus sic: Et *exterminabuntur* aduersarii tanquam exterminantur a
sole *habene*. id est linee et colores yris *curuato arcu nubium*. id est quando
yris curuatur. Melius tamen est ut hec dictio *habene* teneatur datiue sic.

evidence that he lectured on the Bible in Paris himself. He recalls a dispute with the Jews there,[31] and there is an obscure allusion in the *Gloss on the Psalter*, which seems to reflect a personal experience.[32]

What he did when he returned to England, whether he taught at Dunstable and St Albans, and how long he stayed there, we do not know. There is a gap of several years in the evidence. We next find him at Oxford, preaching a sermon appealing for funds for the restoration of St Frideswide's. 'I grieve, brothers, that the place of the church of St Frideswide is terrible now and horrible owing to the ruin of the walls. Why do you not reflect, you laymen, that it was said literally: *Lord I have loved the beauty of thy dwelling* ... The dwelling of the Lord, the holy church, is uncovered and exposed to the attacks and buffetings of the air and the winds ... You are indeed as it were divinely inspired to make a collection on Ascension Day and bring your offerings to St Frideswide.'[33] There was a fire at St Frideswide's in 1190.[34] That Alexander was in Oxford teaching at the time is probable from two other sermons, addressed to the scholars at Oxford,[35] and it is made certain by a

Exterminabuntur aduersarii *ab arcu nubium curuato*, id est sacra scriptura; *curuato*, inquam, tanquam ligneo arcu curuato *habene*, id est ad legem et tensionem corde secundum quam curuatur et lignum. Sed quid? Prodolor! magna est codicum corruptio. Littera enim correcta est *tanquam a bene curuato* et cetera: *CP* ad Sap. 5: 22 (**B**, fols. 41vb-2ra). And again—Magister meus uolens se subducere turbis questionum cor urentium sic exposuit: *Optabam*, id est optarem si optabile esset etc. Sed quid? Aut sciuit hoc esse optabile aut non. Si sciuit hoc esse optabile—scilicet *separari a Christo pro fratribus*, quare hoc non optaret? Si sciuit hoc non esse optabile, ad quid igitur dixit se optare hoc, si non esset optabile?: *CP* ad Rom. 9: 3 (**B**, fol. 79ra).

[31] *SS* i. 31: **R**, fol. 20ra.

[32] Viri etiam magni qui columpne erant ecclesie, qui transierunt iam ad dulcedinem uite claustralium et reliquerunt non pusillos successores laboris eorum, dicere possunt: *organa nostra* scripta sacre scripture quibus utebamur *suspendimus in salicibus* in collis magistrorum modernorum qui sunt in medio Babylonis, ubi et nos quondam fuimus; et tanquam diceretur eis: o uiri magni, quare laborem scolarum reliquistis? Respondent: quia illic scolares *qui duxerunt nos* magistros *captiuos* ad libitum suum utentes nobis imperiose, *interrogauerunt nos uerba cantionum* id est delectabilia tantum: *GP* 72: 22 (MS Bodley 284, fol. 280rb).

[33] Sermon (98): **W**, fols 93^v-4 (see Appendix B).

[34] MCXC. Combusta est ecclesia Sanctae Frideswidae cum maxima parte ciuitatis Oxenfordiae: *Annals of Osney*, ed. H. R. Luard, *Annales Monastici*, iv (RS, London 1869), p. 43.

[35] Sermons 23 and 89: see Appendix B.

story he tells in the *Commentary on the Song of Songs*.
When he was lecturing in theology publicly, he was a violent
partisan of the view that the feast of the Immaculate Conception should not be solemnly celebrated. So he decided
to lecture as if it were an ordinary day. But every year he
was troubled by illness so that he was not able to, whether
by chance or by the divine will. His hearers noted the fact
and secretly rebuked him and he changed his view on the
subject.[36] [He had his critics: Alan of Tewkesbury wrote
c.1192-3 asking for a written account of his teaching on the
Eucharist—'in his quidem: hominem . . . assumptum ad
altaris misterium et quedam alia'.[37]]

Oxford at this period was just beginning to emerge into the
light. Alexander is the first known 'scholastic' theologian
there. It is all the more disappointing that his own works tell
us so little about the methods of teaching. There are a
number of references to his biblical teaching, on Ezekiel, on
Ecclesiastes and[38] on the Psalter. He says he lectured to men
of mature mind and sublime intelligence on the Song of
Songs.[39] But the commentary we have is a monastic produc-
tion. The reference to the lectures on Ecclesiastes may find
a place here because of the allusion to the disputation with
the 'opponens' et 'respondens'. The *disputatio* seems already
to be regarded as a separate exercise from the main exposition:

Dum uero prefui regimini scolarum consueui uersiculum istum exponere
[Eccl. 3: 7] : *Tempus est scindendi*, acutas proponendo questiones, ut

---

[36] Ego ipse, qui hec scribo, dum puplice legerem in theologia, uehemens eram
assertor quod dies conceptionis beate Marie celebrandus sollempniter non esset.
Vnde et quotannis illo die legere puplice decreueram sicut in profestis diebus
consueueram. Sed testor solem iustitie quod repentino morbo uexatus sum
Oxonie singulis annis in illo die, ut nullo modo susceptum magisterii officium
exequi ualerem, siue id casus ageret siue diuina uoluntas. Sed et uiri prudentes
qui me tunc temporis in scolis audierunt, diligenter hoc considerauerunt, me
secreto corripientes eo quod impugnare uelle uidebar celebrantes diem festum
conceptionis beate Virginis: *CCant.* i. 4 (M, fol. 5[rb]).

[37] M. A. Harris, 'Alan of Tewkesbury and his letters', *Studia Monastica*,
xviii (1976), 301: Letter 31;cf. id., 'Influences on the thought of Alan of Tewkesbury', *Journal of Ecclesiastical History*, xxxiii (1982), 8-9.

[38] *SFA* 22 (fol. 26[va]): the four rivers of Paradise; cf. *GP* prol.

[39] Dum in scolis nobile Salomonis opus uiris maturi pectoris et sublimi intelligentie diligenter exponerem, uisum fuit mihi totam Canticorum seriem com-
petenter exponi posse de animo humano et sapientia, ita ut dilectus dicatur
animus, dilecta dicatur sapientia: *CCant.* vi. 24 (M, fol. 192[va]).

subtilis obiciendi modus scindat uirtutem responsionis. Tempus est autem consuendi per solutionis efficatiam ea que disiuncta uidebantur esse per acutam inquisitionis inuestigationem. Opponens enim acute aut mittit iaculum entimematis quo maculas lorice respondentis dissuit et penetrat, aut gladium uibrat sillogismi quo dissecat clipeum solutionis. Respondens uero nunc consolidat clipeum, nunc lorice maculas consuit dissutas prius.[40]

When he was in the schools—he does not say where— he had made an agreement with one of his fellow students that they should enter a monastery together. Alexander fulfilled his part of the agreement, but his friend had entered the service of the king, and 'the philosopher who had studied the *aporismata* of arithmetic far into the night was now tied down by the calculations of the Exchequer'.[41] Alexander appeals to him to fulfil his original intention and paints a gloomy picture of the inconveniences of the court. Peter of Blois mentions a revenue desirable to many that Alexander himself had rejected long before his conversion.[42] It was presumably a benefice of some kind. For him the monastic life was a higher one than that of the teacher: it is between the life of students and the life of saints in triumph.[43] Nevertheless his friends tried to dissuade him from his purpose by saying that envy was rife among monks. The world ascribed the conversion to weakness. But he became like a deaf man and heard not the sounds of the world, and even as a man that heareth not, who before had sinned much by the loquaciousness of his tongue.[44] One friend certainly admired him

---

[40] *In Eccles.* iii. 15: **C**, fol. 128^{ra-b} reading 'disserat'.

[41] Militauimus pariter in castris philosophie et condixeramus nos simul ingressuros fore tabernaculum sapientie. Sed ecce uitis generosa degenerauit in labruscam et philosophus qui aporismatibus arismetice diutius inuigilauerat fisci ratiociniis detinetur: *CCant.* viii. 15 (**M**, fol. 179vb). For a similar agreement see the late twelfth-century letter-collection preserved in MS Donaueschingen 910: A. Cartellieri, *Ein Donauschinger Briefsteller* (Innsbruck, 1898), nos. 68-9.

[42] Diu enim ante conuersionem uestram, desiderabili multis reditu abiecto, abiectus esse in domo domini eligistis: *Ep.* 137 (*MPL* ccvii. 405B).

[43] Vita claustralium media est inter uitam scolarium et uitam triumphantium. Dormi igitur *inter medios cleros* [Ps. 67: 14], hoc est in medio sortium. Est enim quedam sors gratie honestas uite scolarium, sors ultima est delitiosa iocunditas uite triumphantium, media tranquillitas claustralium: *CCant.* ii. 16 (**M**, fol. 79rb).

[44] Et illi *qui querebant animam meam* seducere ante hunc statum *uim faciebant* . . . ne ad hunc statum deuenirem, *et qui inquirebant mala mihi*, id est anime

for his action. We have a long letter from Peter of Blois con-
gratulating him on his conversion, and exhorting him not to
be cast down by the difficulties of the new life, which are
bound to afflict any man with an established position in the
world who enters a monastery.[45]
The monastery he entered was the Augustinian abbey
of Cirencester.[46] It was a royal foundation and one of the
larger and more important Augustinian houses. The Augustinian canons are very difficult to grasp as a body.[47] They
had no rule in the sense that the Benedictines had one.
The so-called rule of St Augustine is short and unpractical, so
that each house had to compose or adapt constitutions.
Few of these have survived; and for Cirencester we have
no information at all. If there can be said to be a central idea
among them, it is the 'linea canonice mediocritatis' put
forward in the sermons of Peter Comestor. 'The mark
(*character*) of your order', he says, 'is moderation in food, in
clothing, in habit, in tonsure, in walking, in psalmody and the
like. Superfluity of such things often breeds intemperance,
excessive austerity sometimes breeds impatience, sometimes
hidden pride. Do thou attend the sweetness of moderation in
three points: it is sufficient, tranquil and secure.'[48] It was this
mee *locuti sunt uanitates* dicendo: 'Summa inuidia regnat inter claustrales *et
dolos tota die meditabantur*' ut me uel sic retraherent a proposito felici. *Ego
autem*, maxime postquam claustrum intraui, *tanquam surdus non audiebam*
strepitum mundanorum, . . . *et factus sum non audiens* qui prius per loquacitatem
lingue nimis deliqueram: *GP* 37: 13-15 (MS Bodley 284, fols. 92vb-3ra). [And
further on:] opinionem uulgi male sentiencis de uita religiosorum *redactus sum ad
nichilum*, dum caput meum iugo religionis supposui. Hoc enim uulgus pusill-
animitati ascribit. *Et nesciui*, id est gessi me tanquam non curarem quid uulgus de
me sentiret: *GP* 72: 22 (MS Bodley 284, fol. 179ra). We get a glimpse of the way
Alexander approached the religious life in the *SFA*, when he says that God
enlivens the soul of a man who proposes to enter it, as he weighs up the customs
of various orders: *SFA* 16 (fol. 19ra).

[45] *Ep.* 137: *MPL* ccvii. 404D-8B. Cf. the similar letter from Geoffrey, sub-
prior of Ste-Barbe-en-Auge (dép. Calvados), to 'master R.': *MPL* ccv. 845C-6C.

[46] *Victoria County History . . . Gloucester* (London, 1907), ii. 79-84. See
further C. D. Ross, *The Cartulary of Cirencester Abbey Gloucestershire* (London,
1964), i, pp. xviii-xl.

[47] J. C. Dickinson, *The Origins of the Austin canons and their introduction
into England* (London, 1950), *passim.*

[48] See two sermons for the feast of St Augustine: 'lineam canonicae mediocritatis extendens, ut sapiens architectus' (32: *MPL* cxcviii. 1797C); 'Character
enim ordinis tui . . .' (31: ibid. 1796A). Cf. Jocelin of Furness, *Vita S. Waldeni*,
iii. 34: *Acta Sanctorum*, Aug. i. 257-8 (*BHL* 8783).

that attracted Alexander. Discretion is the best guide. He did not always find it. He laments that the golden mean of 'regular' discipline has departed; and that there is too much insistence on rules and regulations.[49]

The date of his entry into the abbey can only be determined approximately. The limiting dates are probably after 1197 and before 1202. We have a letter of Pope Celestine III instructing judges delegate the abbots of Combe and Stoneleigh and 'master Alexander of St Albans', which is dated 23 January 1195; and there he is not styled canon.[50] But in a composition before papal judges delegate dated August 1205 he is called 'master Alexander of St Albans, canon of Cirencester'. This composition recites a letter of Innocent III dated 8 May 1203, in which Alexander is again called canon of Cirencester.[51] Allowing time for communication between England and Rome, he can scarcely have become a canon later than the end of 1202. The letter of Peter of Blois makes it probable that he became a canon before 1202. Peter kept adding letters to his collection and *Ep.* 137 was not added until after 1197. This probably means that it was written after that date, but not necessarily, because he sometimes adds older letters. In the letter there is a quotation from Cicero's *De amicitia*, which is taken from Ailred of Rievaulx's tract on the same subject. Peter uses this work in his own *De amicitia*, written between 1198 and 1212; in *Ep.* 207, written between 1208 and 1210; and in *Ep.* 119, which belongs to the group of additions preceding

[49] Per *uittam auream* [12: 6, the golden bowl of AV] designatur regularis disciplina. Sicut enim uitta constringit capillos ne uagis errent discursibus, sic et discipline censura uagos motus animi cohercet. Auro sapientie rutilare debet disciplina fedie. Optima enim moderatrix est discretio. Sed pro dolor! retro iam abiit discipline regularis aurea mediocritas; et nunc pro presidentis arbitrio rigor iuris preponitur equitati, nunc pusillanimitas remissa iuris ordinem subuertit. Vitta cesariem cingens crines ad debite dispositionis consistentiam reducit. Sic et iusticia iusto moderamine reprimere debet excessus delinquentium, relegata procul personarum acceptione: *in Eccles.* v. 11 (C, fol. 183va). *Fedie* is a spelling of p(a)edi(a)e = παιδεἰαc, more often *phedie*: cf. Martianus Capella, *De Nuptiis*, vi. 578, vii. 728.

[50] W. Holtzmann, *Papsturkunden in England*, I. i. 320: *Nachrichten v. d. Akademie d. Wissenschaften in Göttingen*, Phil.-hist. Klasse, xxv (1930), i. 619; cf. J. E. Sayers, *Papal Judges Delegate in the Province of Canterbury 1198–1254* (Oxford, 1971), p. 121.

[51] C. R. and M. G. Cheney, *The Letters of Pope Innocent III (1198–1216) concerning England and Wales* (Oxford, 1967), no. 471; cf. Sayers, loc. cit.

the letter to Alexander. In the address Peter styles himself
archdeacon of Bath. Therefore it is certainly earlier than
1202, since Peter became archdeacon of London in that
year.[52] What is more, Archbishop Hubert Walter's inter-
vention in the affairs of Cirencester c.1200-5 specifically
names 'master Alexander' as one of the four canons with
whom the government of the house should lie.[53]

Alexander soon made friends in neighbouring monasteries.
We have an enthusiastic letter from S., prior of Malmesbury,
to Walter Melidie, canon of Cirencester.[54] He calls himself an
insignificant friend of Alexander, 'the great man whose praises
he wishes to sing'. He has been reading the *Corrogationes
Promethei*. He admired the tone of the preface; it is just
suited to encourage the young. Reading the rest of the book
he was transported back through the pleasant groves of
forgotten youth. He had thought that such a man would have
forgotten these things: a memory that can retain so much is
to be praised. Another and more important friend was
Alfred of Sareshel, who dedicated his *De motu cordis* to the
'greatest Alexander'.[55] It is an attempt to describe the functions of the heart, 'a thing never before attempted by our
[i.e. Latin] scientists'. Alexander is to embrace the work as
his own, since it was chiefly owing to his instigation that it
was begun. None of Alexander's own works have dedications.
But the *Laus sapientie diuine* is sent to the convent at
Gloucester.[56] In the versification of the *Corrogationes
Promethei* he constantly addresses a certain Peter. The name
first occurs in the eleventh line of Genesis[57] and often after-
wards, whenever he wants something to fill up the line. But
there is nothing beyond the name. He may possibly be the
nephew who was sent to master Ralph to learn manners,

---

[52] R. W. Southern, *Medieval Humanism and other Studies* (Oxford, 1970),
pp. 129-32; the letter is found in 'stage IV' of Peter's collection (c.1198).

[53] Ross, *Cartulary* (n. 46 above), no. 327 and p. xx.

[54] P, fol. 240va-b: partly ed. Meyer 1896, p. 657 n. 1.

[55] *De motu cordis*, prol., ed. C. Baeumker (*BGPM* XXIII. 1-2, Münster-i.-W.,
1923), p. 4. See further D. A. Callus, 'Introduction of Aristotelian learning to
Oxford', *PBA* xxix (1943), 229-81, at 235-8; and J. K. Otte, 'The life and writings
of Alfredus Anglicus', *Viator*, iii (1972), 275-91.

[56] *LSD* x. 279-80 (p. 502).

[57] Petre uir est *andros* mulier *gamos*; hec duo produnt: *CPV*, line 11 (MS
Oxford, Bodleian Library, Digby 56, fol. 101).

verse-making and dictamen.[58] Ralph is to send reports on his charge.

Alexander was occasionally concerned with business outside the cloister. An example of his serving as a papal judge delegate we have already referred to. Another case in which he acted as an ecclesiastical judge is preserved in a small formulary probably from Cirencester itself.[59] In the winter of 1204-5 he spoke on behalf of the prior of Lanthony in his dispute with the earl of Hereford.[60] During the Interdict—in September 1212—he was engaged in some royal business which is not further specified: the king gave three marks to master Walter, the clerk of master Alexander Nequam, for taking a message to him at Cirencester.[61] In May of the next year Henricus de Alemannia received 15d. for going as a messenger with some letters to Alexander at Cirencester.[62] In August of the same year he was ordered by the king to accompany John of Hastings, the constable of Kenilworth and a clerk of the archbishop of Canterbury, to inquire into the royal rights in the priory of Kenilworth.[63] There are some words in the *Laus sapientie diuine*, which was written just about this time, suggesting that he repented of whatever he had done:

> Exponi solis radio tibi dulce uidetur,
> tutius est propria uelle latere domo.
> O si magnatum me nunquam curia nosset!
> ha! multis mundi gloria uana nocet.

[58] Quem tibi transmitto, doctor Radulfe, nepotem
suscipe; deuota sedulitate doce . . .
Versibus et rithmis et adhuc dictamine, per te
floreat, et sit in hiis sollicitudo uigil.
moribus informa, uirtutibus imbue, uerbis
exorna, refice dogmate, pinge metris.
(P, fol. 238^{rb-va}).

Printed in full by E. du Méril, *Poésies inédites du Moyen Âge* (Paris, 1854), pp. 170-1 app. Alexander's only attested nephew was Geoffrey Brito, canon of Cirencester c.1230: Ross, op. cit. (n. 46 above), no. 336.

[59] MS Bodleian, Laud lat. 17, fol. 224ra: see Sayers, *Judges Delegate* (n. 50 above), pp. 49-51 (MS O).

[60] H. G. Richardson and G. O. Sayles, *Select Cases of Procedure without Writ under Henry III* (Selden Soc. LX, London, 1941), pp. clxxix-clxxxi.

[61] H. Cole, *Documents illustrative of English History in the Thirteenth and Fourteenth Centuries* (London, 1844), p. 242: *Rotuli Misae*, 14 John.

[62] Ibid., p. 266: *Rotuli Misae*, 14 John.

[63] T. D. Hardy, *Rotuli Litterarum Patentium* (London, 1835), I. i. 103b.

Esse reor tutum claustri latitare sub ala,
o quantum nocuit Cesaris aula mihi![64]

In the same year (1213) he was elected abbot of Cirencester.[65] Mr Russell suggests that his election is partly explained
by the services rendered to the king during the Interdict.[66]
But this is only conjecture. He may equally well have been
the most suitable candidate among the monks; he was almost
certainly 'custos' of the house during the vacancy after the
death of Abbot Richard.[67] A few domestic documents
survive from his years as abbot, relating to the rights and
property of Cirencester; it was in his time that the abbey
was granted an annual autumn fair.[68] On 21 July 1215
Alexander, among others who were leaving for the Fourth
Lateran Council, was issued with letters patent protecting his
rights and property in his absence. On 19 August a boat and
a good lodging were ordered for the abbot of Cirencester
and his train. On 13 September he attested a charter at
Dover with the bishop of Worcester.[69] After this we lose
sight of him. He wrote at least one work after his return, the
Supplement to the *Laus sapientie diuine*, which can be dated
in the second half of 1216. He died early in 1217 at Kempsey,
a manor of the bishop of Worcester, and he was buried in
Worcester cathedral.[70] The Worcester obituary gives the

---

[64] *LSD* iii. 485-90 (p. 406).

[65] D. Knowles, C. N. L. Brooke and V. C. M. London, *The Heads of Religious
Houses, England and Wales, 940–1216* (Cambridge, 1972), p. 160, with references.
See particularly the *Annals of Dunstable*: 'magister Alexander Nequam in abbatem
Cirencestr' . . . electus est (ed. H. R. Luard, *Annales Monastici* [RS, London,
1866], iii. 40-1).

[66] J. C. Russell, 'Alexander Neckam in England', *EHR* xlvii (1932), 263.

[67] Ross, *Cartulary* (n. 46 above), I, no. 233*.

[68] Ibid., nos. 86-7, with references (seisin of temporalities); nos. 533-5 (the
Hagbourne case: 1213/14); nos. 17 and 39 (tallage of Cirencester: 1214); no. 83
(Seven Hundreds of Cirencester: 1215); no. 43 (autumn fair: 1215); no. 465
(lease of a mill: 1213/17); no. 621 (property at Frome); no. 409 (appropriation
of a church: 1216/17).

[69] Ibid., no. 88 (21 July); T. D. Hardy, *Rotuli Litterarum Clausarum* (Record
Commission, 1833-4), 227a (19 Aug.); id., *Rotuli Chartarum* (Record Commission, 1837), I. i. 218b (13 Sept.).

[70] Magister Alexander Nequam abbas Cirec': obiit apud Kemeseye et sepelitur
Wygon': *Annals of Worcester*, ed. H. R. Luard, *Annales Monastici* (RS, London,
1869), iv. 409; cf. J. K. Floyer, 'On a mutilated effigy in the cloisters of Worcester
cathedral, said to represent Alexander Neckam', *Associated Architectural Socie-
ties Reports*, xxiv (1898), 188-96. William Worcestre (s. xv[ex.]) alleges that Nequam

date as 31 March.[71] It can hardly be later than this, since the king approved the appointment of his successor, Walter the cellarer, on 27 April 1217.[72]

The character of a man about whom so little is known cannot be sketched. There are several stories about him in the collections of *exempla*. They cannot be trusted since they simply play on the name Nequam. In the fifteenth century he was credited with the transmission of a miracle of the Virgin concerning Walter, abbot of Tavistock (d. *c*.1168).[73] But there is one story to which attention must be called owing to its date. It comes from a sermon of Caesarius of Heisterbach, which was written about 1220.[74] That Alexander's reputation should have spread so far is remarkable. Caesarius' story is that Alexander was preaching at a monastery and some of the brethren asked him not to make the sermon too long. He cut it to one sentence. We cannot for a moment assume the authenticity of the story, but it may preserve a genuine trait. If he was brusque, however, he was also a jolly man, and he liked his joke and a glass of wine or more. A few extracts from his works will show these traits more clearly than any words of mine. 'A wise man said in joke, but seriously, that the Slavs are not whistlers, because they have

was buried at Worcester 'eo ·quod episcopus de Worcestre nollet ipsum esse supultus apud abbathiam suam de Cirencestre eo quod excommunicatus fuit per episcopum doctore Nekkham de Roma Curia veniente': *Itineraries*, ed. J. H. Harvey (Oxford Medieval Texts, Oxford, 1969), p. 286.

[71] MS Worcester, Cathedral Library, F. 160, fol. 146ᵛ (s. xiv): 'Isti sunt obitus per annum qui debent habere missam cum uno cantore uel cum duobus cantoribus . . . 2 kal. April Alexandri Nequam abbatis Cirencestr' '. For the celebration of Nequam's anniversary at Cirencester itself see Ross, *Cartulary* (n. 46 above), nos. 332, 336.

[72] Knowles, Brooke and London, op. cit. (n. 65 above), p. 160, with references.

[73] MS Cambridge, Sidney Sussex College, 95 (Δ 5 10), fols. 137ʳᵇ-9ʳᵃ (s. xvⁱ: English), has the reference: 'Narrat Alexander Necham libro vᵒ cap. 12 super cantica quod erat quidam prelatus etc.' (fol. 137ᵛᵃ). There is no corresponding passage in *CCant*. v. 12. The story is found in two thirteenth-century manuscripts: MS London, BL, Harley 495, fols. 59ʳᵃ-60ʳᵃ, with the attribution to Nequam, and MS Aberdeen, University Library, 137, fols. 132-5, attributed to William, abbot of Bindon, O.Cist., Dorset. See Herbert, *Cat. Rom.* ii. 535.

[74] Caesarius of Heisterbach, sermon for the fifth Sunday in Lent (Passion Sunday): excerpt quoted by A. E. Schönbach, 'Studien zur Erzählungsliteratur des Mittelalters, IV: über Caesarius von Heisterbach', *SB Vienna*, cxliv. 9 (1902), 77.

no vines. He would have got nearer the reason if he had said it was because they do not drink wine.'[75] The first book of the *De commendatione uini* describes the stages of drunkenness with such gusto that he has been called a 'glühender Verehrer der Bacchusgabe'. To study, he says, he must always have wine at hand. May he never be without it.[76] For all his versatility he was not conceited; and as a fitting end to this chapter we may quote two pieces from his latest works. In the one he shows a mixture of truculence and humility which is rather touching; in the other, the prayer at the end of the *Super mulierem fortem*, he bids a modest farewell to his book.

> Lima mordaci, sed prudens sepius utor,
>   cor rapio multis quos bene corripio;
> sed nec parco michi sub lima iudiciali,
>   cum uerbis mores corripiendo meos.
> corripio mores, uersus emendo, reuoluo
>   sermonem, pingo uerba colore suo.
> perscrutor sensum, sermonem rebus adapto,
>   uix michi cum faleris uerba nouella placent.
> Barbariem uito uerborum, turgida semper
>   sperno, sedent animo publica uerba meo.
> scinthasis (? *leg.* syntaxis) ipsa docet ut nubat mobile fixo,
>   substet materies, forma uenustet eam.
> si male conueniat uirgo sociata marito
>   et sociam querulus respuat ille [*cod.* illa] suam,
> coniugium soluo, celebro diuorcia, legem
>   incidens, socio nubat ut illa nouo.
> O si barbariem uiciorum sic reprobarem,
>   ut uicium Soloes lingua latina fugit.
> Vt sit limatus sermo desidero, mores
>   uix sub iudicium conuoco, uerba uoco.
> Si tempus studiis dandum feliciter arto,
>   si male dilato que breuianda forent,
> dissimulo, sileo, conniueo: corripiendam
>   producens, gemitus edo, dolore tremo.
> Carminibus parco propriis, carpens aliena
>   inuideo si quis nobile condat opus.
> Que mens commendat os damnat, singula prudens
>   que sunt apposite dicta reseruo michi.
> Singula dampno, licet multo sint digna fauore
>   et furtim scriptis insero multa meis.

[75] *SS* iii. 13: **R**, fol. 54[vb].
[76] *DCV* i. 123–4: **P**, fol. 215[ra] (Esposito, p. 455, lines 4–5).

Sed tamen improbus est censor, me iudice, scripto
quisquis in alterius ingeniosus erit.[77]

Fortasse tuo, liber, superstes eris Alexandro. Prius enim me uermes
commedent, quam te tinea corrosura sit. Vermibus debetur corpus
meum: te demolientur tinee. Tu speculum es animi mei, tu meditacio-
num mearum interpres, propositi nostri certissimus es iudex, affectuum
mentis mee fidelis es nuncius, tu dulce solacium meroris, tu testis
consciencie uerax. Tibi tanquam fideli depositario cordis archana commendaui. Restituis fideliter michi ea que fidei tue commisi. In te
meipsum lego. Venies, uenies in manus alicuius pii lectoris, qui pro me
preces effundere dignabitur. Tunc quidem tuo libelle domino proderis,
tunc tuo Alexandro gratissimam recompensabis uicissitudinem. Vincet,
nec inuideo, laborem meum pii lectoris deuotio, qui te nunc gremio
repositurus, nunc pectori suo admoturus, nonnumquam capiti, tanquam
dulce ceruical, suppositurus, quandoque te letis manibus leniter con-
trectaturus, pro me affectuose dominum exorabit Iesum Christum,
qui cum patre et spiritu sancto uiuit et regnat deus per infinita seculorum secula. Amen.[78]

A NOTE ON ALEXANDER'S NAME

The earliest form of Alexander's name is 'Alexander de sancto Albano'
from his birthplace. This is found in the address of the letter of Peter
of Blois (*Ep.* 137); in the letters of Celestine III and Innocent III
appointing him papal judge delegate; and in other documents where
he is a judge;[79] in manuscripts of the *De naturis rerum*; in one manuscript of the *Commentary on the Athanasian Creed* and in the Lambeth
manuscript of the *Questiones.*[80] According to Madox it was on his
seal.[81] There are a few places where he is simply called 'magister
Alexander canonicus Cirencestrie', as in the manuscript of the *Speculum
speculationum* (R) and in the Paris manuscript of the *Laus sapientie
diuine* (P); or 'magister Alexander abbas Cirencestrie', as in J, fols. 74va,
75vb, and a Cambridge manuscript of *LSD.*
The commonest form by far is 'magister Alexander Nequam'. It was
sufficiently well established in his lifetime to be used by clerks in the
royal chancery on official documents. It is found on the roll of Letters
Patent in 1213 and on the Misae Roll in 1212 and 1213.[82] It is the

---

[77] *SD* i. 1033–64: **P**, fol. 222vb.

[78] *SMF*: **J**, fol. 125ra. Translation in Thorndike, ii. 203–4, who renders
'capiti tamquam dulce ceruical suppositurus' as 'sometimes place you as a sweet
pillow beneath his head'.

[79] See nn. 50–1 and 59.

[80] See Appendix A ad loc.

[81] T. Madox, *Formulare Anglicanum* (London, 1702), no. xlv (= Cheney,
no. 471: n. 51 above), p. 26. The seal is now lost.

[82] See nn. 63, 61 and 62 above.

form used by Alfred of Sareshel in the dedication of the *De motu cordis*.[83] It is the form normally used in thirteenth-century quotations: Caesarius of Heisterbach and Matthew Paris both say 'Alexander cognomento Nequam';[84] Roger of Wendover is playing on the name when, speaking of another Alexander of St Albans, he has the rubric: 'De consiliis iniquis magistri Alexandri Nequioris'.[85]

The forms 'Necham' and 'Nekham' appear side by side in the fourteenth century in the library catalogue of Peterborough abbey.[86] At the end of the fourteenth century Walsingham writes 'Nequam', following Matthew Paris, in the *Gesta Abbatum*, but in a little tract he wrote on the famous men of St Albans he put 'Nekham'.[87] It becomes fairly common in manuscripts in the fifteenth century. A good example is Oxford, St John's College, 178 (*Corrogationes Promethei*), where the thirteenth-century title at the head of the work is 'Prologus magistri Alexandri Nequam' (fol. 105) and the fifteenth-century list of contents has 'Prologus magistri Alexandri Nekham' (fol. 1). This was no doubt the form with which Leland and Bale were familiar. In Hearne's careful edition of the *Collectanea* we can see how Leland writes Necham over Nequam.[88] Their acceptance of it gave it the authority of print.

> *Eclypsin patitur sapientia. Sol sepilitur*
> *Cui si par unus minus esset flebile funus.*
> *Vir bene discretus et in omni more facetus*
> *Dictus erat Nequam: uitam duxit tamen aequam.*
>
> MS Lambeth Palace Library 23, fol. i:
> 'Epitaphium Alexandri | Nechami ex uet:
> manuscript:' (*c*.1700; and see Floyer, loc.
> cit. [n. 70 above], p. 192).

---

[83] See n. 55 above.

[84] nn. 74 (Caesarius) and 14 (Matthew Paris).

[85] Roger of Wendover, *Flores Historiarum*, ed. H. O. Coxe (London, 1841), iii. 229. On another master Alexander of St Albans, a royal clerk (Alexander Caementarius), noted by Wendover, s.a. 1209, see F. M. Powicke, 'Alexander of St Albans: a literary muddle', *Essays in History presented to R. L. Poole*, ed. H. W. C. Davis (Oxford, 1927), pp. 246-60.

[86] M. R. James, 'Lists of manuscripts formerly in Peterborough abbey library', *Bibliographical Society Supplt.* no. 5 (1926), nos. 87-8, 90, 92 (Necham); 110, 157, 160, 218 (Nekham).

[87] MS London, BL, Cotton Claudius E. IV, fol. 333: ed. H. T. Riley, *Annales Monasterii S. Albani a Iohanne Amundesham . . . conscripti* (RS, London, 1871), ii. 296-306, at 306.

[88] J. Leland, *De rebus britannicis collectanea*, ed. T. Hearne (2nd edn., London, 1774), iv. 15.

II

THE AUTHENTICITY AND CHRONOLOGY OF HIS WORKS

THE chronology and authenticity of the works may conveniently be considered together. There is in most cases no doubt about the authenticity. It is sufficiently guaranteed by the manuscripts and by cross-references from one work to another. There is further an independent source of information in a *Florilegium* entirely composed of extracts from Alexander's writings.[1] It was probably put together at Cirencester about the middle of the thirteenth century. The early grammatical works are not drawn upon, but all the theological works are used; and it is particularly valuable for some of the lesser of these. It will, therefore, only be necessary to discuss authenticity when there is any doubt. But the chronology is more difficult, and we can do little more than indicate a rough sequence.

We know from the letter of Peter of Blois[2] that Alexander had some reputation as a writer before he became a canon. On what writings was it based? All his surviving major theological works were written after his entry to Cirencester. We may with some confidence place the *De nominibus utensilium*, the *Commentary on Martianus Capella* and the Fables in this earlier period. Of these the first and last belong purely to the school and its more elementary stages. They may have been written either at the time when he taught the *artes* in Paris or after his return to England. Paris seems more probable. For there is an allusion in the *De nominibus utensilium* to the school at the Petit Pont, of which he was a member;[3] and, more significant, the work is found in a number of continental manuscripts. It is well known that the

---

[1] CUL Gg. 6. 42 = G. See below, pp. 118, 147.

[2] *Ep.* 137: cf. pp. 9–10 above. Peter's phrase is 'litteratura uestra' (*MPL* ccvii. 405A).

[3] Of a good wine Alexander says 'subtilitati Paruipontane ueritatis equiparetur': *DNV* (Scheler, p. 68).

works of English writers of the twelfth century very rarely had any circulation outside England.[4] By the same argument the Fables may be assigned to the Paris period. They were certainly remembered there a generation later. There is a quotation from one of them in a sermon preached before the University by Odo of Châteauroux.[5]

The *De nominibus utensilium* contains a reference to some early writings: 'Multa etiam talia ad propositum pertinentia in aliis meis literis persecutus sum, unde non me, sicut quamplurimos, iuuat palinodia'.[6] These 'litere' have not been found, and it is not easy to say what they were. Possibly it was the same sort of work as the *De nominibus utensilium*, which is itself once called 'epistole'.[7] In one manuscript a versified vocabulary entitled *Duodecim decades* or *De utensilibus domi* is ascribed to him.[8] In another manuscript it is ascribed to John of Garland, and in six others it is anonymous. The work itself contains no evidence of authorship. It is easy to see how such a work could have been ascribed to Alexander, simply owing to the resemblance to the *De nominibus utensilium*. Similarly the *Phale tolum* of Adam de Paruo Ponte is sometimes given to Alexander.[9] It has been suggested that the 'magister N.' who wrote a commentary on it was Nequam.[10] But he is never called 'magister Nequam'. The *Commentary on Martianus Capella* contains nothing that shows to what period it belongs.[11] But it is almost entirely concerned with mythology, and there is not the same moralization as in the *De naturis rerum*. It may be put here provisionally. The mythological work

[4] The other work found outside England in a number of manuscripts is *CP*; but most of these are English. P is English. I have not seen MS Cambrai, Bibl. Mun., 976, which contains *CAth*.

[5] M. M. Davy, *Les Sermons universitaires parisiens de 1230–1231* (Paris, 1931), p. 194; cf. Hauréau, *Notices*, vi. 205–6.

[6] *DNV*: Scheler, p. 163.

[7] MS London, BL, Add. 8092, fol. 1: 'Incipiunt epistole magistri Alexandri Nequam de utensilibus domorum'; cf. p. 127 below.

[8] See p. 148 below.

[9] L. Minio-Paluello, 'The *Ars Disserendi* of Adam of Balsham *Paruipontanus*', *MARS* iii (1954), pp. 118–19, with references.

[10] MS Cambridge, Gonville and Caius College, 136 (76), pp. 21–30: see P. Meyer, 'Les manuscrits français de Cambridge, IV', *Romania*, xxxvi (1907), 485–8.

[11] See p. 128 below.

known as *Mythographus tertius* has sometimes been ascribed to Alexander, but it is now known to be the work of Alberic of London.[12] In two of the three manuscripts in which it is ascribed to Alexander it is followed by his *Commentary on Martianus Capella*, which draws largely from it, and this may have given rise to the confusion.

Of his other grammatical writings the first part of the *Corrogationes Promethei* was probably based on lectures, but it was not put into its present shape until after he became a canon; the *Sacerdos ad altare* is also later.

There are a few traces of Alexander's lectures at Oxford. Material from them is probably incorporated in some of his later writings. The *Commentary on the Athanasian Creed* may have been written when he was there. It seems to contain no indication even of relative date. But in one of the manuscripts he is called 'magister Alexander de sancto Albano', which is a sign of early date.[13] There are some *questiones* in a Lambeth manuscript, which are attributed to him. But their genuineness cannot be determined until the *questio* literature of the period has been more carefully sifted. He certainly wrote a *questio scolastica* on the Last Judgement. There are extracts from it in the *Florilegium*, and it is perhaps the *questio* in the list of his works in the *Registrum Anglie*.[14] But no complete manuscript has yet been found.

We reach surer ground with the sermons, though the authenticity of all of them is not established beyond doubt.[15] There are extracts from seventy-one in the *Florilegium*, and of these thirty-three are known from that source alone. But the compiler certainly did not make excerpts from all the sermons. The chief manuscript collection is in Bodleian Wood empt. 13 (W), which contains fifty-five sermons. In all probability only the first forty-two are genuine. Nos. 43-5 are sermons for Advent; three genuine Advent

[12] E. Rathbone, 'Master Alberic of London, mythographus tertius Vaticanus', *MARS* i (1941), 35-9; see further p. 148 below.

[13] MS London, BL, Harley 3133, fol. 100 (s. xiii¹). The same manuscript has a marginal annotation (fol. 98ᵛ), probably added later, which refers to *GP* 22: 4 (MS Bodley 284, fol. 41ʳ⁻ᵛ).

[14] See p. 125 below.

[15] See Appendix B.

sermons are at the beginning of the manuscript. Nos. 43-4 are also attributed to John of Liège; no. 45 has not been found elsewhere, but its style is unlike that of Alexander. No. 46 is found anonymously in two Paris manuscripts.[16] No. 47 and probably no. 48 are by Maurice of St Victor.[17] Nos. 49-50 are by Peter Comestor.[18] Nos. 51-3 have not been found elsewhere, but the context and their style make them suspect. The only other large collection is in Cambridge, Corpus Christi College, 217. It is an important manuscript of theological works by writers of the late twelfth century. It contains a group of thirty-one sermons, which are all found in W except three. Of these one is in the *Florilegium*, no. (96), and the other two, (96a), (96b), in none of the other manuscripts. In the smaller collections context and internal evidence are more reliable guides than the attributions of the manuscripts themselves. Thus in Cambridge, University Library, Ii. 1. 24, there are two groups of seven and five sermons attributed to Alexander.[19] Of the seven one is on the same text as a sermon in the *Florilegium*, no. 65; but the piece in the *Florilegium* does not occur in it, and the others have not been found elsewhere. It gives the impression of a homogeneous group in a barer and simpler style than Alexander's. In the group of five the first four are unlike Alexander, and only the fifth, no. 28, is certainly by Alexander. In the important Cirencester manuscript of his works, Jesus College 94 (J), two sermons have been added. They are marked: 'Sermo magistri Alexandri abbatis Cyrencestrie'. The first is certainly by Peter Comestor;[20] and the second, which is also anonymous in Harley 325, is probably not

---

[16] MSS Paris, BN, lat. 3803, fol. 18, and 13586, p. 351: See Hauréau, *Notices*, ii. 322.

[17] Schneyer, *Repertorium*, iv. 169, nos. 3 and 5, with references.

[18] No. 49 consists of two excerpts from Peter Comestor: *MPL* cxcviii. 1806CD and *MPL* clxxi. 476D-8C, abridged (= Schneyer, iv. 637-9), plus another, unidentified excerpt (fol. 136ᵛ). But contemporary marginalia read 'Ex sermone magistri Alexandri abbatis Cirencestris qui sic incipit, *Domum tuam domine decet sanctitudo*' (Ps. 92: 5) and 'Item ex sermone eiusdem qui sic incipit *Apprehendunt vii mulieres uirum unum*' (Is. 4: 1) (both W, fol. 136). No. 50 is by Peter Comestor (*MPL* cxcviii. 1778C-82D: Schneyer, iv. 641-2).

[19] Nos. 61-7; and 68-70, sermon 'Ecce odor', 28. The sermon 'Ecce odor' (Gen. 27: 27) may be by Geoffrey Babion: Schneyer, *Repertorium*, ii. 152, no. 18.

[20] Peter Comestor, sermon 35: Schneyer, *Repertorium*, iv. 638, no. 35; cf. J, fols. 74ᵛᵃ-5ᵛᵃ.

by Alexander.[21] On the other hand Merton 180 contains a group of five genuine sermons of which only the third is ascribed to Alexander in the manuscript.[22] The first is only found in this manuscript, but contains a valuable cross-reference to a sermon otherwise known from extracts in the *Florilegium*; the second is only found in the extracts of the *Florilegium*; and the rest are known from other manuscripts. Similarly in an anonymous collection of sermons in Peterhouse 255 there are six by Alexander. One of them would otherwise only be known from the extracts in the *Florilegium*. It seems most probable that other sermons are lurking in sermon collections of the first half of the thirteenth century.

It is quite clear that none of these manuscripts contains a complete collection of the sermons. But there is evidence that Alexander did make some sort of a collection. In the list of his works in the catalogue of Henry of Kirkestede there is an entry: 'Sermones ab aduentu domini Pr. Post susceptam.' Bale amplified this incipit to 'Post susceptam praedicandi functionem'.[23] Few as the words are, they do point to the preface of a collection. The Wood manuscript (W) begins with Advent sermons and roughly follows the liturgical year, though in many places the order is seriously dislocated. The Corpus manuscript is with one exception in proper liturgical order from Trinity Sunday to Whitsunday. Even as we have them the sermons seem to have been edited by Alexander himself. We find cross-references from one sermon to another, which in the Wood manuscript are all references back; and there are appeals to the reader as well as to the hearer, for example:

Quare uero dicatur assumpcio si scire desiderat lector, querat sermonem quem composui iam reuoluto anni circulo in laudem et honorem beatissime et intemerate uirginis Marie, qui sic incipit: *Que est ista que ascendit* etc.[24]

---

[21] No. 60: J, fol. 75vb.

[22] Nos. (103), (104), 2, 13, 11.

[23] *Catalogus*, 4 (cf. n. I. 16 above); Bale (1559), i. 273.

[24] No. 19 (W, fol. 55), referring to no. 18; cf. no. 41, referring to no. 36, and no. (103), referring to no. (101). In no. 28 there is a general reference: 'alibi in aliis sermonibus nostris diffiniuimus' (W, fol. 80^{v}). Other appeals to the reader are 'Attende lector, attende auditor' (W, fol. 77^{v}) and 'cum igitur audis, o lector' (W, fol. 117).

The reference is to the immediately preceding sermon in the manuscript. All but one of the sermons preserved entire were apparently delivered before he became a canon. The exception is no. (98), to the monks of St Peter's, Gloucester, found in a manuscript which belonged to Thomas de Bredone, abbot there from 1223 to 1228. In one at least of the extracts in the *Florilegium* he also seems to speak as a regular or prelate to monks.[25] In the other sermons to monks he is a teacher and a secular. He recalls the imperfection of his state when he addresses them. They preach by their works, we ('nos scolares') only by word.[26] The only place mentioned is Oxford. There is sermon no. 26 addressed to the citizens of Oxford. There is the appeal, no. 33, for funds for the rebuilding of St Frideswide's. There is the heading to no. 2 in the Merton manuscript: 'Alexander in primo aduentu scolaribus Oxonie'. And in the same collection there is a reference to a sermon 'de primo aduentu quem feci scolaribus Oxonie, qui sic incipit: *Dixit Deus, fiat lux*'.[27] It seems reasonable, therefore, to suppose that the other sermons addressed to 'scolares' or 'scolares et laici' were also preached there while he was teaching.

We now come to the works written while Alexander was a canon. This was the period of his great literary activity. It is disappointing not to be able to fix accurate dates. Our starting point is a passage in the *De naturis rerum*:

Si quis autem diligentiorem explanationem principii Geneseos inspicere desiderat, legat opus nostrum, quod *in laudem beatissime uirginis* scripsimus, et opus morale quod intitulaui *Solatium fidelis anime*. Desiderans uero pleniorem expositionem super initium Iohannis, quaerat opus nostrum rudes informans in multis, quod nuncupauimus *Corrogationes Promethei*.[28]

The work in praise of the most blessed Virgin has not yet been recovered.[29] But there are extracts from it in the

[25] No. (105) (G, fol. 88^v): Extra consortium spiritualis collegii eicitur qui temerarie in prelatum suum insurgit. Si contemptui uobis sum, quia minister sum, parcite michi saltem, non dico quia pater sed quia frater uester sum.

[26] No. 18: W, fol. 53; see below, p. 87.

[27] No. (103), referring to no. (101).

[28] *DNR* i. 2 (p. 16: Wright 'pleniorum').

[29] *LBV*: see p. 130 below. See further *DNR* i. 1 (p. 10 app.) and *SMF*: 'dulcissima est historialis intelligentie ueritas, quam expositione luculenta declarauimus in opere nostro quod in laudes gloriose dei genetricis feliciter consumauimus' (J, fol. 99vb).

Florilegium, one of which does contain an exposition of the beginning of Genesis.[30] A *Solatium fidelis anime* is contained in a thirteenth-century manuscript at Canterbury, and it is clearly the work referred to here.[31] The style and manner is that of Alexander. In the preface the author says he is going to pay special attention to tropology. It contains an exposition of the beginning of Genesis. The passages from the *Solatium* in the *Florilegium* are found in it. It was written after he became a canon. He is addressing religious as a religious himself,[32] and he refers to his teaching in the schools in the past tense:

In scolis autem legentes consueuimus dicere lignum uite dici gratiam, lignum uero scientie boni et mali usum liberi arbitrii.[33]

The *Corrogationes Promethei* was one of his most popular works, and it is preserved in a large number of manuscripts. That it was written after he became a canon is shown by references to his teaching on grammar[34] and theology, in particular by a passage at the beginning of the notes on Ezekiel, which reminds us of a charge made against Abailard:

Ezechiel paucis se prebuit facilem, nostris tamen contrectari manibus in claustro, qui in scolis nobis se ultro optulit, non reformidat.[35]

The versification of Part II of the *Corrogationes* may be dealt with here, though it may well be somewhat later. No such work is mentioned by the bibliographers. But there is the following entry in the Syon catalogue (E 46): 'Magister Alexander abbas Cirencestrensis de quorundam terminorum explanacionibus omnium librorum Biblie in metro'.[36] An

[30] G, fols. 24ᵛ-9ᵛ.

[31] See pp. 130-1 below; cf. J. C. Russell, 'Alexander Neckam in England', *EHR* xlvii (1932), 267. *SFA* is referred to in an excerpt from *LBV*: 'Qui autem moralem expositionem istorum desiderat legat, si placet, opus illud tropologicum, quod inscripsimus *Solacium fidelis anime*' (G, fol. 29).

[32] *SFA*, caps. 20 and 23: MS Canterbury Cathedral Lit. B. 6, fols. 24ᵛᵃ and 29ʳᵇ.

[33] *SFA*, cap. 21: fol. 26ᵛᵃ.

[34] Possumus et nos dicere, ut in scolis dicere consueuimus, quod do, das componitur indo, indis, indidi: B, fol. 17ᵛᵇ.

[35] B, fol. 33ᵛᵇ.

[36] M. Bateson, *Catalogue of the Library of Syon Monastery Isleworth* (Cambridge, 1898), p. 48; cf. M. R. James, 'Lists of manuscripts formerly in Peterborough abbey library', *Bibliographical Soc. Supplt.* no. 5 (1926), p. 64, no. 239.

anonymous work answering to this description is found in three manuscripts.[37] That this is in fact a work of Alexander is made probable by the quotations from it in the *Vocabularium* of William Brito. William quotes verses by Alexander Nequam nineteen times, and they are all found in the anonymous work.[38] We have another example of Alexander versifying his own work in the *Laus sapientie diuine*.

We can get a *terminus ante quem* for the composition of the *De naturis rerum* and *Super Ecclesiasten*. In it he tells the story of two falcons and an eagle. The eagle kills one of the falcons, but in the end the other lures the eagle on to destruction. At the end he says:

Euentus autem quem iam scripto commendaui testes sunt inuictissimi ciues Rotomagenses, quibus falco generosus, regie uictor auis, certum uisus est presagium dedisse Francorum insidias euadendi potenter.[39]

This must have been written before the fall of Rouen on 24 June 1204, and recalls the famous siege of 1193. There are two remarks on tournaments, which were introduced into England in 1194, though they were doubtless known to Alexander before that.[40] The *terminus post quem* is the autumn of 1187, given the 'planctus super Ierusalem', in which he laments its capture by the 'Mahometans', and upbraids the Christian princes: 'Insurgunt in se mutuo principes cristiani. ha sui! ha sancte ecclesie! ha Cristi nimis obliti!'[41]

The *Gloss on the Psalter* refers to the Third Crusade itself:

Dum uero tempore Saladini principes nostri terram promissionis aduenerunt, gentes Machometine *effuderunt sanguinem . . . in circuitu Ierusalem*. Immo potius in circuitu Acharon, ut nomine tamen Ierusalem quodcumque castrum Syrie designetur.[42]

This work also may be assigned to the early part of Alexander's

[37] See pp. 133–4. below.

[38] L. W. and B. A. Daly, '*Summa Britonis' siue Guillelmi Britonis 'Expositiones uocabulorum Biblie'*, 2 vols. (*Thesaurus Mundi*, 15–16, Padua, 1975), pp. xxviii, 859 and ad loc.

[39] *DNR* i. 27 (pp. 80–1). Wright (pp. xiii–xiv) argued for the same date on the basis of 'Brompton's Chronicle', which is however no earlier than the fifteenth century.

[40] *In Eccles.* iii. 7 and v. 2: C, fols. 102ra, 170va.

[41] *In Eccles.* iii. 16: C, fol. 125rb-va.

[42] *GP* 78: 3 (MS Bodley 284, fol. 192rb).

monastic career. This is a fair inference from the way in which Alexander speaks of the attempts of his friends to dissuade him from entering a monastery.[43] It may be earlier than the *De naturis rerum*, because in that work, speaking of the four rivers of paradise, he says: 'De his alibi in opusculis nostris reperies'; and this may refer to the prologue to the *Gloss on the Psalter*.[44] Similarly in the *Gloss on the Psalter* he says he will not here pursue the matter of how the first hour of the second day is given to the moon, because it is not pertinent.[45] He does pursue it in the *De naturis rerum*.[46] The only definite cross-reference it contains is to one of his sermons.[47] The *Speculum speculationum* contains references to the *Gloss on the Psalter*,[48] the *De naturis rerum*,[49] the *Commentary on Proverbs*[50] and the *Commentary on the Song of Songs*.[51] The only existing manuscript, which may come from Cirencester, styles him 'magister Alexander canonicus Cirencestrie'. From this it seems reasonable to infer that he had not yet become abbot. It gives us a relative date for the commentaries *on the Song of Songs* and *on Proverbs*. The *Laus sapientie diuine* can be put just before he became abbot. In the best manuscript he is called 'canonicus';[52] and there is a reference to the death of Willelmus de Montibus, which occurred in 1213.[53]

In this last period we have one work which is dated. In the *Suppletio defectuum* of the *Laus sapientie diuine* Alexander

---

[43] See p. 9 above.

[44] *DNR* ii. 2 (p. 128): cf. MS Bodley 284, fol. iii[ra].

[45] Nolo hic prosequi quia non spectat ad propositum: *GP* 47: 1 (MS Bodley 284, fol. 118[vb]).

[46] *DNR* i. 11 (p. 48).

[47] *In finem* . . . Transmittit etiam nos in secundum aduentum . . . quod quidem in sermone composito a nobis de primo aduentu planissime disseruimus, qui sic incipit *Nox precessit* etc. [sermon 58] : *GP* 18: 1 (MS Bodley 284, fol. 30[rb]).

[48] *SS* i. 32 (**R**, fol. 20[vb]), referring to *GP* 8: 2 (MS Bodley 284, fol. 11). Alexander retracts an opinion on the tetragrammaton: see the cross-reference in an older manuscript of *GP* ad loc.—'Istud retractat in libro qui intitulatur Speculum speculationum' (**J**, fol. 6[vb] margin).

[49] *SS* iii. 5 (**R**, fol. 51[ra]), referring to *in Eccles*.

[50] *SS* iii. 81 (**R**, fol. 68[va]), referring to *CProv*.

[51] *SS* iv. 6 (**R**, fol. 78[ra]), referring to *CCant*.

[52] **P**, fol. 189[vb].

[53] *LSD* v. 837–48 (p. 460). See further H. Mackinnon, 'William de Montibus: a medieval teacher', *Essays in medieval history presented to Bertie Wilkinson*, edd. T. A. Sandquist and M. R. Powicke (Toronto, 1969), pp. 32–45, at p. 33.

says he is writing in the year in which King John died (12 October 1216) and Honorius became pope (18 July).[54] Two other works seem to belong to the same period, the *Corrogationes noui Promethei* and the *Super mulierem fortem*. In both he assumes the tone of a superior giving instruction.

The verses in praise of wine and the other miscellaneous verses were presumably composed at different times. The bulk of what has so far been found is contained at the end of the *Florilegium* and in **P**. It is here that much remains to be found. The author of the *Distinctiones monasticae* quotes some verses, most of which are only known from this source.[55] Among them is a couplet from a *Passio sancti Albani*, a work we might have expected Alexander to write. But so far this is the only trace of it.[56]

There remains the *Sacerdos ad altare*, so called by its discoverer C. H. Haskins from its opening words. Only one manuscript has been found, Caius 385, which is of the second half of the thirteenth century.[57] It contains a large collection of grammatical works, mostly, but not all, by John of Garland. The *Sacerdos ad altare* is the first piece. It has no heading or title, but begins with a list of chapters (from which one has fallen out). Each chapter of the text is followed by a gloss in a smaller and much abbreviated hand. The text is bad. The manuscript came to Caius from Roger Marchall in the fifteenth century, and at that period a list of contents was drawn up, in which the tract was attributed to John of Garland.[58] The first modern scholar to examine it seriously was Haskins, and he suggested that the true author was Alexander.[59] His conclusion has not been accepted without reserve, though no serious arguments have been brought against it. Paetow inclined to claim it for John of Garland, and Manitius treated it as strictly anonymous, not even

[54] Scripsimus hoc anno quo rex in fata Iohannes | cessit, quo fulsit Cinthius orbis apex. [And again:] Cinthius est et erat qui factus Honorius orbem | ornat et est summi summus honoris honor: *SD* ii. 1211-12, 17-18 (**P**, fol. 229rb).

[55] See p. 57 below.

[56] W. R. L. Lowe and E. F. Jacob, *Illustrations to the 'Life of St Alban'* (Oxford, 1924), p. 38 app.

[57] Pl. I, and see p. 136 below.

[58] Emden, *BRUC* 392-3.

[59] Haskins, pp. 356-76.

mentioning it among Alexander's works.[60] Haskins argued
that the style and date were both fatal to the claims of John
of Garland, but that there were various things in style and
matter to make it likely that Alexander was the author.
He showed that parts of the text were copied from passages
in the *De nominibus utensilium* and the *De naturis rerum*;
and that in the gloss there were borrowings from the *Corrogationes Promethei*. Further examination only tends to emphasize the connection of the author with the works of Alexander,
and the style is reminiscent of him. Haskins collected some
characteristic turns of phrase, but missed the anaphora of
sic in the passage: 'sic sic a regulis gramatice transeat quis ad
maximas dialectice', which is one of his most common tricks
of style.[61] Haskins also did not quite make clear the extent to
which the *Corrogationes Promethei* is used in the gloss.[62]
There are also a number of pieces from the *De naturis rerum*
in it.[63] It has always been assumed that the text and the
gloss are by the same person. This is difficult to prove, but is
pretty certainly true. Apart from the fact that Alexander's
works are used in both, the gloss is homogeneous; and the
author seems to have regarded each section of text and gloss
as a *capitulum*, since there are a few cross-references in the
following form: 'OPVS [this is the lemma], nomen indeclina-
bile ut supra in capitulo primo'.[64] There is nothing in the
gloss which is inconsistent with the date of the text.

As for the date, Haskins, arguing from the way tournaments
were referred to and the list of law books, put it before 1194,
but admitted that the line could not be drawn sharply. It is
now clear from the general chronology of the works that this
is too early. For though the exact dates of the *Corrogationes*

---

[60] L. J. Paetow, *'Morale Scolarium' of John of Garland* (University of California
Memoirs, IV. ii, Berkeley, 1927), pp. 131-2 n. 14; J. E. Sandys, *History of
Classical Scholarship* (3rd edn., Cambridge, 1921), p. 550, attributing the *SA* to
John of Garland; Manitius, iii. 12.

[61] Haskins, p. 374, lines 51-2 and n. 16.

[62] *SA*, p. 15a ('cassilide'), quoted by Haskins, p. 364 n. 38, is from *CP* on
Tobias 8: 2 (**B**, fol. 25vb).

[63] See respectively *SA*, p. 31a ('aera')/*DNR* praef. (p. 2 n.); *SA*, p. 37a ('fal-
cones')/*DNR* i. 26 (p. 77); *SA*, p. 43b ('Argus')/*DNR* i. 39 (pp. 90 f.); *SA*, p. 44a
('aues Phasidos')/*DNR* i. 42 (p. 95).

[64] *SA*, p. 25a, referring to 9b; cf. p. 11a—De talibus *dictionibus de quibus
dubitatio esse solet quo accentu sint regende* dicemus inferius capitulo 3°. The
italicized words are from *CP* I (**B**, fol. 16: Meyer 1896, p. 665).

Promethei and the *De naturis rerum* are uncertain, they fall within the period *c*.1200-4. A later date is supported by a piece of evidence in the work itself, which escaped the notice of Haskins. The *Doctrinale* is cited by name at least four times[65] and we know it was finished *c*.1199.[66] It is referred to as the *Doctrinale nouum*, a title of which I have been unable to find another instance. But fortunately the manner of quotation leaves no doubt that the references are to the work of Alexander de Villa Dei. A lower limit is fixed by the list of law books. There is no mention of the first official collection of decretals, the *Compilatio tertia* of 1210, though the student is advised to study the decretals of Alexander III, the collections of which were unofficial.[67] We may therefore put forward the first decade of the thirteenth century as the date of the *Sacerdos ad altare*. And this date seems to me the most convincing argument for the authorship of Alexander. It is surely improbable that at that time someone else would be as familiar with Alexander's works as the author of the *Sacerdos ad altare*. And it is in accordance with his habits to use his own works if he has to deal with the same subject again. In the preceding discussion we have necessarily concentrated on the points of connection with his work; and the impression may have been given that *SA* is almost a cento from his other writings. This is not so. The repetitions are considerable, but they do not affect the independence of the work.

How far Alexander revised his own works is a question that can only be decided if and when the works are edited. It was a practice common enough. There are two recensions at least of nearly all the works of Giraldus Cambrensis. One example of such a revision is too obvious to be overlooked, and is moreover of some interest. In the Jesus College

---

[65] Cetera etheroclitorum genera patent in capitulo de etheroclitis super *Doctrinale nouum* ibi, Hec tibi signabis—*SA* 23b/*Doctrinale*, 364-84; significationes [uesper, uesperus] patent in nouo Doctrinali—*SA* 26a/*Doctrinale*, 441-4; [compound nouns] patet super Doctrinale ibi, Rectos compone—*SA* 34a/*Doctrinale*, 316-20; [comparison] patet super Doctrinale nouum—*SA* 51b/*Doctrinale*, 458-98.

[66] Manitius, iii. 757.

[67] H. Kantorowicz, 'A medieval grammarian on the sources of the law', *Tijdschrift voor Rechsgeschiedenis*, xv (1936-7), 25-47.

manuscript of the *Gloss on the Psalter* (J) there are a number of marginal additions.[68] A few are simply corrections of the scribe's omissions, or rewritings of words ill-written in the text. The majority are real additions. This can be shown not only from the nature of the additions themselves, but also from the fact that none of them are found in Lambeth 61. They are all in the text in Royal 2 C. XI and in Bodley 284. There are fewer additions in the later part of the gloss, but one cannot follow the diminution in Jesus 94, because there is a large gap in the middle of the manuscript. The hand that made the additions is a striking one. It is current, but not quite like the ordinary charter hand of the day. The exaggerated top in some of the *as* and the curving round to the right of the ends of the ascenders are noteworthy. In the same manuscript the *Commentary on Proverbs* and the *Super mulierem fortem* also have some marginal additions. They are mainly in the hand of the text. The concept for them was written in the bottom margin in brown crayon. But a few are in what seems to me the same hand as that which made the additions to the *Gloss on the Psalter*. Now since the manuscript is contemporary with Alexander and was at Cirencester in the thirteenth century, as the *ex libris* shows, it would be cowardly not to suggest that these additions are written in the hand of Alexander himself.[69]

[68] See the frontispiece.

[69] Some forty manuscripts survive from Cirencester (*MLGB*, pp. 51-2). Many are of the twelfth century and have inscribed in the front the names of the abbot, the cantor and the canon who wrote them. The annotator of J has not been noticed in any of these other manuscripts.

III
THE GRAMMARIAN

THE earliest grammatical work of Alexander is the *De nominibus utensilium*, which is a list of words strung together to form sentences. It touches most sides of daily life, but is not very systematic in its arrangement. We begin with the household utensils and some foods. We pass to the traveller on foot and on horseback, his clothes and the trappings of his horse. Then comes the house and especially the bedroom with its furniture, including the perch for hawks, falcons and other birds. We return to cooking and the preparation of meat; and there is a characteristic passage on the qualities of wine, which is to be as strong as the buildings of the Cistercians and as subtle as the doctrine ('ueritatis') expounded by the school of Petit Pont.[1] The castle is described with its defences, provisions, arms and defenders; then the granary, farmyard birds and stables. We pass to weaving with its reminder of the life to come; and to the cart and chariot. The hall is next described and its roof and door. We turn to the farmer and the things he needs; then ploughing and a little on farming. Next comes the ship and its fittings with the famous reference to the use of the magnet as a guide to seamen. His words imply a needle mounted on a pivot. It is the earliest reference to the use of a compass outside China.[2] The last section is on the scribe and his tools and the jeweller and his. At the end is a short piece on 'instrumenta ecclesiastica', which may be an interpolation. The *DNV* is an elementary book designed to teach boys the Latin equivalents of many of the ordinary words of daily life. John of Garland defines his *Dictionarius* as a book which contains the words that every student is bound to keep not only in a wooden (book-)chest but in the

[1] Scheler, p. 68: for the 'subtilitas' of Petit Pont cf. John of Salisbury, *Metalogicon*, IV. ii, ed. C. C. J. Webb (Oxford, 1929), p. 167.

[2] Scheler, pp. 164-5: cf. *DNR* ii. 98 and see further E. O. von Lippmann, *Geschichte der Magnetnadel bis zur Erfindung des Kompasses (gegen 1300)* (Berlin, 1932), pp. 21-2.

cupboard of his mind ('cordis').[3] The introductory glosses, which usually accompany the *De nominibus*, nearly all speak of its 'causa' as the instruction of boys, thus making its elementary purpose plain.[4]

It is not the first medieval work of the kind. It was preceded by the *Phale tolum* of Adam de Parvo Ponte, so called from its opening words.[5] The main difference between the two is that Adam's work is largely a collection of obscure and glossematic words. Alexander's is more practical and sober. The words he gives are in the main those in common use. His house, for instance, is a real house of the time.[6] That he was satisfying a need is evident from the popularity of the book, and from the imitation of the form by John of Garland. The manuscripts that have survived are typical small school-books: rubbed, worn and much glossed. It is not possible at present to say much of its sources. Like other books of its kind the *DNV* was 'improved' by those who used it; and the two editions we possess are not based on a sufficiently wide use of the manuscripts. An examination of the words in the first section will show that most are ancient and a few purely medieval ('artaui', 'salarium', 'salsarium'). But the proportion varies. A surprising number come straight from the classical poets. Robinson Ellis noticed that lines or parts of lines from Horace, Lucan, Juvenal and even the *Ciris* and *Moretum* are embedded in it.[7] One of the staples was naturally enough Isidore's *Etymologiae*.

Though it is much later, the *Sacerdos ad altare* may be considered here.[8] For it is essentially a work of the same

[3] L. J. Paetow, *'Morale Scolarium' of John of Garland* (University of California Memoirs, IV. ii, Berkeley, 1927), p. 129, with references.

[4] It is doubtful whether Alexander wrote a gloss on the work himself. The glosses in the manuscripts seem to vary greatly, the most constant being the interlinear French glosses. For these see further *Anglo-Norman Dictionary* (London, 1983: *The Modern Humanities Research Association*), fasc. III, p. vii, articles by T. Hunt. The most systematic gloss, beginning 'Cum rerum notitia', is clearly late. The more interesting fragment in MS Oxford, Bodleian, Laud Misc. 497, (Meyer 1868, p. 298) is related to that in MS London, BL, Add. 8092, fols. 1-16.

[5] Scheler, pp. 75-93: *inc.* 'Phale t(h)olum . . . cum prospicerem . . .'

[6] T. H. Turner, *Some Account of Domestic Architecture in England* (Oxford, 1851), i. 3.

[7] R. Ellis, 'A contribution to the history of the transmission of classical literature in the middle age, from Oxford MSS', *American Journal of Philology*, x (1889), 159-62.   [8] See Haskins, cap. XVIII, and p. 136 below.

kind, only a little more advanced. Its plan has perhaps been a little obscured by the interest taken in the list of textbooks it contains. The first four chapters deal with the priest's vestments, the church and its fittings and the monastery; five to seven with the king and his court; eight to eighteen with the student and the books he should read; and nineteen to twenty with the scribe.[9] These last two chapters are presumably put here to represent the technical equipment of the student. Except for them it covers ground not dealt with in the *De nominibus*. We may say we are on a higher social level—the king sitting on his throne crowned and sceptred, his hunting-dogs and birds, the exercises and amusements of the courtiers, and the menagery. The incidents of monastic life are reflected in the directions for the care of guests. The doorkeeper must be polite and well brought up and present a cheerful countenance to visitors. Dry wood is to be used for the fire and green is to be kept for the kitchen, since it is more suitable for roasting as well-instructed cooks know. Care is to be taken that the fire does not smoke, so as not to spoil the enjoyment of the guests, 'lest they be compelled to cry whom it beseems rather to smile'. The beds are to be made up of fresh straw, 'lest troublesome fleas cause the guests to pass sleepless nights'. Its glossarial character is not quite so much on the surface as in the *De nominibus*, and it is more smoothly written. Each chapter of text is followed by a long and elaborate gloss. Chapter Two covers one column in the manuscript and is followed by thirteen pages of gloss. But this does not give the true proportion, because the gloss is in a much smaller hand and is much abbreviated. It is only to a slight extent concerned with the elucidation of the text, and is mainly a series of disquisitions on points of grammar. The sources of a good deal of these seem to be Isidore's *Etymologiae*, the *Panormia* of Osbern of Gloucester and Alexander's own *Corrogationes Promethei*.

Hauréau[10] connected the *Phale tolum* with the introduction

---

[9] Caps. 1-7, 9 and 19 are unprinted, except part of 7 in Haskins, p. 362; 8, 10-18 are in Haskins, pp. 372-6; 20 is in Haskins, p. 361, except for the last two sentences. The list of law books with their gloss (cap. 17) is printed by Kantorowicz, op. cit. (n. II. 67 above, pp. 31-7.

[10] Hauréau, *Notices*, iii. 199-216.

of new methods by the school of Petit Pont, which John of
Salisbury attacks so fiercely in his *Entheticus*:

> Incola sum modici pontis, novus auctor in arte,
> dum prius inventum glorior esse meum.[11]

Alexander was a member of this school and in this was
continuing its tradition. His whole attitude rather shows
how unfair John's attack was. There was a real dearth of
elementary treatises; and if education was to be more widely
spread, a supply of them was needed. Alexander's own account
in the *Sacerdos ad altare* is tantalizingly vague. 'After the
boy has learnt his ABC and is imbued with the other boyish
rudiments, let him then learn Donatus and that useful compendium of morals, which the common herd thinks is the
work of Cato, and let him pass from the *Eclogue* of Theodolus
to the *Eclogues* of the shepherds, first however having
read certain little books necessary for the instruction of
beginners.'[12] This covers up in a general phrase what we most
want to know. We shall see in a moment that he says his
Corrogationes Promethei are intended for the instruction of
beginners.

Our knowledge of the actual courses in the Schools at this
period is very meagre. It is difficult to know how seriously
to take the division of the seven liberal arts. Everyone refers
to it and thinks in terms of it, though in fact it was being
gradually undermined.[13] It is probable that grammar and
rhetoric were taken together rather than interrupted by logic
and dialectic. Grammar teaches one to speak correctly,
rhetoric to speak elegantly and to the point so as to persuade.[14]
In the two main textbooks, Donatus and Priscian, the figures
and tropes are included in grammar, and they had a grammatical and a rhetorical application.

Alexander's grammatical teaching is contained in the

---

[11] *Entheticus*, 49–50: ed. R. E. Pepin, 'The *Entheticus* of John of Salisbury:
a critical text', *Traditio*, xxxi (1975), 139.

[12] Haskins, p. 372, lines 5–9.

[13] G. Paré, A. Brunet, P. Tremblay, *La Renaissance du XIIe siècle: les écoles
et l'enseignement* (Paris and Ottawa, 1933), p. 101. Alexander himself describes
the seven arts in *LSD* x. 37–166.

[14] Sicut autem grammatica docet recte loqui, ita rethorica docet loqui ornate
et apposite ad persuadendum: *DNR* ii. 173 (p. 284).

Corrogationes Promethei.[15] The title of the work is fortunately fixed for us by the mention of it in the *De naturis rerum*. The many variations in the manuscripts are easily explained by the obscurity of the real title. Meyer's explanation of it as 'collections of a man condemned to idleness'[16] seems more satisfactory to us than most of the explanations given of the fancy titles so fashionable at this period. But it may be doubted whether it is the true one. For though it answers to one of the ways in which Prometheus was moralized, it is not the only moralization. He was also thought of as a person who gave men instruction in the arts. In his *Historia scholastica* Peter Comestor says that Prometheus the brother of Atlas is said first to have made men—'tum quia de rudibus doctos fecit, tum quia legitur fecisse imagines hominum'.[17] Taken in conjunction with Alexander's own description of the *Corrogationes Promethei* as 'opus nostrum rudes informans in multis',[18] this rather suggests that it means the collections of an instructor in the rudiments.

The work is divided into two parts. The first, after a chapter on grammar as an *ars*, deals with the 'figure locutionis' and the 'figure constructionis', accents and orthography. This part never was finished, at least it contains two unfulfilled promises. Talking of 'refert' at the end of the section on 'antitosis', he says he will leave it for the tractate on impersonal verbs;[19] and later on he says that, God willing, he will treat of caesuras below. But neither appears.[20] The second part sets out to explain the difficult words in the Old and New Testament; but it tends to become more and more a set of *glosule* on select passages. The beginners are sometimes forgotten as he follows up points that interest him. The work is a formal unity. In dealing with some subjects such as the accents of words, there are references from the second to the first part.[21] P. Meyer thought that the first part

[15] Meyer 1896, pp. 641–82; cf. pp. 131–3 below.

[16] Meyer 1896, p. 653.

[17] *Historia Scholastica*, 86: *MPL* cxcviii. 1124C. Cf. John of Garland, *Integumenta Ovidii*, i. 63–4, ed. F. Ghisalberti (Messina and Milan, 1933), p. 40 and app.

[18] *DNR* i. 2 (p. 16).   [19] **B**, fol. 12[rb].

[20] **B**, fol. 18[ra]. There is a very short section on caesuras in one manuscript of *CP*: Cambridge, Pembroke College, 112, fol. 67; but it is probably an interpolation.

[21] See for example *CP* on Gen. 44: 4 (**B**, fol. 20[vb]: Meyer 1896, p. 672), referring to the section on orthography (**B**, fol. 13[va]).

was meant to be *en quelque sorte* the introduction to the second. It is quite true that in commenting on the Bible no less than on the classics, tropes and figures were used and that the classical originally set the model to the biblical. Yet by this time the two were not in very close connection. The use of the theologian was not necessarily that of the grammarian; and Bede's little tract *De schematibus et tropis*[22] was more useful to the former, since all its examples were taken from the Bible.

When we speak of students of the trivium, of grammar, dialectic and rhetoric, we are apt to forget that this means students hearing set texts read and explained. As far as grammar is concerned these texts were the *Institutiones* of Priscian and the *Ars Minor* and *Barbarismus* of Donatus. The instruction was systematic in that it followed Priscian and Donatus, but in the exposition new matter might be introduced by the master at any point as he went along. There were attempts to codify the new and old. The best-known example is the *Summa super Priscianum* of Petrus Helias, written about the middle of the century.[23] But the masters continued to lecture on Priscian and to develop their own doctrines. Alexander belongs to the generation after Petrus Helias and wanted to make the learning of his day more widely available. He is not writing for those who have neared the summit of the art of grammar. For it is idle to try to help the light of the sun; he wants to teach the less-instructed ('minus instructos informari uolo').[24]

When we examine Part I of the *Corrogationes Promethei* it

---

[22] Bede, *De arte metrica*, II, i-ii: *De schematibus et tropis*, ed. C. W. Jones (*CCSL* CXXIIIA Turnhout, 1975), pp. 142-71. English manuscripts of the early thirteenth century include London, Lambeth Palace, 122, fol. 215[ra] and 199, fol. 249[ra] (both following the *Tropi* of William de Montibus), Cambridge, Corpus Christi College, 217, fols. 10[va]-11[vb], Oxford, Bodleian, Rawl. C. 22, p. 231 (excerpts). For the value of the study of tropes and figures and its current neglect see John of Salisbury, *Metalogicon*, i. 19, ed. C. C. J. Webb (Oxford, 1929), pp. 46-8.

[23] See R. W. Hunt, 'Studies on Priscian in the eleventh and twelfth centuries, I: Petrus Helias and his predecessors', *MARS* i. 2 (1943), 1-38, with references. Petrus Helias' *Summa* xvii-xviii is edited by J. E. Tolson (Cahiers de l'Institut du Moyen Âge Grec et Latin, XXVII-XXVIII, Copenhagen, 1978). For an explanation of his name see *CP* on Nahum 1: 1 (**B**, fol. 36vb): 'Naum adest qui dicitur Helchisei, s. filius, sicut dicitur Petrus Helie'.

[24] *CP* I: **B**, fol. 1rb (Meyer 1896, p. 658).

appears to be mainly lecture notes on Donatus and Priscian
worked up in a more literary form. For the 'figure locutionis'
Alexander has followed the *Barbarismus* of Donatus, taking
over the order, the elements of the definitions and most
of the examples. For the 'figure constructionis' etc. Priscian
is the basis, though he is not so slavishly followed as Donatus.
It is not easy to demonstrate the connection of the *Corrogationes Promethei* and glosses on Priscian, since only extracts
of Alexander's work are available in print and since no gloss
on Priscian has been fully edited. The only course is to
choose a few examples. The gloss on Priscian which I have
chosen for comparison is one which is derived from the
lectures of an unknown master at Paris not far in date from
Alexander's period of study there. It is the gloss which I
have called *Promisimus*.[25]

Corrogationes Promethei
Bodley 550, fol. 14ᵛᵃ⁻ᵇ

Queritur utrum dici debeat *offa*
uel *ofa*. Respondeo: regulariter
debet dici *ofa*, et est prima naturaliter correpta. Vnde Marcialis
[xii. 48. 17]: 'Me meus ad tenues
inuitet amicus ofellas. Hec michi
quam possum reddere cena placet'.
Iuuenalis   tamen   auctoritate
poetica geminauit *f* cum dicit
[ii. 33]; 'patruo similes effundet
offellas' [*rectius* effunderet offas].
Sunt tamen qui dicunt dicendum
esse *offa*, et est dictio compo-
sita, ut aiunt, et dicitur *offa*,
quia *ob*est *f*anti. In eius dictione
didiminutiuo [*sic*] *ofella* non est
nisi unum *f*.

Simile, ut aiunt, accidit in hac
dictione *mamma*, in qua sunt duo
m. In hac autem dictione *mamilla*
non est nisi unum *m*.

Promisimus
Laud lat. 67, fol. 43ᵛ (*on Priscian,*
Inst. *ii. 8*)

Obbicitur de *offa*, quod *f* in ea
geminatur, et est dictio simplex.
Quidam dicunt compositam, ex
ob et *for faris*; quia nocet fanti;
et habet duo *f* naturaliter, quamuis   tantum   unum   habeat   in
diminutiuo—scilicet *offelle* Qui
uero dicunt esse simplicem dicunt
non habere nisi unum *f* naturaliter,
quod patet in eius diminutiuo,
scilicet *ofella*, ut [Juvenal, xi.
144]: 'frustis imbutus ofelle'.
Offa producitur ut [*cf.* Juvenal,
ii. 34] 'quales effuderet offas'.
Habet ergo, ut dicunt, *f* accentua-
liter, ut possit in metro produci
—sicut *relligio, relliquias*.

²⁵ R. W. Hunt, 'Studies on Priscian in the twelfth century, II: the school of
Ralph of Beauvais', *MARS* ii (1950), 1–56.

Similiter etiam, ut aiunt, in hac dictione *nummus* geminatur *m*, sed in hac dictione *numisma* non est nisi unum *m*.

Vnde Horatius [*Ep.* II. 1. 234] : 'Retulit acceptos, regale numisma, Philippos'. Sed dicimus quoniam in utroque dictorum exemplorum errant, quia *mammillam* regulariter esset dicendum, similiter *nummisma*. Sed Horatius poetica licentia unum *m* subtraxit, sicut in hac diccione *reliquias* non esset nisi unum *l*. Virgilius tamen causa metri dixit: 'Relliquias Danaum' [*Aen.* i. 30].

ibid., fol. 19rb

Constat etiam quoniam dicendum est sincérum, non síncerum. Vnde [Hor. *Ep.* I. 2. 54] : 'Sincerum nisi uas, quodcunque infundis ace(s)cit'. Vnde sicut *occipud* dicitur quasi *occi*dua pars *capi*tis, ita *sincipud* dicitur quasi *sinc*era pars *capi*tis. Et fit compositio a *sin*, quod est con, et *(c)èra*.

Dicitur item *hic* et *hec sínceris* et *hoc síncere*, quasi *sine carie*. Est autem caries-ei putredo ligni. Vnde in Ep. ad Philippenses [1: 10] : 'Vt probetis potiora et sitis sínceres et sine offensa'.

Sed illud Virgilii in *Moreto* occurrere uidetur huic opinioni, ubi ait [41-2] : 'subsedit *sincére* foraminibusque liquatur | Emundata Ceres'. Ponitur autem ibi *sincéres* pro impura portione farine. Est igitur sincére impurum; et fit compositio a *sin*, quod est con, et *ceros*, quod est equiuocum ad purum et ad cornu. Vnde ceróma -tis dicitur unguentum ...

Qui dicunt esse compositum, dicunt non esse mirum si in primitiuo geminet *f* et non in deriuatiuo, sicut *nummus* geminat *m*, *numisma* uero non—ut 'asper quid ualeat nummus?'
Item Horatius: 'Rettulit acceptos, regale numisma, Philippos'. Similiter: 'Quem genitum manie lactauit *mamma* nouerce'. Item [Juvenal, vii. 159-60] : 'leua quod parte *mamille* | nil salit' etc.

ibid., fol. 63ra (*on Priscian*, Inst. *iv. 19*)

Sincerus a *sine* et *cera*; et est tractum a melle, quod tunc pura est cera quando est sine melle.

Hic et hec sincěris et hoc -re correpta penultima a *sine* et *carie*, quod est putredo. Quod autem sine putredine est, purum est. Tamen produci potest penultima, si fiat deriuatio a cera,

secundum quod Virgilius in *Moreto* [41-2] : 'Subsedit *sincére* forami nibusque liquatur | Emundata Ceres'. Et sic secundum diuersa componentia diuersa sortitur tempora.

The resemblances in these two passages clearly reflect the same tradition of teaching and a common stock of examples. Those in the second piece are already found in the *Summa super Priscianum* of Petrus Helias,[26] a Parisian work of the preceding generation. It is interesting to see the *questio* form in a grammatical work: 'queritur utrum', 'obicitur de', 'respondeo', 'solutio' and so on. Much work has now been done on the development of the *questio* in theology, but the writings of the artists remain to be examined.[27] It does look as if we have here the *questio* emerging from lectures on a single book. Probably it was due to the example of the theologians rather than the other way about.

The development of grammatical doctrine at this time is at present very imperfectly known. In Thurot's great treatise,[28] owing to the limitation of accessible material, no author is used between Petrus Helias and Robert Kilwardby, except the verse writers like Alexander de Villa Dei and Eberhard. But the two main tendencies are plain: the emergence of purely medieval works, mostly in verse, which gradually ousted the older books from their pride of place as the foundation of grammatical instruction; and the increasing interest in the logical aspects of grammar and in the investigation of meaning. They both appear quite early: parts of the *Doctrinale* go back to the eleventh century.[29] But the evolution is gradual. In the work of Alexander Nequam we can see these tendencies. There are many tags of grammatical verse, some of which appear in almost the same form in the *Doctrinale* and *Graecismus*. We have in the *Sacerdos ad altare* what must be some of the earliest quotations of the *Doctrinale* itself.[30] The logical bias is there too. Alexander

---

[26] Thurot, 'Notices' (n. 28 below), p. 435.

[27] See Meyer 1896, pp. 665-6. We still know very little about *questiones* in the Arts Faculty: see A. Kenny and J. Pinborg in *The Cambridge History of Later Medieval Philosophy*, ed. N. Kretzmann, A. Kenny and J. Pinborg (Cambridge, 1982), pp. 23-6.

[28] C. Thurot, 'Notices et extraits de divers manuscrits latins pour servir à l'histoire des doctrines grammaticales au Moyen Âge', *Notices et extraits des manuscrits de la Bibliothèque Impériale* (Paris, 1868), xxii. 2 (reprinted Frankfurt-am-Main, 1964 [Minerva]).

[29] S. A. Hurlbut, 'A forerunner of Alexander de Villa-Dei', *Speculum*, viii (1933), 258-63.

[30] See n. II. 65 above.

says that it is clear that grammar is an 'ars intelligendi', therefore they describe it inadequately who say that grammar is the 'ars recte scribendi et recte proferendi'. They have left out what is most important in the art. They should add 'et recte intelligendi'. He goes on to distinguish it from dialectic. Dialectic deals with truth and falsehood, grammar with congruity and incongruity.[31] His insistence on the 'recte intelligendi' shows that it had not won the universal acceptance that it had in the thirteenth century. Any attempt at placing Alexander would be premature, but it is to Paris or at any rate France[32] that he looks.

Alexander has left no works directly on rhetoric. But in his writings there are plenty of traces that he went through the mill, and there are a few incidental references to its doctrines. 'I have used the artificial rather than the natural order in treating of angels before time' he says in the *De naturis rerum*.[33] In the *Super mulierem fortem* he alludes to the well-known theory of the three styles exemplified in the *Eclogues*, *Georgics* and *Aeneid* of Virgil.[34]

One of the main exercises in rhetoric was writing verses on set themes.[35] We have a good example of this in Alexander's rendering of the first six *Fables* of Avianus in elegiac couplets.[36] As Rutherford says (though he is speaking of an earlier time, his words will apply to the Middle Ages): 'The fable was put into schoolboys' hands to be analysed, to be rewritten, to be extended, to be abbreviated, and to be turned upside down by a thousand rhetorical tricks. Given a fable, write down its moral. Given a moral, write out a fable to illustrate it. Given certain animals, compose a fable in which they act in character . . . Poor lads! Poor masters!

[31] *CP* I: **B**, fol. 2[ra] (Meyer 1896, p. 660).

[32] See the references to 'magistri . . . in partibus Galliarum' (*CP* I: **B**, fol. 18[ra]) and 'magistri . . . Parisienses' (*CP* in Tobit 8: 2: **B**, fol. 25[va]).

[33] *DNR* i. 4 (p. 29).

[34] Mantuanus uates bucolicum *carmen gracili modulatus* est *auena*; *egressus siluis uicina coegit ut quamuis auido parerent arua colono* in Georgicis. In Eneide *horrentia Martis* arma descripsit. Stilorum uero trina uarietas ethice et ethonomie et politice fideliter deseruiunt: **J**, fol. 88rb; cf. Sermon 30 (**W**, fol. 86[v]). Cf. the lines added to the *Æneid*: Mynors, p. (xii).

[35] Cf. Peter of Blois, *Ep.* 101: Scio mihi plurimum profuisse, quod cum in arte uersificatoria paruulus erudirer, praecipiente magistro mihi materiam non de *fabulis* sed de historiarum ueritate sumebam (*MPL* ccvii. 314A).

[36] See pp. 128–9 below: *Novus Avianus*.

The system flourished, and no wonder, for the boy who best caught the trick was there to fill his master's shoes when the old man slipped them off, and to add another subtlety to his definition of the μῦθος or shed new light on the traditional ἦθος of the ass.'[37] Three versions of the fable of the Eagle and the Tortoise have been preserved, headed COPIOSE, COMPENDIOSE and SUCCINCTE respectively.[38] These headings in themselves are enough to betray their school origin. We may compare Geoffrey de Vinsauf's versions of the story of the Snowchild.[39] The *Novus Esopus* probably belongs to the same category, though it may be that Alexander simply wished to give an up-to-date versification of the fables.[40] There are forty-three fables, all based on the ordinary *Romulus* except six.[41] These six present a problem. One of them, the fable of the Gnat and the Bull, is in Ademar's collection. The other five have so far been found nowhere else, though it has been thought that two of them may be of ancient origin.[42] The style is more vigorous and lively than most of Alexander's verse.

[37] W. G. Rutherford, *Babrius* (London, 1883), p. xl.

[38] *NA* ii: L. Hervieux, *Les Fabulistes latins*, iii. *Avianus et ses anciens imitateurs* (Paris, 1894), pp. 463-4.

[39] Geoffrey of Vinsauf, *Poetria Nova*, 713-17, 733-6: ed. E. Faral, *Les Arts poétiques du XIIe et du XIIIe siècle* (Bibliothèque de l'École des Hautes Études, CCXXXVIII, Paris, 1923), pp. 219-20.

[40] See p. 129 below: *Novus Esopus*. But what Alexander quotes as 'Esopus' is Galfridus Anglicus: *CNP* 678 (**P**, fol. 234rb), from Galfridus xii. 3-4, 10-11 (ed. L. Hervieux, *Les Fabulistes latins* [2nd edn., Paris, 1894], ii. 321).

[41] *Novus Aesopus*, i-xlii, is edited by Hervieux, op. cit., pp. 392-416. Nos. iii, vii, xi, xiv and xxxviii, and the fable of the Bear and its Cubs ([xliii]: see p. 129 below), are not based on 'Romulus', for whom see n. 42. For no. iii, the Gnat and the Bull, see 'Ademar', ed. G. Thiele, *Der illustrierte Aesop in der Handschrift des Ademar* (Leiden, 1905), no. 36 and pl. XI (fol. 200).

[42] G. Thiele, *Der lateinische Aesop des Romulus* (Heidelberg, 1910), pp. cxxxi-cxxxii. Nos. xi and xxxviii may be ancient.

IV

ALEXANDER'S USE AND KNOWLEDGE OF THE CLASSICS

THE discussion of the classical knowledge of any medieval author is beset with pitfalls. If the author is one intensively studied like Chaucer, much knowledge will certainly be attributed to him which he did not possess; but when the author's works are still for the most part in manuscript, obvious and important things are easily missed. There are a large number of direct quotations in Alexander and enough have been collected to make a beginning;[1] and it is to be hoped that the picture will be true in its main lines. But even one or two quotations overlooked may make a great difference.

Before we examine his actual knowledge, we must try to find out Alexander's attitude towards the classics. He uses the common phrases about the liberal arts being the hand-maid of theology. But when he talks of the liberal arts he has the sciences in mind. He is trying to guard against what he calls vain curiosity; and his words do not necessarily apply to the poets. Here there was less danger and temptation for him. No aesthetic delight was likely to lead him astray. He allows that there is much that is of use to be found in the figments of the poets,[2] and that moral instruction lies hid in their stories.[3] In the *Sacerdos ad altare* he prescribes a large number of the classics, more and less than appear in his quotations. The emphasis is there laid on the usefulness of the books. Partly in accordance with this view and partly following the fashion of the time he ornamented his writings with verses from the poets and sentences from the prose-writers of antiquity. But he would certainly have condemned any undue exaltation of them.[4]

---

[1] About 400 classical verse quotations have been noted; there are certainly others to be found.

[2] *DNR* ii. 11 (p. 134).   [3] *DNR* ii. 107 (p. 189); cf. ii. 137 (p. 217).

[4] See Sermon 31 (W, fols. 88–90ᵛ); cf. the words of Sapientia, 'Vt quid

In considering the knowledge shown in his quotations we are confronted with the question whether an author derived his knowledge of the classics from his reading of the texts themselves or from florilegia. The answer can only be that it depends on the author. It is just as wrongheaded to say that a knowledge of the classics was almost entirely derived from florilegia as it is to assume from an occasional citation of Ovid that an author had read Ovid. His citations and his methods of citing must be critically examined. It is natural to find that a compiler like Vincent of Beauvais lightens his labours by taking many of his extracts from a ready-made florilegium. But this is a simple case. In independent works where occasional citations of classical authors appear, it is much less easy to decide. Peter of Blois may derive many of his quotations from the *Policraticus* of John of Salisbury, but it would be foolish to assert that he was not well read himself. Again in every age there is a mass of current quotation. He who quotes 'There are more things in heaven and earth' may not be consciously quoting Hamlet. The difficulty in dealing with authors of the twelfth century is that we hardly know what the current quotations were, and that the contents of the florilegia have only been examined for authors whose works were not in general circulation. We know that medieval authors tended to quote pithy moral sayings and that these are the very things that the compilers of florilegia excerpt. Thus we find much agreement between the quotations of Ovid's *Metamorphoses* in Alexander and in a florilegium. But it is unjustifiable to argue from that that he derived his knowledge of the *Metamorphoses* from a florilegium. In general with an author so obviously learned as Alexander it is fair to start from the assumption that he has read the works from which he quotes; and then make limitations.[5]

The florilegium is not the only source of indirect knowledge. Another is the tags used by grammarians. Thus when we find a quotation from the *Moretum* in the *De nominibus* philosophie uestes audet quis comparare uestimentis scripture celestis? Artes liberales se gloriantur ancillas esse theologie. Quid Quintilliani flores, quid Ciceronis collores conferre presumis uenustati sermonis pagine celestis?': *CCant.* iv. 20 (**M**, fol. 124va).

utensilium, we do not necessarily conclude that Alexander knew the poem, because that passage was a regular *auctoritas* to illustrate the quantity of a word.[6] There are similar tags which belong to most subjects. No inference can be drawn from them; and the man who uses them may well be unaware of their real authorship. In the chapter on 'yle' in the *Speculum speculationum* Alexander quotes, or rather misquotes; 'ex insensibili ne credas sensile nasci'.[7] This is derived from Lucretius, ii. 188, a verse regularly cited by the twelfth-century scientists: it appears in the *Philosophia* and *Dragmaticon* of William of Conches and in Daniel of Morley.[8] It would be very surprising if William knew Lucretius; and it probably came from Priscian, *Inst.* iv. 27.[9] We shall see that Alexander's acquaintance with the Christian poets is scarcely evident. In the *Commentary on the Athanasian creed* we find: 'Vnde Prudencius—Prima petit campum dubia sub sorte duelli | pugnatura Fides'.[10] In the *Gloss on the Psalter* he quotes a line from Arator's versification of Acts.[11] Again he quotes five times the lines: 'Quo fugis Enchelade, quascumque accesseris horas, | sub Ioue semper eris'.[12] No author's name is given, but once he says 'gentilis' and twice 'poeta'. It is a fragment of the *Gigantomachia* of Claudian preserved in Jerome's *Commentary on Isaiah*.[13]

Paring off excrescences of this kind is easy when one has

---

[6] *DNV* (ed. Scheler, p. 162, lines 20–1); cf. *Moretum*, 43.

[7] *SS* iii. 9: **R**, fol. 52[vb].

[8] William of Conches, *Philosophia Mundi*, i. 21 (*MPL* clxxii. 54C); id., *Dragmaticon*, i. ed., G. Gratarolus (Strassburg, 1567; reprinted Frankfurt-am-Main, 1967), p. 28; Daniel of Morley, ed. K. Sudhoff, *Archiv f. Gesch. Naturwissensch.* viii (1918), 1–40, at p. 10. Gerald of Wales cites it as Plautus: *Speculum Ecclesiae*, i, prol. (ed. J. S. Brewer, *Giraldi Cambrensis Opera* [RS, London, 1873], iv. 3).

[9] H. Keil, *Grammatici Latini* (Leipzig, 1855), ii. 132.

[10] *CAth.* (MS London, BL, Harley 3133, fol. 93), quoting *Psychomachia*, 21–2 (ed. M. P. Cunningham [*CCSL* CXXVI, Turnhout, 1966], p. 152). This was an *auctoritas* in discussions on the priority of faith: cf. G. Englhardt, *Die Entwicklung der dogmatischen Glaubenspsychologie in der mittelalterlichen Scholastik* (*BGPM* XXX. 4–6, Münster-i.-W., 1933), pp. 405 (Simon of Tournai), 463 (Stephen Langton).

[11] *GP* 118: 25 (MS Bodley 284, fol. 253ra), quoting *De Actibus Apostolorum*, i. 408; ed. A. P. McKinlay (*CSEL* LXXII, Vienna, 1951), p. 36.

[12] *SFA* 2 (MS Canterbury Lit. B. 6, fol. 3ra); *GP* 44: 6, 67: 2 and 138: 24 (MS Bodley 284, fols. 112[va], 162[ra], 284[rb]); *in Eccles.* iv. 4 (C, fol. 144[va]).

[13] Jerome, *In Esaiam*, VIII. xxvii. 1: ed. M. Adriaen (*CCSL* LXXIII, Turnhout, 1963), p. 345, reading 'Deo' for 'Ioue'.

been fortunate enough to light on the intermediate source. It will be well to give a few instances of quotations where the intermediate source has not been found. Three times Alexander quotes together two lines on the same subject:

> Dumque sitim sedare cupit, sitis altera crescit.
> Quo plus sunt pote plus sitiuntur aque.[14]

The first line is from Ovid, *Met.* iii. 415, and the second from *Fasti*, i. 216. Quite often a line occurs several times without the mention of any author. The line of Martial, v. 42. 9— 'Quas dederis solas semper habebis opes'—is quoted seven times,[15] and the author's name is never mentioned; so that we suspect Alexander's source was not the original. We should perhaps say the same of Ovid, *Fasti*, i. 419—'Fastus inest pulchris sequiturque superbia formam'—which is quoted six times.[16] But here the author is mentioned in the *Corrogationes noui Promethei*, where Alexander puts in the margin the names of the poets from whom he borrows lines. It is hard to decide how much stress to lay on an odd phrase. Alexander was fond of the phrase 'remigio alarum'. Was he consciously imitating Vergil every time he used it? Surely not.[17] But there are examples where he may sometimes be conscious of the quotation, and sometimes not. Writing a note on Isaiah he says—

Sirene. Hec sirena. In liberalibus utimur libentius hoc nomine *sirenes*. Vnde Boetius [*DCPhil.* I, pr. i. 11] : 'Sirenes usque in exitium dulces'.[18]

The same phrase from Boethius occurs at least twice in the *Commentary on the Song of Songs* without any indication that it is a quotation.[19]

---

[14] Sermon 36 (**W**, fol. 105: order reversed); *SFA* 5 (MS Canterbury Lit. B. 6, fol. 5[va]); *DNR* ii. 116 (p. 196).

[15] Sermon 10 (**W**, fol. 27); 26 (**W**, fol. 74); *SFA* 17 (MS Canterbury Lit. B. 6, fol 20[rb]); *GP* 75: 6 (MS Bodley 284, fol. 184[rb]); *DNR* ii. 187 (p. 331); *in Eccles.* iv. 3 (**C**, fol. 144[va]); *CCant.* v. 10 (**M**, fol. 144[va]).

[16] *SFA* 12 (MS Canterbury Lit. B. 6, fol. 14[vb]); **G**, fol. 67; *DNR* i. 39, ii. 155 and ii. 183 n. (pp. 92, 247, 287); *SMF* (**J**, fol. 124[vb]); *CNP* 607 (**P**, fol. 233[vb]).

[17] *DNR* i. 23 (p. 72); i. 39 (p. 92); ii. 57 (p. 165). Similarly 'degeneres animos' (*Aen.* iv. 13) is used at *Novus Avianus* ii. 25 (L. Hervieux, *Les Fabulistes latins*, iii. *Avianus et ses anciens imitateurs* [Paris, 1894], p. 464).

[18] *CP* on Isaiah 13: 22: **B**, fol. 31[vb].

[19] *CCant.* ii. 10 and vi. 10: **M**, fols. 47[vb] and 168[ra].

There are very few instances of a quotation being attributed to the wrong author. Four times Alexander quotes the line of Boethius, *DCPhil.* v, m. i. 3 'Tigris et Euphrates uno se fonte resoluunt', and every time he attributes it to Lucan.[20] He may have found the line in a florilegium, misattributed. The other instances are rather different. They are ascriptions of medieval lines to ancient authors. Twice Martial is given

> Gaudia perpetuis compenso breuissima penis,
> talia consequitur gaudia talis amor.[21]

These lines are part of an epitaph of 'Ganymedes Chrysopolita', which is almost certainly medieval.[22] Alexander gives a line of the *Pamphilus* to Ovid: 'Arbore de dulci dulcia poma cadunt'.[23] This attribution is in two of his latest works. The line is anonymous in one of the earlier ones, the *Solatium fidelis anime*,[24] and I doubt if he really thought the *Pamphilus* was by Ovid. There is one quotation of 'Ovid' in the *Gloss on the Psalter* that I have not been able to find. It is: 'Distentos ramos auro pallere uideres'.[25]

Let us now turn to the particular authors he quotes. We will begin with that group of elementary books, of which the composition is fairly fixed.[26] They were no doubt all learned by heart. There are several quotations of the *Disticha Catonis*, but never by name. Once one is introduced by the phrase 'In puerilibus nempe rudimentis accepimus'.[27] It is noticeable that in quotations of the other books of the group which occur—the *Ecloga* of Theodulus, the *Elegies* of Maximian, the *De raptu Proserpinae* of Claudian[28]—the source is

[20] *LBV* (**G**, fol. 29); *CP* I (**B**, fol. 18rb); *CCant.* i. 16 margin (**M**, fol. 30rb); *SD* ii. 481 n. (**P**, fol. 226rb).

[21] *SFA* 4 (MS Canterbury Lit. B. 6, fol. 4va); *CNP* 509-10 (**P**, fol. 233va).

[22] Walther 7894.

[23] *Pamphilus*, 350, ed. E. Evesque in G. Cohen, *La Comédie latine en France au XIIe siècle* (Paris, 1931), ii. 207. Evesque dated the *Pamphilus* to *c.*1200; but see the quotation in *Metalogicon*, iv. 30, p. 197 [= Evesque, line 71].

[24] Attributed to Ovid in *CNP* 996 (**P**, fol. 235va) and *SD* ii. 378 (**P**, fol. 225vb). Anonymous in *SFA* 7 (MS Canterbury Lit. B. 6, fol. 8vb).

[25] *GP* 67: 14: MS Bodley 284, fol. 163va.

[26] B. L. Ullmann, 'Classical authors in certain mediaeval *florilegia*', *Classical Philology*, xxvii (1932), 38–40; M. Boas, *Disticha Catonis* (Amsterdam, 1952), pp. lxxx-lxxxiii.

[27] *CCant.* vi. 11 (**M**, fol. 170rb), quoting *Disticha Catonis*, i. 11.

[28] For example Alexander quotes Theodulus (ed. Osternacher) 13 in *DNR*

never given except when he is incorporating a line in his own verse. The *Achilleis* of Statius, often a member of the group, comes after Horace and Ovid in the list in the *Sacerdos ad altare*; and in the one quotation I have noted, it is named.[29]

For the rest it will be convenient to follow the order of the *Sacerdos ad altare*.[30] From the *Thebaid* of Statius we pass on to the *Aeneid* of Vergil, Lucan and Juvenal. All these are quoted freely, Lucan the most. Some thirty-seven passages of the *Pharsalia* are quoted, including at least one from each book. There are many quotations of the *Satires, Epistles* and *Ars Poetica* of Horace. But we have to go over into the grammatical works to find anything of the *Odes*[31] and *Epodes*.[32] The 'Elegies' of Ovid—that is the *Heroides*—the *Metamorphoses* and the *Remedium Amoris*, are often quoted. But there are more quotations from the *Ars amatoria* than from the *Remedium amoris*. Alexander also quotes from the *Fasti*, which some of his contemporaries thought should not be read.[33] The *Amores* may be included in the 'carmina amatoria'. The *Tristia* and the *Fasti* are not on the list, but are quoted from, the latter frequently. There are two quotations from the *De medicamine faciei* in the *Corrogationes noui Promethei*, which is rare.[34] Quotations from the *Bucolics* and *Georgics* are supposed not to be very common in the twelfth century. Alexander evidently enjoyed the *Georgics* and remembered the technical precepts. In the *Commentary on the Song of Songs* he says:

ii. 164 (p. 273), 44 in *GP* 29: 5 (MS Bodley 284, fol. 62vb), 323 in Sermon 18 —all anonymous—but 323 by name in *SD* ii. 430 (**P**, fol. 226ra). He quotes Maximian (ed. Petschenig) ii. 49 in *DNR* i. 51 (p. 102) and i. 133-4 by name in *CNP* 759-60 (**P**, fol. 234va). He quotes Claudian, *De raptu Proserpinae*, prol. 1-2, in *DNR* ii. 19 (p. 139).

[29] *In Eccles.* i. 5, citing *Achilleis*, i. 136-7: **C**, fol. 97rb.

[30] Haskins, pp. 372-6. At p. 372, line 14, read 'flagitium' (with the lemma of the gloss) and line 28 ? 'cocus'.

[31] See respectively *CMC* i. 1 (MS Bodleian Digby 221, fol. 37rb) and *CP* I (**B**, fol. 16vb) for *Odes*, III. xxi. 22 and I. xxiv. 1-3.

[32] *DNV* (Scheler, p. 160) alludes to *Epodes*, ii. 33.

[33] See for example Alexander of Villa Dei, *Ecclesiale*, prol. 55-6, ed. L. R. Lind (Lawrence, 1958), p. 11; cf. D. Reichling, *Das 'Doctrinale' des Alexander de Villa Dei* (Berlin, 1893), p. xxvii.

[34] *CNP* 711-14 and 729-32 (**P**, fol. 234rb) = *De medicamine faciei*, 23-6 and 45-8.

Et attende quia in uinee cultu opus est cautela discretionis, quia uitem,
si maturius putes plura sarmenta, si serius fructus plurimos consequeris,
si tamen in hac parte fidem adhibere uolueris auctoritati Palladii.[35]

He adds a note: 'Hoc ideo apponitur quia Virgilius in *Georgicis*
contrarium uelle uidetur'. The prose-writers that follow we
pass over for the moment. Martial is quoted quite freely.
The last poetical work is the tragedy ('tragediam') of Seneca.
It may be a slip for 'tragedias'. But the tragedies of Seneca
were apparently unknown in the twelfth century.[36] As far
as the poets are concerned therefore the list scarcely exag-
gerates his knowledge. And there are some authors whom he
quotes that are not mentioned in it. For as one would expect
he quotes various poems of Claudian. There is one quotation
of Terence,[37] but it is probably indirect. There are only
two quotations of Persius.

The most interesting addition is the *Appendix Vergiliana*.
We have already mentioned the grammatical citation of the
Moretum. But we can show that he had some real knowledge of
part of it. There is the curious story which he tells in the *De
naturis rerum* of his misconception of the plot of the *Culex*
before he had seen the book.[38] And there is a passage in the
Suppletio defectuum where he mentions some of the others. He
is on his favourite topic of mixing the playful with the serious:

> Demulcet fidibus crinitus Apollo canoris
>   Numina; Virgilii musa iocosa iubet
> 'Pone merum et talos, pereat qui crastina curat,
>   Mors autem uellens, uiuite, ait, uenio'.
> *Copa*, liber *Culicis*, *Est et non*, *Ver erat*, atque
>   'Iam nox hibernas' digna fauore canunt.[39]

---

[35] *CCant.* vi. 14, citing *Georgics*, ii. 362 ff.: M, fol. 175ra. The Palladius reference has not been found.

[36] 'Tragediam ipsius et declamaciones legere non erit inutile': Haskins, p. 373.
R. W. Hunt subsequently found evidence that the *Troades*, or part thereof, was
available in the first half of the thirteenth century, in England: see R. H. Rouse,
'New light on the circulation of the A-text of Seneca's Tragedies', *JWCI* xl (1977),
283–6, with references.

[37] *In Eccles*. iii. 16, citing *Eun*. 265 ('comicum illud'): C, fol. 127rb. Gerald of
Wales cites the same line: *Epp*. xxxi (ed. J. S. Brewer, *Geraldi Cambrensis Opera*
[RS, London, 1861], i. 319).

[38] *DNR* ii. 109 (pp. 190–2); cf. B. L. Ullmann, 'Classical authors in certain
mediaeval *florilegia*', *Classical Philology*, xxvii (1932), 4.

[39] *SD* i. 895–900: P, fol. 222ra.

Here we have references to the *Copa*, *Culex*, *Est et non*, *De rosis* and *Moretum*. The manuscripts of the *Appendix Vergiliana* fall into two divisions containing different poems.[40] Alexander evidently had one containing the *Culex*, *Copa*, *Moretum*, *Est et non*, *Vir bonus* and *De rosis*.

There is no mention in the *Sacerdos ad altare* of the Christian poets, which is a reflection of the way they went out of fashion in the later twelfth century. And there is little to show that Alexander knew them. One quotation of Prudentius we have already dealt with. One alleged by Pitra I have not succeeded in identifying.[41] Sedulius is quoted once in the *Corrogationes Promethei*.[42] Arator is quoted in the *Gloss on the Psalter*.[43]

The quotations in Alexander's works do not allow us to decide how far the prose works mentioned in the list represent what he had actually read. The only ones there mentioned which are freely used are Seneca's letters and Solinus, *De mirabilibus mundi*. He once quotes Valerius Maximus,[44] who is not in the list. His acquaintance with Petronius, though he knew he contained 'many things not fit to be heard', remains unproved.

In any consideration of Alexander and the classics, the legendary aspects cannot be passed over in silence, difficult and controversial as the subject is. Oriental legends, folklore, romance and faint recollection of the ancient glories of Rome are so interwoven that it is almost impossible to disentangle the skeins. Alexander was fond of setting down

---

[40] *Appendix Vergiliana*, ed. R. Ellis (Oxford Classical Texts, Oxford, 1907), p. ix.

[41] At *Clauis Melitonis*, xlv, the Latin commentators adduced by Pitra include *Distinctiones Monasticae*, lib. i: 'Et Alexander Nequam, in *Passione sancti Albini* [*sic*], "Omnimodis penis patientia pugnat inermis | Plus tamen est armis omnia posse pati"': *Spicilegium Solesmense* (Paris, 1855), ii. 319. Pitra comments: 'unum Alexandro certe in eo loco praeluxisse Prudentianum—*Maxima uirtutum Patientia pugnat inermis | Armatosque solet uincere sepe uiros*' (p. 319 n. 9). [Difficulties remain.—MG]

[42] *CP* on Heb. 1: 3: **B**, fol. 90[ra]. The passage does not appear in Sedulius' commentary on the Pauline Epistles: *MPL* ciii. 253.

[43] See n. 11 above.

[44] *CProv.* i. 1 (J, fol. 60[ra]): '*Dii boni* inquit Valerius loquens de filiis degenerantibus a meritis parentum *quas tenebras e quo lumine nasci passi estis*' (*Memorabilia*, III. v, ed. C. Kempf [Teubner, Leipzig, 1888], p. 139, reading 'fulmine').

little pieces of folklore. He gives us the first reference to the three days borrowed by February from March,[45] and an early mention of the Man in the Moon.[46] He refers to the custom of throwing relics of saints into the fire to save a town from burning.[47] Nor was he less interested in romance. He tells the story of Ogier the Dane at length.[48] He alludes to the story of the four sons of Aymon,[49] and to Charlemagne's siege of Vienne and the combat of Roland and Oliver. This last is first told in Bertran's *Girart de Vienne*, written *c*.1180.[50] He mentions Roland's tomb at Blaye.[51] His whole description of England is coloured by the fabulous figures of Geoffrey of Monmouth, and he has a list of the *Mirabilia Angliae*.[52]

It is in this setting that we should turn to his stories about classical personages. The earliest reference is in the *Corrogationes Promethei*. Commenting on the text *whose works are unsearchable* he says, 'that is owing to their number, as if he were to say: they have found so many works that the power of finding them is not given to posterity. For who can find the treasure of Octavian? Who the baths ('thermas') of Maro? the things that Aristotle hid in his tomb?'[53] The treasure of Octavian was a famous matter in the twelfth century and goes back to the story of Gerbert's search in the Campus Martius told by William of Malmesbury in that amazing burst of stories in the *Gesta regum*.[54] What

---

[45] *DNR* i. 191 (p. 348); cf. P. Meyer, 'Les jours d'emprunt d'après Alexandre Neckam', *Romania*, xxvi (1897), 98–100.

[46] *DNR* i. 14 (p. 54).

[47] Vnde minus commendabilis est consuetudo quorumdam qui reliquias sanctorum mittunt in ignem, ut sic uilla uel ciuitas ab incendio liber[ar]etur: *GP* 59: 11 (MS Bodley 284, fol. 149rb).

[48] *DNR* ii. 158 (pp. 261–4); cf. *LSD* v. 649–50 (p. 455). See Bédier, *Les Légendes épiques* (2nd edn., Paris, 1917), ii. 321–7.

[49] *DNR* ii. 184 (p. 326); cf. Bédier, op. cit. (Paris, 1921), iv. 219.

[50] *LSD* iii. 737–40 (p. 412): cf. Meyer 1896, p. 678 n. 4; and *Girart de Vienne*, xcii–clxxiv, ed. W. G. van Emden (Société des Anciens Textes Français, Paris, 1977), who dates the work *c*.1180 (pp. xxx–xxxiv).

[51] *LSD* iii. 764 (p. 413).

[52] *LSD* v. 722–86 (pp. 457–8); cf. some common material in Nennius, *Historia Britonum*, caps. 67–76.

[53] *CP* on Baruch 3: 18: **B**, fol. 33vb (Meyer 1896, p. 678).

[54] *Gesta Regum*, ii. 169–70: ed. W. Stubbs (RS, London, 1887), i. 196–201. See also *SMF*: 'Quid Octouiano [*sic*] confert thesaurus ille qui materia est fame loquacis?' (**J**, fol. 95vb).

Aristotle hid is related at length in the *De naturis rerum*:
'About to go the way of all flesh that philosopher ordered
all his more subtle writings to be laid with him in his tomb,
so that they might be of no service to his successors. And by
some natural force or artificial power, not to say by a trick
of magic, he so made his own the ground near his tomb
all round, that even in those days no one could enter it.
But why did he write works of which he envied others the
use? Some say that the place will yield before the wiles
of Antichrist and they think he will inspect the writings
placed there. As they say, his messengers will carry the secrets
of Aristotle to the sight of him who will be the idol of
abomination and desolation. But who dares to give credence
to things uncertain?'[55] No parallel has been found to this
story. In general the stories told about Aristotle are a mere
appendage of the Alexander legend. People sought to fill
up the gaps in the story of their relationship from their
imagination, just as the writers of the apocryphal Infancy
gospels invented stories about the childhood of Christ,
with no felicity. Our Alexander does not tell many of the
Alexander legends. But one of his references is interesting.
On his death-bed Alexander divided his empire among his
twelve successors. These are the twelve peers that were
attached to Alexander that his glory might not be less than
that of Charlemagne.[56]

The baths of Vergil he refers to again incidentally in the
Laus sapientie diuine.[57] But he tells other stories in the
De naturis rerum, and it is perhaps by these that he is best
known. They are introduced in the chapter on the places
where the liberal arts have flourished.[58] He begins with
Egypt and Greece and goes on to Italy. Italy is famous in
arms and in letters, witness Julius Caesar and Cicero. Happy
were the days when rulers gave themselves up to the study

[55] *DNR* ii. 189 (pp. 337–8); cf. W. Hertz, *Gesammelte Abhandlungen* (Stuttgart
and Berlin, 1905), p. 371. The story is quoted by Higden, following *DNR*, loc.
cit.: *Polychronicon*, iii. 24, ed. J. R. Lumby (RS, London, 1871), iii. 366–8.

[56] *DNR* ii. 189 (p. 338); cf. Hertz, op. cit., pp. 57–60. Another Alexander
legend mentioned is the glass diving-bell: *DNR* ii. 21 (p. 142).

[57] *LSD* iii. 271 (p. 401).

[58] *DNR* ii. 174 (pp. 309–10); cf. J. W. Spargo, *Virgil the Necromancer* (Harvard
Studies in Comparative Literature, X, Cambridge, Mass., 1934), with references,
reviewed by R. M. Dawkins in *Medium Aevum*, iv (1935), 113–22.

of philosophy. Cordova produced Seneca and Lucan. Naples was of use to Vergil. He then tells of the golden leech, the meat-market, the garden with the wall and bridge of air, and the *Saluatio Romae*. There is not a word of comment or explanation. There is no corresponding section in the *Laus sapientie diuine*. But in the lines devoted to Rome in Distinctio V he again describes the *Saluatio Romae*.[59] Here not only is there no mention of it being the work of Vergil but there are considerable discrepancies in detail, especially in the omission of the bronze horseman. Perhaps the explanation is simply that he was following a different source. The stories of Vergil suddenly appear at the end of the twelfth century. The stories themselves are mostly old and analogies with stories told about Apollonius of Tyana can be found. But it has yet to be shown how they came to Europe and why Vergil's name was attached to them.[60] It seems to me the answer is to be sought on this side of the Alps and in connection with the rise of Romance.

[59] *LSD* v. 291–314 (p. 447).
[60] Vergil is called 'philosophus': *CCant* ii. 17 (M, fol. 54[rb]). This is the old idea that all philosophy is contained in the *Aeneid*; cf. John of Salisbury, *Policraticus*, ii. 15, ed. C. C. J. Webb (Oxford, 1929), i. 90.

V

THE VERSIFIER AND STYLIST

MEDIEVAL poets rarely collected their own works, especially their minor works. Baudri de Bourgeil is an exception. The authenticity of the *Alexandreis* has never been in doubt; but it is only in recent years that the minor poems of Gautier de Châtillon have been recovered.[1] The case of Alexander is analogous. The longer poems are well established as his work; but the shorter ones are a puzzle, and the manuscript tradition gives us only partial clues. The principal manuscripts are Cambridge, University Library, Gg. 4. 42 (G: the *Florilegium*) and Paris, Bibliothèque Nationale, lat. 11867 (P). To these we should add MS Madrid, Biblioteca de Palacio, II. 468, which has not been fully examined.[2] [This manuscript belonged to Bale, who calls it 'Liber noster Oxoniensis'.[3]] According to his description it contained the *Laus sapientiae diuinae, De commendatione uini*, i–iii, *Nouus Auianus, Nouus Esopus* and an *Exhortatio ad religiosos*. Among these manuscripts there is a fair measure of agreement. The *Laus sapientie diuine*, the *Suppletio defectuum* of that work, the *Corrogationes noui Promethei*, the *De commendatione uini*, the *Nouus Auianus*, the poems to Abbot Thomas and master Ralph, with some of the miscellaneous verse, are common to G and P; and except for the miscellaneous verse there is no reason to doubt that these are Alexander's work, and that they constitute the bulk of his verse. Of the poems in only one of these manuscripts the

---

[1] K. Strecker, *Moralisch-satirische Gedichte Walters von Chatillon* (Heidelberg, 1929).

[2] For G and P see below, pp. 147 and 140–1 respectively. MS Madrid, Biblioteca de Palacio, II. 468 (s. xiv) is described by W. von Hartel 'Bibliotheca latinorum hispaniensis, VI: Privatbibliothek Sr. Majestät des Königs', *SB Vienna*, cxiii (1886), 505–6; a microfilm is now available in the Bodleian Library, Oxford. I am deeply indebted here to my colleague, Dr R. H. P. Wright.

[3] *Index Britanniae Scriptorum*, edd. R. L. Poole and M. Bateson (Oxford, 1902), pp. 26–7.

Ridmus de curia in **G** is probably genuine and the fragments in **P** after *De commendatione uini*, i–ii, also appear to be genuine.

The hymns were printed from **P** by Dreves in *Analecta Hymnica*, xlviii, nos. 275–83, but in an unsatisfactory manner. For he says that they are followed by hymns of other authors, implying that they are continuous in the manuscript and that he has kept the order of the manuscript.[4] A glance at the contents of **P** shows that the hymns are in fact in three groups, and we shall find that the order of the edition is not always that of the manuscript:

P, fol. 238[ra–rb]	*Incipiunt oraciones de sancta Maria*
	Iubileas excitent . . . (no. 275)
	Alia oracio
	Salue uirgo generosa . . . (no. 276)
	Alia oracio
	Ad pedes benignitatis . . . (no. 277)
fols. 238[va]–9[ra]	Paradisus uoluptatis . . . (no. 278).
	Hec columpna nubis lucens . . . (no. 279)
	De sancta Maria Magdalena
	Voluptatum sitim . . . (no. 284)
	Item de sancta Maria
	Magdalenes inclita . . . (no. 285)
	Item de eadem
	Cordas cordis intendamus . . . (no. 286)
	Item de eadem
	Vniuerse uota . . . (no. 287)
[fol. 239ra	Alan of Lille: *AH* lii, nos. 283–4
fol. 239[ra–rb]	Philippe de Grèves: *AH* l, nos. 363–5]
fol. 240[ra–va]	Stella maris stilla mellis . . . (no. 280)
	Gaude sacrarium . . . (no. 281)
	Letare uirginum . . . (no. 282)
	In te concipitur . . . (no. 283)

In effect Dreves attributed to Alexander all the hymns for which there were no other claimants. Apart from the hymns of Alan and Philippe the only ones known from other sources are 'Letare uirginum' (no. 282), which is found in an English manuscript,[5] and 'In te concipitur' (no. 283), of which a

---

[4] *AH* xlviii. 262–73. Dreves used **P**, which he sometimes emends unnecessarily: e.g. no. 277. 5b 'seua seuus'; no. 280. 4b 'estque'; no. 281. 4b 'merces itineris'; no. 281. 5, line 9, 'filium'; no. 283. 2b, line 4, 'uernare', 4a, line 5, 'quod'; no. 286. 5a 'feruens'.

[5] MS Cambridge, University Library, Add. 710, fol. 121[r–v]: see R. J. Hesbert, *Le Tropaire-Prosaire de Dublin* (*Monumenta Musicae Sacrae*, Rouen, 1970), pp. 174–5.

variant version is found in an Oxford manuscript.[6] Dreves's
attribution may well turn out to be right in the end.[7] The
presence of the hymns in **P** makes some sort of a case for
Alexander's authorship. The fact that they are all addressed
to Our Lady and St Mary Magdalen is in his manner. But it
is hard to prove their authenticity. The rhythmical verse of
Alexander is so fragmentary that there is no firm basis for a
stylistic argument. There are occasional phrases that remind
one of Alexander, for example the characteristic anaphora of
sic in 'sic sic regi propinare | Gaudet amor flens amare', and
'Quam felices habuit | Successus ad uota', a phrase that is
constantly on his lips.[8] But parallels are not as easy to find as
one might expect. The hymns are more restrained than his
usual addresses to Our Lady, perhaps owing to the difficulties of finding rhymes. At present, then, we cannot get
beyond a certain probability.[9]

The minor verses are summarily listed below (pp. 141-5).
A few are quoted elsewhere in Alexander's work. No. 12
figures as a 'uulgare prouerbium' in the commentary *in
Ecclesiasten*. No. 19 is quoted in the *Solatium fidelis anime*
as 'certain well-known verses which I learnt in my youth,
which pleased me then and do not displease me now'. No 17
is in the *Laus sapientie diuine*. No. 20 is a trick verse known
from other sources as an example of a line into which as
many false quantities as possible are packed. Another
fragment, otherwise unknown, is quoted in the *Speculum
speculationum*:

Notum est item quia deus ipse dicitur gratia. Vnde et de gratia memini
me dixisse—

> gratia dat gratis nature munera grata,
> dat seruat nutrit multiplicatque data.[10]

---

[6] MS Oxford, Bodleian, Digby 2 (s. xiii[2]: English), fols. 4[v]-5: printed *AH*
xx. 140.

[7] This is still the position of V. Saxer: 'Les hymnes magdaléniennes attribuées
à Philippe le Chancelier sont-elles de lui?', *Mélanges Éc. Franç. Athènes et Rome*,
lxxxviii (1976), 157-97, at pp. 172-7.

[8] Nos. 284, verse 4, and 285, verse 8.

[9] The hymn 'Splendor patris fons sol Ares | languent oculi solares' (G,
fol. 237[r-v]: not otherwise recorded) may also be by Alexander.

[10] *SS* iv. '50' (15): **R**, fol. 81vb.

More valuable are the quotations in the *Distinctiones mona-sticae*. This is an alphabetical collection of distinctiones of which extracts were printed piecemeal by Cardinal Pitra in his *Spicilegium Solesmense*, ii–iii.[11] The work is anonymous, but it is clear from internal evidence that the author was an English Cistercian, probably from one of the Lincoln-shire houses. It was probably written early in the thirteenth century. It is interesting because of the large number of medieval Latin verses that are cited as illustrations, and still more so because the name of the author is often given and credit can be attached to the attributions. There are five quotations from Alexander. One is from the poem in praise of the English (no. 5). The others are new: one is from a life of St Alban; two seem to come from the same poem attacking lawyers.[12] There are a few further traces of his verse. At the end of a thirteenth-century manuscript from Lanthony there is one couplet headed *Versus Alexandri Nequam*:

> Veruex et pueri puer alter sponsa maritus
> cultello limpha fune dolore ruunt.

The next couplet is on a similar theme by one W. Walding:

> Fur cruce furta luit ueruecis, sponsaque fune,
> ense duo pueri, tercius amne puer.

Such verses may or may not be his.[13] Once his name was attached to a line by Primas, but there was here an obvious reason for the confusion.[14]

The subjects of the poems are all-embracing. There are occasional poems, of which we could wish for more. There

[11] R. W. Hunt, 'Notes on the *Distinctiones Monasticae et Morales*', in *Liber Floridus Paul Lehmann* (St Ottilien, 1950), pp. 355–62, with references.

[12] See most conveniently MS Bodleian Library, Rawl. C. 22 (*SC* 15408), pp. 183 (at BELLVM), 192 (at CALAMVS), 210 (at LEX), 219 (at LAQVEVS).

[13] MS Oxford, Corpus Christi College, 59 (s. xiii[2]: Lanthony), fol. 120[V]: printed by C. Brown, 'A thirteenth-century manuscript from Llanthony priory', *Speculum*, iii (1928), 587–95, at 593; detailed description of this manuscript in M. T. Gibson, N. F. Palmer and D. R. Shanzer, 'The manuscripts of Alan of Lille, *Anticlaudianus* in the British Isles', *Studi Medievali*, forthcoming.

[14] MS London, BL, Royal App. 85, fol. 41[V] (margin): 'Vnde magister Alexander Nequam Si ruit ad cautem | ratis est dictura "tu autem"'. See Primas, no. 4, line 15: ed. W. Meyer, 'Die Oxforder Gedichte des Primas II', *Göttingen. Nach-richten* (1907), ii. 124.

are the remains of rhythmical poems on the shortcomings
of the age. There is a long encyclopaedic poem, the *Laus
sapientie diuine*, and a long moral poem, the *Corrogationes
noui Promethei*. With most of these we deal elsewhere,
but something must be said of the last. A short piece of it
only has been published and it is so far hardly intelligible.[15]
As for the title, Prometheus is presumably again the teacher.
He says (333-4: **P**, fol. 232vb):

> Sed scribens aliis scribo michi, disco docendo;
> sic michi, sic aliis utilis esse uolo.

The *Corrogationes noui Promethei* falls into three
main parts. The first (1-204) is an account of the way
an abbot should rule a monastery. Love should be the
guiding force. If monks have to be reproved it must be
done compassionately. The abbot must be the teacher
by precept and by example. He must not be too anxious
to fill the chests with gold. We then turn to the monks.
They have passed to a better life and must put aside all
carnal cares. They must receive those whom the spirit
moves, not only their relatives (177-8):

> Stent foris agnati cum cognatis tibi, fratres
> elige, quos sanctus *spiritus intus alit.*

They must persevere in the life they have chosen. They have
put their hands to the plough and cannot turn back. The
second part (205-1178) is an account of the vices—anger,
envy, detraction, hatred, gloom (tristicia), sloth, sleep, luxury,
lust, gluttony, drunkenness, ambition, daintiness at table, the
right measure of hospitality, excessive use of candles, display
in dress, vainglory, hypocrisy, avarice, flattery and pride.
The order is roughly governed by the way one vice is related
to another. Detraction comes of envy and envy produces
hatred. Gloom is an effect of hatred and sloth is the off-
spring of gloom. There is a wealth of examples, mainly
classical and scriptural, to illustrate each vice. On sloth there
is a dialogue in which Amphitrio tries to rouse Birria from
bed, which no doubt derives from the *Geta* of Vitalis of

---

[15] See pp. 138-9 below.

Blois.[16] Where it is appropriate, Alexander always gives a picture of the physical effects of each vice. As an example we will take anger, which is perhaps the most picturesque (231-42: **P**, fol. 232rb-va).

> Ira succensus rictus obliquat in amplos
> os, capud indignans circulat ipse suum.
> intonat ore minas, pugiles facit esse lacertos
> aut sistris ipsum ludere uelle putes.
> si res exposcit, sua brachia flectit in arcum,
> aut suram sure subicit ipse sue.
> corporis ingenui turbatur gloria forme,
> et nouus adueniens inficit ora color.
> degenerare rosas uernantes cerne genarum,
> abscedit frontes lacteus ille nitor.
> ira frequens florem cogit marcere iuuente,
> et faciem rugis exarat illa nouis.

The monks are almost entirely forgotten. Of sloth alone he says that it is particularly well known in monasteries. The frame of the third part (1179-1624) is the ages of man. But it is not used systematically. After insisting on the sordid origins of human life and the uncertainties and difficulties and disappointments of bringing up children, he describes the games of boyhood, youth and manhood—playing with tops, dicing, hunting hares and does, hawking, wrestling, chess, boar-hunting, fighting at tournaments and boxing. It ends with an elegy on the loss of youth (1515-52: **P**, fol. 237va):

> Leta iuuenta uale tibi feci, tota recessit
> etas precedens, leta iuuenta uale.
> Leta iuuenta uale, pueritia transiit, etas
> precedens abiit, leta iuuenta uale . . .

and so on, which is reminiscent of the *Apostropha ad urbem Romam*;[17] and a description of the coming of old age.

The poem has neither beginning, middle, nor end. There is no introduction, there are none of the *transitus*, or bridge-passages, which we find in the *Laus sapientie diuine*. Indeed

---

[16] Cf. *Geta*, 61-84, ed. E. Guilhou in G. Cohen, *La 'Comédie' latine en France au XIIe siècle* (Paris, 1931), i. 37. *Geta*, 46 (p. 36), is cited in *DNR* ii. 187 (p. 329) and elsewhere.

[17] *LSD* v. 325-44 (p. 448).

it is hard to see what connection there could be between the three parts as they stand. Even if we had no further evidence we should be almost bound to say it was incomplete or unfinished. Fortunately we have a little evidence, though the interpretation of it is not easy. In the *Florilegium*, besides the verse extracts, there are two extracts in prose, headed 'Ex libro qui intitulatur *Corrogationes noui Promothei*';[18] and Leland saw at Barnwell a 'Prometicus Alexandri Nequam carmine prosa intermixta'.[19] There is nothing improbable in such a work. To take books he certainly knew, Alexander had models in Martianus Capella, Boethius and Bernardus Silvestris. But it does not seem possible to reconstruct the work. For one of the prose extracts in the *Florilegium* is simply a slight amplification of a passage in the *Corrogationes Promethei*; and the other one would expect to find there also on Judges 16: 4, though in fact it is not there. The incipit given by Leland is probably part of a hexameter, but it is not among the verses we have. It is disappointing that the quotations in Ringstead's *Postilla on Proverbs* are of no help. They are all found in the verses we have in **P**. Probably Ringstead had a similar manuscript.[20] There are no chronological references. But reading the verses one has the impression that they are late. Alexander says (1025-6: **P**, fol. 235[va]):

> En me, qui cepi maturo carmine crimen
> suggillare tuum, ludere, palpo, putas.

There are a good many verses simply taken over—with acknowledgement—from classical poets,[21] a thing which is more common in the *Suppletio defectuum* than in the *Laus sapientie diuine*. In the second part some of the descriptions of the vices seem to derive from the *De naturis rerum*, though they are not strictly versifications of it. For example, the scheme of the first chapter on the envious in

---

[18] G, fols. 72[v]-3, 147[v]-8.

[19] Leland, iii. 15: 'in bibliotheca Bernwellensi' (Can. Reg.: Cambs): *inc.* 'Sponte sua genius pater . . .'

[20] See below, p. 123.

[21] The longest are *CNP* 511-16 from Ovid, *De remedio amoris*, 139-44; *CNP* 711-14, 729-32, from Ovid, *De medicamine faciei*, 23-6, 45-8; *CNP* 735-48 from Ps.-Ausonius, *De rosis*, 35-50.

the *De naturis rerum* (ii. 189: pp. 336-9) is illustrations from the Bible, illustrations from the pagans and a description of the physical manifestations of envy. The arrangement in the *Corrogationes noui Promethei* is the same, though it is shorter and less vivid. The formal resemblance of the elegy on youth to a passage in the *Laus sapientie diuine* has already been noticed. These are subjective considerations, but they incline one to put the *Corrogationes noui Promethei* after 1214.[22]

Alexander's favourite metre was the elegiac couplet. The ancients knew better than to write encyclopaedic poems in it. Each couplet is a unity in itself, and it becomes very monotonous in a long poem. It is only when dealing with the most intractable matter that he allows himself to run on from one couplet to another, for example *Suppletio defectuum*, ii. 1111-14 (**P**, fol. 228[rb]):

> Tunc facit excursum lunatio Iulia, legem
>   inmutans solitam, lucibus xter[23] enim
> quolibet annorum cicli regnauerat, at tunc
>   a numero dicto est diminuenda dies.

But the couplet became the fashion in the twelfth century. The *Aurora* of Petrus Riga with its thousands of verses is mainly written in it. But the most influential writer to use it was Matthew of Vendôme in his *Tobias*. It was he who developed the rules for the art of writing verses, and there were few after him who escaped his influence. Alexander had something to say and his subject-matter held him in check—

> Aspera sermoni plano seruire coegi
>   et clausi uictor ardua lege metri.[24]

But he seizes any opportunity for writing fine verses, if he has to touch on a conventional theme. For example he

---

[22] Raby seems inclined to assume the first part was written while Alexander was waiting for expected preferment: *A History of Christian-Latin Poetry from the beginnings to the close of the Middle Ages* (2nd edn., Oxford, 1953), p. 384.

[23] This is, of course, to be pronounced as the letter 'x'. It is only in astronomy that the device is used for numbers.

[24] *LSD* iv. 394-5 (p. 429); cf. *LSD* ii. 29-30 (p. 373).

compresses the four seasons into a couplet, which is further
adorned by a *chiasmus*:

> Colligit autumpnus quae feruens decoquit aestas,
> quae uer producit semina nutrit hiems.[25]

The fountain which changes the sex of anyone who enters it
recalls the manners of the court, and we have a set passage
(*LSD* iii. 175-86; p. 399):

> Curia magnatum uirtutum deicit artem,
>   in qua nunc uirgo, nunc puer Iphis erit,
> immutat mores, animos effeminat, orbem
>   confundit, leges abrogat, aera sitit,
> lucrum uenatur, indignos promouet, arcet
>   iura, colit fraudes, ui rapit, arte nocet.
> regnat ibi uitium quod nomen traxit ab aula,
>   liuor edax, fastus, ambitus, ira, Venus.
> spes fructus cruciat, auraeque fauor popularis
>   illam demulcet sollicitatque timor.
> Curia se curis agitat, ferit alta securis,
>   rebus securis ha! peritura furis.

The two couplets composed only of nouns and verbs are
typical, as is the pentameter made up of five nouns. The last
couplet is an *unisonus*. Such rhymes are used sparingly and for
special effect. Alexander had a fondness for trick rhymes, as
here 'se curis', 'securis' (noun) and 'securis' (adjective).[26] The
only long piece we have in hexameters is *De commendatione
uini*, Book I.[27] Here he is amusing himself and using ornamental
varieties. The first section is simply *leonini*, the second
leonini unisoni and the third and fourth *caudati* with some
unisoni. Better done is the 'Latine Rithme of the middle
times, in praise of the English Nation, with some close

---

[25] *LSD* ii. 107-8 (p. 375). Cf. the 'compendious' version in Matthew of
Vendôme, *Ars Versificatoria*, i. 108: ed. E. Faral, *Les Arts poétiques du XIIe et
du XIIIe siècle* (Bibliothèque de l'École des Hautes Études, 238, Paris, 1923),
p. 147.

[26] He uses the same rhymes in the *Ridmus de curia* (no. 48).

[27] *DCV* i. 31-2 has been ascribed to Serlo of Wilton by B. Hauréau, *Notices
et extraits de la Bibliothèque Nationale*, xxix. 2 (Paris, 1891), p. 260 n. 3, and
F. J. E. Raby, *A History of Secular Latin Poetry in the Middle Ages* (2nd edn.,
Oxford, 1957), ii. 171. The error arises from the presence of three lines of Serlo
in the margin of G (fol. 224^v): 'Et breue sit dedecus . . .', ed. J. Oberg, *Serlon
de Wilton: Poèmes latins* (Stockholm, 1965), p. 124. In P the lines have gone
(fol. 214vb), but the name 'Serlo' remains.

cautions' (no. 5), which was first printed in Camden's *Remains* without the name of the author.[28] As Camden further observed: 'Its quilted, as it were, out of shreds of divers poets, such as Scholars do call a Cento'. Here Alexander borrowed the idea of the goliardic strophe with *auctoritas*, that is to say three lines of goliardics with a quotation in the fourth. Instead we have three hexameters *caudati* and every fourth is an *auctoritas*.

We have so little of the rythmical verse that it is hardly safe to generalize. But in the fragments we have, verbal tricks and slight innovations in form seem rather to cover up an emptiness of content. No. 2 is a variant on the goliardic strophe with *auctoritas*. Strophes 1 and 3 are made up of four goliardics and an *auctoritas*, strophes 2 and 4 are made up of three goliardics and a hexameter which is not strictly an *auctoritas*. The *Ridmus de curia* (no. 48), which is mainly interesting because it is macaronic, is a bewildering variety of measures. There seems to be no attempt at correspondence. In the hymns ascribed to Alexander there is something of the same irregularity.[29]

To examine the style of an author whose works are for the most part unprinted is impossible. But it seemed worth while to make a few observations and set down one or two characteristic turns of speech. They are not necessarily peculiar to Alexander, but by their recurrence they are his. In general his style is highly coloured and very rhetorical. Leland was right when he said: 'Vsus est autem Asiatico quodam dicendi genere; nempe copioso, luculento et florido'.[30] Alexander may say that a moral treatise is better put in simple words to the absolute exclusion of rhetorical ornament.[31] He certainly did not follow this himself, at least not if rhetorical ornament is to bear an ordinary meaning.

---

[28] W. Camden, *Remains concerning Britain* (reprinted London, 1870), p. 18. See p. 142 below.

[29] In no. 13, for example, 4a and 4b do not correspond: *AH* xlviii, no. 287.

[30] J. Leland, *Commentarii de scriptoribus britannicis*, cap. CCXVIII: ed. A. Hall (Oxford, 1709), p. 241.

[31] *DNR* prol. (p. 2): 'exclusis penitus ornatus rhetorici lenociniis'.

ANADIPLOSIS

The most striking thing about his style is the extent to which he uses anadiplosis;[32] and it is for rhetorical effect. It is a figure which nearly all writers use to some extent. But if medieval writers did use it more freely than classical ones, few can have used it as much as Alexander. The commonest word doubled is *sic*, for the purpose of introducing the moralization. So in the *De naturis rerum*:

Stellarum fulgor scintillans de nocte gratum mortalibus exhibet solatium. *Sic sic* et nocte huius conuersationis uirorum, quorum opera lucent coram deo et hominibus, dulce est solatium.[33]

And again in the sermon *Quem queritis* (no. 24):

'Tunc obseruancior equi | fit populus' (Claudian, *IV Hon. Cons.* 297), cum uiderit ipsum auctorem parere sibi. *Sic sic* retorquetur os turturis ad ascellas. *Sic sic* recte dependent lingule mitre pontificalis super humeros.[34]

Verbs are not often redoubled: e.g. '*fallitur* itaque, *fallitur* decrepitus' (*DNR* i. 4, p. 32); 'sentio, sentio' (*CCant*. i. 5: M, fol. 6[va]). Most of the examples are of adverbs, adjectives and pronouns. To the same search for emphasis belongs 'certo certius est quod', as in the sermon *Venit mater* (no. 19):

Quacunque forma uerborum utamur, *certo certius est quod* iugiter nobis confert [Virgo] subsidium.[35]

DEGREES OF COMPARISON

Play on the degrees of comparison is common at the period.[36] Alexander's favourite is *felix*:

Felice sum felicior dum illum uideo quem reges optauerunt uidere et non uiderunt (*in Eccles*. iii. 9: C, fol. 104rb).

---

[32] E. Woelfflin, 'Die Gemination im Lateinischen', *Ausgewählte Schriften* (Leipzig, 1933), pp. 285–328. A fair number of examples are to be found in St Bernard, e.g. *In Cant*. viii. 9 and xi. 7: ed. J. Leclercq, *S. Bernardi Opera* (Rome, 1957), i. 41 and 59.

[33] *DNR* i. 6 (p. 37); cf. ibid., pp. 9, 37 (again), 55, 63, 72, 73, 75, 81, 82, etc.

[34] W, fol 71; cf. Sermon 22 (W, fols. 64[v], 65) and Sermon 40 (W, fol. 115). The phrase about the turtle-dove and the pendants of the mitre is a favourite: see *GP* 9: 12 and *GP* 22: 4 (MS Bodley 284, fols. 13[ra] and 41[vb]).

[35] W, fol. 56.

[36] See A. Hilka and O. Schumann, *Carmina Burana* (Heidelberg, 1930),

And again in the *Solatium fidelis anime*:

Nonne *feliciorem felicissimo* te censeres, si pedem aut brachium martiris alicuius haberes?

Finally in the sermon *Grata est* (no. (136)):

Felices illos esse censeo qui cum Christo crucifiguntur . . . *Felicibus feliciores* sunt qui in monumento iocunde tranquillitatis quiescunt . . . *Felicissimi* uero sunt qui iam resurrexere.[37]

Alexander makes comparatives out of names,[38] a thing familiar to us from Shakespeare's 'to out-Herod Herod': 'Thrasonem representaret, nisi quia Thrason Thrasonior est' (*DNR* ii. 190: p. 344).

EXCLAMATIONS

Rhetorical questions are Alexander's besetting sin. His arguments are difficult to follow because they are so full of them. Questions and exclamations are legion,[39] for example: 'o dedecus' (*DNR* ii. 124, 191), 'o pudor, o dedecus' (*DNR* ii. 121), 'o dolor, o dedecus, o morum subuersio' (*DNR* ii. 155), 'o dolor, o gemitus' (*SMF*: J, fols. 80va, 84rb). His pen runs away with him and he cannot check it:

Difficile nempe est transire a mundo ad heremum, a theatro ad claustrum, a regno ad tugurrium, a potestate ad iugum, a sericis ad sagum, a plumis ad stramentum, a carnibus ad pulmentum, a piscibus ad olera, ab inpunitate ad uerbera, a diuiciis ad pauperiem, a crapula ad abstinentiam, a luxu ad continentiam, a copia ad inopiam, a gloria ad ignominiam, a deliciis ad contumeliam.[40]

In his edition of the *De naturis rerum* Wright observes that in the manuscripts there are marginal notes 'which are the same in the different copies where they occur and which therefore belong to the book and not to any particular

ii. 54, on 35.1. Cf. *DNR* i. 10 (p. 47); and, with accusative and infinitive, *CCant.* ii. 22: 'Tunc certo certius erit uerissimum esse quod dominus in euuangelio dicit' (M, fol. 59va).

[37] G, fol. 108: cf. *CCant.* i. 7 and ii. 18 (M, fols. 13ra and 55vb); *SMF* (J, fol. 93vb); *SFA* 17 (Canterbury Lit. B. 6, fol. 20ra).

[38] Cf. Hilka and Schumann, op. cit. (n. 36 above), ii. 32, on 19.5.

[39] See for instance *DNR* ii. 173 (pp. 283-8).

[40] Sermon (130): G, fol. 62^r-v.

manuscript; indeed one or two of them bear evidence of
having come from the author himself'.[41] This is surely an
understatement. The manuscripts in which they all occur
with insignificant variations are so good and in some cases
contemporary with the author, that there can be no doubt
that all the notes come from him. Further there are notes of
the same kind in the manuscripts of the *Commentary on the
Song of Songs*, which is similar in form to the *De naturis
rerum et super Ecclesiasten*. Their disposition is the same
in the manuscripts of both works. They are put in the margin
and framed with red, red and green or red and blue, and
attached to the text by conventional signs over the word
to which they refer. Doubtless they owed their preservation
to this clear arrangement. For they survive more or less
intact in MS Oxford, Corpus Christi College, 245 (*DNR*),
which is a manuscript of the fifteenth century. In a care-
lessly written manuscript like Bodley 356 (*CCant.*) they
lose their frames and tend to 'creep' into the text;[42] but still
most survive. This is also true of the rubrics.[43] The notes are
of three sorts: the rarest give the author of a phrase or the
verse on which a phrase is based (e.g. *DNR* ii. 167, 173); the
commonest are explanations of words and phrases. The rest
are warnings to the reader that others hold different views or
are wrong: quite often generally—as 'Multi tamen in physica
sentiunt contrarium' (*DNR* ii. 153); sometimes more
particularly—as 'Anselmus cantuariensis et nonnulli alii
sentiunt contrarium' (*DNR* i. 3); or that Macrobius was
wrong about the length of the 'annus magnus' (*DNR* i. 6).
The only other works so annotated are the poems.[44] There
the notes are of the first kind.

---

[41] Wright, p. lxxvii.

[42] Compare the marginal notes in MS Balliol 39, fols. 32rb ('Dum grex . . .')
and 39vb ('sinchresis . . .'), with the corresponding passages in MS Bodley 356
(fols. 21rb and 27rb), where these notes have been absorbed into the text. On the
other hand the note in MS Balliol 39, fol. 22ra (Statius, *Thebaid*, i. 16-17),
appears in MS Bodley 356, fol. 12ra, as marginalia marked to be inserted into the
text.

[43] Two missing rubrics are noted in MS Bodley 356, fols. 7ra, 8va. The former
is supplied in the bottom margin.

[44] These notes are unfortunately not in the inferior manuscript (London,
BL, Royal 8 E. IX) from which Wright edited the *LSD*.

VI

THE SCIENTIST

ALEXANDER has long been recognized as a leading repre-
sentative of the scientific current in English thought of the late
twelfth and early thirteenth centuries.[1] His chief scientific
works, the *De naturis rerum* and the *Laus sapientie diuine*,
have long been in print, and the unpublished *Suppletio defectuum* does not add much that is really new. But scattered
among his other works there are a number of passages which
help us to gauge more accurately the extent of his knowledge.
The twelfth century was a time of great scientific revival. Its
main sources were the translations made in Spain and Italy
from the Arabic and Greek; and Alexander was one of the
first scholars in the West to combine the knowledge of the
translations of Aristotle made from both languages.[2] There
was always a considerable interval between these early
translations and their assimilation. It is not therefore surprising that Alexander had a very imperfect grasp of Aristotelian
theories. Yet, as far as he could, he was determined to follow
'our philosopher'[3] Aristotle. Apart from complaints on his
brevity and obscurity,[4] which were a stock theme, going back
to Chalcidius' *Commentary on the 'Timaeus'* and repeated
again and again in the twelfth century,[5] he has nothing but
praise, often extravagant praise for him. He calls him the
great, the most acute Aristotle, the most excellent philosopher, the guide, head and honour of the world.[6] He thinks
it superfluous to commend his genius because it is useless

[1] Thorndike, ii. 188–204.
[2] A. Birkenmajer, 'Le rôle joué par les médicins et les naturalistes dans la
reception d'Aristote au XIIe et XIIIe siècles': *Extrait de la Pologne au VIe Congrès
Internationale des Sciences Historiques, Oslo 1928* (Warsaw, 1930), p. 5.
[3] *LSD* i. 675 (p. 373).
[4] *DNR* i. 2 (p. 17); cf. *DNR* ii. 189 (p. 338).
[5] See M. Grabmann, *Mittelalterliches Geistesleben* (Munich, 1936), ii. 73 and
app.
[6] *LSD* iv. 218 (p. 425); *DNR* i. 9 (p. 46); *CCant.* i. 9 (M, fol. 16ra); *LSD* i.
299–300 (p. 364).

to help the sun with torches;[7] and he goes so far as to call him the guiding spirit of the earth.[8]

The only works of Aristotle of which Alexander has a real grasp were within the corpus of the old and new logic.[9] He frequently quotes from them both on matters of logic and dialectic and for their incidental scientific references. It seems that most of his knowledge of Aristotle's views comes from such passages. Traces of the scientific works themselves are very slight, and it is not certain that all the quotations are taken directly from them. There is a curious passage in the *Commentary on Ecclesiastes* that suggests that such works could only be studied in secret.[10] It is true that in the *Sacerdos ad altare*, after mentioning the books that make up the *Organon*, he goes on: 'Let [the student] also inspect the *Metaphysics* of Aristotle and his *De generatione et corruptione* and his book *De anima*'.[11] But we cannot point to any passage in Alexander's writings that show he used any of them. In the *Speculum speculationum* the chapter 'Quod anima humana non sit ex traduce' begins: 'Gaudeat autem philosophus sua consideratione animam sic describens, *anima est corporis organici perfectio uitam habentis in potentia*'.[12] This is the definition of the soul from the *De anima*.[13] But in the form here given it does not

---

[7] *DNR* ii. 174 (p. 309).

[8] 'Terre numen': *SD* ii. 982 (**P**, fol 228[rb]); cf. *LSD* ii. 32 (p. 374); *LSD* iii. 115 (p. 397); *SS* i. 12 (**R**, fol. 9[ra]).

[9] For the texts of the *logica uetus* and *noua* see most conveniently *Aristoteles Latinus, Codices*, i, edd. G. Lacombe *et al.* (Rome, 1939), pp. 43-9.

[10] Possunt et *uidentes per foramina* dici subtilium rerum inuestigatores acuti, qui per subtiles et tenues rimas inquirunt rerum naturas. Rectores ergo scolarum *claudunt hostia in platea* dum clandestinas lectiones paucis paucis legunt auditoribus. *In humilitate uocis molunt*, dum suppressa uoce legunt: *in Eccles.* v. 11 (**C**, fol. 182[va]: over an erasure). Alexander felt strongly on this subject—'Eos autem indignos censeo nomine doctorum, qui nec aliis prosunt, nec in se proficiunt. Cernes nonnullos sua sibi reseruare secreta usque dum pro proprie mentis arbitrio tempus nanciscantur idoneum, quo suas in medium proferant subtilitates': *in Eccles.* v. 1 (**C**, fol. 168[ra]). A few years later (1210) Aristotle's scientific writings were indeed banned in the University of Paris: B. G. Dod, 'Aristoteles Latinus', in *The Cambridge History of Later Medieval Philosophy* (Cambridge, 1982), edd. N. Kretzmann *et al.*, p. 71, with references.

[11] Haskins, p. 373: at line 40 read 'secunde' for 'secundo'.

[12] *SS* iii. 89: **R**, fol. 71[vb].

[13] C. Baeumker, 'Die Stellung des Alfred von Sareshel (Alfredus Anglicus) und seiner Schrift *De motu cordis* in der Wissenschaft des beginnenden XIII. Jahrhundert', *SB Munich*, ix (1913), 1-64, at p. 38; cf. R. de Vaux, *Notes et*

agree with any of the known translations and is nearer that in Chalcidius.[14] Hauréau stated that the *De anima* was cited in the *De nominibus utensilium*.[15] But no one else has found it since. There is a tantalizing sentence in the *Commentary on Martianus Capella*. Commenting on the word 'endelichiam', he transcribes Remigius' note and adds: 'De hac Aristoteles multa disputauit et de origine anime subtiliter inquisiuit'.[16] On the other hand there is a quotation in the *De naturis rerum* apparently taken direct from the *De celo et mundo*;[17] and in the *Speculum speculationum* there are two quotations from the *vetus ethica*, which agree pretty well with the printed version. They are introduced by the phrase: 'Damnat item theologia illud Aristotilis dicentis in *Ethica*'.[18] It has been asserted that Alexander knew the *Historia animalium* and the *De Generatione animalium*.[19] The passages refer to the torpedo-fish and the mule.[20] In both it is true that he cites Aristotle as his authority. But these works were first translated by Michael Scot probably after Alexander's death, and certainly years after the *De naturis rerum* was finished. Even if the translations had been available earlier, comparison of the nearest parallels shows that Alexander was not quoting directly or from memory. The source therefore of these passages remains to be identified.

textes sur l'avicennisme latin au confins des XIIᵉ-XIIIᵉ siècles (Bibliothèque Thomiste, XX, Paris, 1934), p. 67 n. 1.

[14] Chalcidius, *In Timaeum*, ccxxii: ed. J. H. Waszink (London and Leiden, 1962), p. 235, lines 8-9.

[15] B. Hauréau, *Histoire de la philosophie scholastique* (Paris, 1880), II. i. 63, on the basis of MS Paris, BN, lat. 15171 [presumably in the extensive gloss—MG].

[16] *CMC* ii. 213: MS Bodleian Digby 221, fol. 87vb.

[17] *DNR* i. 6 (p. 39): cf. *De caelo et mundo*, ii. 7.

[18] *Virtutes accepimus agentes prius, quemadmodum in aliis arti*bus. *Fabricantes fabri sunt et citharizantes cithariste. Sic et iusta*, inquit, *facientes iusti sumus, cast casti, fortia fortes*: *SS* iv. '50' [15] (**R**, fol. 81vb); cf. *Ethica Nichomachea*, ii. 1, ed. R. E. Gauthier (*AL* XXVI. 1-3, Leiden and Brussels, 1972), pp. 5-6. And again—'Bene igitur dicitur quoniam ex iusta comparatione [*sic*] iustus fit quis': *SS*, loc. cit. (fol. 81vb); cf. *Ethica*, ii. 3, ed. cit., p. 11.

[19] S. D. Wingate, *The Medieval Latin Versions of the Aristotelian Scientific Corpus* (London, 1931), pp. 74-5, with references.

[20] For the torpedo-fish ('narcos') see *DNR* ii. 44 (p. 156); *LSD* iii. 497-8 (p. 406). For the mule see *DNR* ii. 159 (p. 265); *LSD* ix. 191-6 (p. 490). The Latin sources for the torpedo-fish are Cicero, *De natura deorum*, ii. 50; Pliny, *Historia Naturalis*, ix. 67; Claudian, *Carmina Minora*, xlix; Isidore, *Etymologiae*, xii. 6. 45.

There are other quotations attributed to Aristotle, which are not to be found in his works. One, a rather garbled version of the well-known definition of the world (God) as a sphere whose centre is everywhere and whose circumference is nowhere, comes from the *Liber XXIV philosophorum*,[21] which he quotes elsewhere as Hermes Trismegistus.[22] The most interesting is from the Neoplatonic *Liber de causis*:

Quidam autem inani philosophia gloriantes dicunt Aristotilem dixisse, *Omne esse superius aut est superius eternitate et ante ipsam, aut est cum eternitate, aut post eternitatem et supra tempus*. Et ut dicunt: Esse quod est ante eternitatem est causa prima, quoniam est causa rei. Sed esse quod est cum eternitate est intelligentia (id est angelica natura), quoniam est esse quod secundum beatitudinem unam non patitur neque destruitur. Esse uero quod est post eternitatem et supra tempus est anima, que est in orizonte eternitatis inferius et supra tempus. Huiusmodi autem uerba reor esse minus digna commendatione quia fere heresim sapiunt.[23]

The book was translated by Gerard of Cremona, but this is one of the earliest instances of its use. Alexander's comment is noteworthy, since the book was later included in the Aristotelian corpus and was regularly read in the universities. There are several references to a *Liber de eligendis* or *Liber eligendorum*, which I have not yet identified.[24]

There is no need to underline the meagreness and uncertainty of these quotations. The question therefore arises how Alexander could be such an ardent Aristotelian. The way to an answer has been pointed by Birkenmajer in the paper already cited.[25] He has shown that the first men to

---

[21] *DNR* ii. 173 (p. 299): cf. *Liber XXIV Philosophorum*, ii, ed. C. Baeumker (*BGPM* XXV. 1-2, Münster-i.-W., 1928), p. 208.

[22] Vnde Hermes Trismegistus—Monas monadem genuit, que in se suum reflectunt ardorem: Sermon 95 (**W**, fol. 116ᵛ); cf. *Liber XXIV Philosophorum*, i, ed. cit., p. 208. See also *SS* i. 3 (**R**, fol. 6ʳᵇ): 'Hermes tamen Trimegistus ait—Monas monadem genuit in nullo differentem nisi quia monas est'.

[23] *SS* ii. 35 (**R**, fol. 31ᵛᵃ); cf. *Liber de causis*, 2, ed. R. Steele, *Opera inedita R. Baconi*, xii. 162.

[24] Vnde ut dicit philosophus *in libro de eligendis*—philosophari melius est quam ditari, et tamen egenti magis eligendum est ditari: *CP* in Phil. 1: 23 (**B**, fol. 85ᵛᵇ); cf. *SS* iii. 54 (**R**, fol. 64ᵛᵇ). Further references are: 'Vnde ut ibidem *in libro de eligendis* dicit philosophus—melior est iusticia iusto' (*SS* i. 12: **R**, fol. 9ʳᵃ); and 'Vis rationabilis legens iam *librum eligendorum* non Aristotilis calamo sed manu Sapientie scriptum' (*SMF*: **J**, fol. 94ʳᵇ).

[25] n. 2 above.

utilize the new scientific Aristotle were the medical writers of the school of Salerno, especially Urso and Maurus.[26] He drew attention to a mention of Urso hidden in the *Laus sapientie diuine*:

> Obtusus, liquidus, mundans, grauis, alteritati
> parens, diaphanus, albet ut Urso docet.
> Rumpere liuor edax, liceat mihi uera fateri
> laudassent tantum saecula prisca uirum.[27]

This is apparently the only place where Urso is mentioned by name. But I have found that long passages in the *De naturis rerum* have been taken straight from Urso's commentary on his *Aphorismi*. The changes, which are very slight, may be explained by variants in the manuscripts and by Alexander's efforts to improve the style of Urso, which is often awkward. To take an example, the first part of *DNR* ii. 98 is taken from the commentary on Aphorism 26, with very few changes.[28] Two other chapters and part of a third have been copied out from Urso;[29] and he is the source of other passages, where the borrowing is not verbal.[30] In the *De naturis rerum* Urso's *De commixtionibus elementorum* is apparently not used; but in *Laus diuine sapientie*, iv, Alexander's most systematic treatment of the theory of the elements, the examples given of things in which various elements dominate are the same and in the same order as

[26] For Urso see B. Lawn, *The Salernitan Questions* (Oxford, 1963), pp. 31–4, 217 *et passim*; for Maurus, ibid., pp. 30-1 *et passim*. M. H. Saffron has suggested that Nequam's knowledge of the *Articella* and Salernitan doctrine may derive from the Parisian lectures of Giles de Corbeil: 'Maurus of Salerno: twelfth-century *Optimus Physicus*, with his commentary on the 'Prognostics of Hippocrates', *Trans. American Philosophical Society*, NS lxii. 1 (1972), 10. I am indebted here to Piero Morpurgo.—MG.

[27] *LSD* iv. 234-7 (p. 425); reading 'mundans' from MS Cambridge, Trinity College, R. 3. 1, fol. 15rb.

[28] Compare the passage 'Rerum aliae . . . summersa aquam' (*DNR* ii. 98: pp. 181-3) with Urso's commentary on Aphorism 26, ed. R. Creutz, 'Die medizinisch-naturphilosophischen Aphorismen und Kommentare des Magister Urso Salernitanus, *Quellen u. Studien z. Geschichte der Naturwissenschaften u. d. Medizin V*. i (1936), pp. 57-8.

[29] *DNR* ii. 59 (p. 166) and ii. 79 (p. 175) both draw on Urso's commentary on Aphorism 32, ed. cit., pp. 65 and 64. *DNR* ii. 153 (pp. 236-7) draws on the commentary on Aphorism 38, pp. 68-9.

[30] Compare the following: *DNR* i. 16 (p. 56)/commentary on Aphorism 33, pp. 65-6; *DNR* ii. 4 (pp. 128-9)/commentary on Aphorism 43, p. 85.

Urso's in the *De commixtionibus elementorum*.[31] Urso's
work grew out of his medical teaching. Maurus introduced
current scientific problems into his medical works. According to Birkenmajer he started the fashion of discussing
general questions in his commentary on the *Isagoge* of
Johannitius: the book which forms the introduction to the
'ars medicinae'.[32] All the books comprised in the 'ars' are
mentioned with other more advanced works in the *Sacerdos
ad altare*; and in the *De naturis rerum* Alexander quotes from
the *Tegni* of Galen, the *De dietis uniuersalibus* of Isaac and
the *Pantegni* of Constantinus Africanus once each.[33]

The subjects discussed in the preliminary part of the
commentary on Johannitius' *Isagoge* are 'hyle', the elements
and the mingling of the elements, the humours and the
degrees.[34] These topics represent the centre of Alexander's
interests. In the *Speculum* he treats of 'hyle' at considerable
length,[35] and the theory of the elements, humours and degrees
forms the basis for the majority of his explanations. As an
example we may take his discussion on the peacock:

Cum enim [pauo] frigidae et siccae complexionis sit, grauia in eo
dominari elementa uerisimile est. Sed cum auis sit, uidetur quod leuia
elementa in ipsa predominantur. Vt enim dicit Ysaac . . . Superficies
enim leuium predominantur in auibus . . . in ambulabilibus media
leuium dominantur, ultima leuium in reptilibus; et ita preabundant
leuia elementa in omnibus [*sc.* auibus] secundum magis et minus.[36]

---

[31] *LSD* iv. 810-19 (p. 439): cf. *De commixtionibus elementorum* (MS
Cambridge, Trinity College, O. 2. 50, fols. 90vb-91ra).

[32] Birkenmajer, op. cit. (n. 2 above), pp. 4-5. See now P. O. Kristeller,
'Bartholomaeus, Musandinus and Maurus of Salerno and other early commentators of the *Articella*, with a tentative list of texts and manuscripts', *Italia Medioe-
vale e Umanistica*, xix (1976), 57-87; and (better) id., 'The school of Salerno:
its development and its contribution to the history of learning', *Bulletin of the
History of Medicine*, xvii (1945), 138-94.

[33] See respectively: *DNR* ii. 161 (p. 267), 'Ut dicit . . .'/cf. Galen, *Microtegni*,
II, de uentre, 4 (Venice, 1523: II. iii^r [= *Articella*]); *DNR* i. 39 (p. 93)/Isaac
Israeli, *De dietis uniuersalibus*, cap. xxix (Lyons, 1515), fol. lxiiia and cap. xlviii
(ibid.), fol. lxxvi; *DNR* ii. 157 (p. 257)/cf. Constantinus Africanus, *Pantegni*,
iv, practice 37 (Lyons, 1515), fol. 96.

[34] Maurus, *Super Isagogen Ioannitii*, is unpublished: see MS Paris, BN, lat.
18499, fols. 1-55 (s. xiii), ad loc.

[35] *SS* iii. 9: **R**, fols. 52va-3vb.

[36] *DNR* ii. 39 (p. 93). Alexander's text has much in common with an
anonymous 'introduction to medicine' found in MS Oxford, New College, 171,
fols. 1ra-16vb: cf. here fol. 2va, 'Dicit igitur Isaac etc.'.

The scholastic *disputatio* is often near the surface, as in the question of the crowing of the cock and the cock's comb: 'Solet queri ab iis quos agitat talis labor, quare gallus cantu suo horas distinguat. Ad hoc respondent . . . Queritur item . . . Ad hoc respondent . . . Et item . . .'[37]

Alexander certainly knew something of the earlier scientific writings of the twelfth century. One chapter of the *De naturis rerum* is taken almost verbally, again without acknowledgement, from the *Questiones naturales* of Adelard of Bath:

Quedam animalia, ut boues, cerui, capre cibum ad dentes reuocant propter defectum caloris, ut iterato comminuti facilius digerantur.

Quandoque tamen ruminationis causa est instrumentorum penuria, ut in bidentibus.

Preterea tam modici caloris sunt, ut sepum admodum melancholicorum animalium habeant.

Alia, que calidiora sunt, pinguedinem habent molliorem utpote magis decoctam, quam communi usu unctum uocant.[38]

There are other passages which recall Adelard.[39] Rather surprisingly there are no clear indications of any use of William of Conches. It may be due to chance that the order of topics of the first chapter of *De naturis rerum*, Book I, are the same as those of the *Philosophia* of William of Conches.

The bestiary was being eagerly cultivated in England at the end of the twelfth century. Gerald of Wales produced the first recension of the *Topographia hibernica* in 1188, and when it was read to Archbishop Baldwin the archbishop asked Gerald where he got the moralization of animals from. Gerald proudly answered that he had made them up himself;[40] and in every subsequent recension the number of them was increased.[41] In his *Pantheologus*, finished about the same

---

[37] *DNR* ii. 75 (p. 121).

[38] *DNR* ii. 162 (p. 268): cf. Adelard, *Quaestiones Naturales*, vii, ed. M. Müller (*BGPM*, XXXI. 2, Münster-i.-W., 1934), pp. 12–13.

[39] See respectively *DNR* ii. 76 (p. 174)/*Quaestiones Naturales*, v (ed. cit., p. 11) and *DNR* ii. 153 (p. 238)/*Quaestiones Naturales*, xxiii (ed. cit., p. 30).

[40] *De rebus a se gestis*, ii. 20: *Giraldi Cambrensis Opera*, ed. J. S. Brewer (RS, London, 1861), i. 79–80; cf. *Epistola ad capitulum herefordense*, ibid., pp. 409–10.

[41] *Giraldi Opera*, ed. cit., vol. v, p. xiii.

time, Peter of Cornwall introduced many such moraliza-
tions.[42] The illustrated bestiary was just taking on a fixed
form.[43] It was in such an atmosphere that Alexander had
to write. It would have been surprising if he had not made
some use of the work of his contemporaries, and it can
be shown that he borrowed a good deal from Gerald. The
clearest instances are the eagle and the osprey:

Aquila enim pullos suos radiis solaris fulgoris exponit, ut illos qui
irreverberata luminum acie iubar solare sustinent educat et sibi reseruet
tanquam auite nobilitatis immitatores . . . Sic sic uiros contemplatiuos
in lucis aeterne gloriam oculos considerationis et deuotionis figentes
commendat diuine benignitatis miseratio.

And again—

Aufrisius habet namque unum pedem uncis armatum unguibus, reliquus
uero natatui idoneus est. Hec igitur auis opus est nature aut ludentis
aut prodigiose aut prouide.[44]

The greater number of the chapters on animals are taken
from Isidore's *Etymologiae*, Solinus and Cassiodorus' *Variae*.
Alexander does not appear to have used Pliny's *Natural
History*. The passages taken from these authors, which are
quoted verbatim, are nearly always marked in the margin
with the author's name.[45] The borrowings from Gerald, like
those from Urso and Adelard, are not indicated. It was the
fashion only to acknowledge what one took from those who
were authorities. One story is taken from Apuleius' *De deo
Socratis*;[46] Apuleius is named. Thus in many chapters

[42] The *Pantheologus* was finished c.1189: see R. W. Hunt, 'The disputation
of Peter of Cornwall against Simon the Jew', in *Essays presented to F. M. Powicke*,
edd. R. W. Hunt *et al.* (Oxford, 1948), p. 144 and app.; and id., 'English learning
in the late twelfth century', *TRHS*, 4th ser., xix (1936), 19–42, at 33–4 and 38–42.

[43] M. R. James, *The Bestiary* (Roxburghe Club, Oxford, 1928).

[44] For the eagle see *DNR* i. 23 (pp. 71–2)/*Topographia Hibernica*, i. 13
(ed. cit., v. 39); for the osprey [aurifrisius] *DNR* i. 58 (p. 108)/*Topographia
Hibernica*, i. 16 (ed. cit., v. 49). Alexander will then have his information about
the barnacle from Gerald. The question is not decided by E. Heron-Allen, *Barnacles
in Myth and Nature* (Oxford, 1928).

[45] See respectively *DNR* ii. 151 (p. 232)/Solinus, 27. 23–5; *DNR* i. 65 (p. 114)/
Isidore, *Etymologiae*, xii. 7. 16; *DNR* ii. 72 (p. 171)/*Etymologiae*, xvii. 8. 14;
DNR ii. 105 (p. 187)/*Etymologiae*, xii. 4. 10; *DNR* ii. 114–19 (pp. 194–8:
serpents, quoting Lucan)/*Etymologiae*, xii. 4; *DNR* ii. 133 (p. 215)/*Etymologiae*,
xii. 2. 9.

[46] *DNR* ii. 126 (p. 206); cf. *De deo Socratis*, prol. iv, ed. P. Thomas (Teubner,
Leipzig, 1908), pp. 3–4.

Alexander is using the same sources as the *Bestiary*, but in a more critical spirit. The *Physiologus* itself he does not appear to use. None of the more fantastic animals are given, and where they overlap Alexander often attacks some of the errors. It is probably the *Physiologus* or its derivatives that he has in mind when he says of the weasel: 'Falso autem opinantur qui dicunt mustelam ore concipere, aure effundere partum'.[47] And where the *Physiologus* says that the weasel can bring its young to life again he tones the statement down: 'Tantum autem habet herbarum medicinalium delectum, ut foetus suos reanimare ab imperitis putetur; sed reuera ipsis mederi nouit, etiam cum fere usque ad mortem lesi sunt'.[48] Many of the most interesting stories, as that of the escape of the knight's parrot,[49] are apparently his own. The time has not yet come for a final statement of Alexander's indebtedness here. In particular no one has attempted to see how much may be the fruit of his own observation. It has been shown recently that Gerald and the author of *The Owl and the Nightingale* derived much more than is commonly allowed from personal observation.[50] The same will probably be true of Alexander—'Dum uisu recreor studium commendo potentis | nature, que tam nobile finxit opus'.[51]

We cannot here deal with all of Alexander's scientific interests. To do so one would have to be endowed with the same encyclopaedic turn as Alexander himself.[52] But we must say something about his knowledge of astronomy. To the reader of the *De naturis rerum* it appears to be a number of disjointed facts, which are repeated more than once, such

---

[47] *DNR* ii. 123 (p. 201); cf. *The Bestiary* (n. 43 above), fol. 28^{r-v}. See also *LSD* ix. 175-8 (p. 490).

[48] *DNR* ii. 123 (p. 201). Compare his treatment of the beaver and its hunters: *DNR* ii. 140 (pp. 220-1); contrast *The Bestiary* (n. 43 above), fol. 8^v.

[49] *DNR* i. 37 (p. 89).

[50] U. T. Holmes, 'Gerald the Naturalist', *Speculum*, xi (1936), 110-21, with references. See now R. Bartlett, *Gerald of Wales* (Oxford, 1982), pp. 133-44.

[51] *SD* i. 549: **P**, fol. 220vb.

[52] For the section on jewels—*DNR* ii. 85-97 (pp. 177-81) and *LSD* vi. 129-324 (pp. 466-71)—see J. Evans, *Magical Jewels of the Middle Ages and the Renaissance* (Oxford, 1922), pp. 61-3; cf. C. Meier, *Gemma Spiritalis: Methode und Gebrauch der Edelsteinallegorese vom frühen Christentum bis ins 18. Jahrhundert*, II. iv (Münstersche Mittelalter-Schriften: forthcoming). In the section on herbs the order of Macer, *De uiribus herbarum*, is followed with scarcely a change: ed. L. Choulant (Leipzig, 1832), pp. 28-123.

as: the sun is a hundred and sixty-times and a fraction larger than the earth.[53] The list of books given in the *Sacerdos ad altare* is not impressive. He only mentions the *Canons* of Ptolemy and Alfraganus' compendium of Ptolemy, which was translated early in the twelfth century.[54] He quotes Alfraganus once in the *De naturis rerum* and the same quotation occurs twice in the *Gloss on the Psalter*.[55] We find the sentence, 'circulus solaris circulus est egresse cuspidis', which probably comes from the same work.[56] More knowledge is to be found in the *Suppletio defectuum*, of which we shall speak shortly, but the elegiac couplet makes an extraordinarily obscure vehicle for conveying information on the subject. At the end of the section on planets and equinoxes Alexander mentions an author whom I have not yet succeeded in identifying. He says:

> Si predicta legis uigilanter habes Heremannum
> carminis auctorem iudiciique mei.[57]

There are two Hermanns, who wrote or translated astronomical works, Hermannus Contractus, a monk at Reichenau (1013-54),[58] and Hermann of Carinthia (*fl.* 1140).[59] But neither of these authors, to judge from their works so far identified, is referred to here. Like Roger Bacon Alexander criticized some of the calculations used in the computus, in particular an error in the calculation of the rise of the moon—'Future ages will groan for it':

> Nondum causa tamen in lucem prodiit unde
> sit quod ab accensu tercia prima datur.
> Aures demulcet responsio, que prothoplasti
> attendit uisum, fictio uana nimis.

[53] *DNR* i. 8 (p. 44); ii, prol. (p. 126); *SS* ii. 50 (R, fol. 41ra).

[54] Haskins, p. 374, lines 56-8.

[55] *DNR* ii. 49 (p. 159), from Alfraganus, *Breuis ac perutilis compilatio* (Ferrara, 1493; Hain 823), differentia iii: 'quod terra cum uniuersis partibus suis tam terrestribus quam marinis sit ad instar sphere'. Cf. *GP* 23: 2 and 135: 6 (MS Bodley 284, fols. 43va and 277va).

[56] *DNR* i. 13 (p. 51). Cf. Alfraganus: 'Vnusquisque autem egresse circulorum cuspidis uocatur circulus egresse cuspidis' (ed. cit., differentia xii). See further A. Birkenmajer, *Vermischte Untersuchungen* (*BGPM* XX. 5, Münster-i.-W., 1922), pp. 215-16.

[57] *SD* ii. 1251-2: P, fol. 229rb.

[58] Manitius, ii. 756-78.   [59] Haskins, cap. III.

A coitu distat nonnumquam quarta relucens,
    immo quinta, tamen prima notatur ibi.
Obliquus liber est ortus, casus celer eius
    sub radiis, trina Cinthia luce latet.
Sic fit ut a coitu uideat iam quinta recedens,
    cum uulgi primam censeat error eam.
En iam uulgaris manifeste compotus errat:
    hunc cur errorem non reuocare student?
Terminus id paschalis agit, ne forte uacillet
    inmutatus: ob hoc secla futura gement.
Vrgens articulus hunc errorem reuocabit,
    o utinam ueri cogeret istud amor.[60]

On astrology Alexander is cautious.[61] The seven planets have an influence on things below, which is given them by God. But they do not drive the free will into the necessity of doing this or that. For if it were so the will would not be free, and sin would have to be imputed not to the soul but to the operation of a necessary law of higher bodies. So when Saturn is in Aquarius floods occur, provided that no other planet hinders them, if it pleases the divine will.[62] In the *Laus sapientie diuine* this is simply paraphrased.[63] But in the *Suppletio* various practices connected with astrology are sharply condemned:

Zoile decanos et apotelesmata linquo,
    catholice fidei queque nociua fuge.
Seruiat anticiis oroscopus, at michi numquam,
    et que uicina est infera porta pigro.[64]

THE *LAVS SAPIENTIE DIVINE*

Wright called the *Laus sapientie diuine* 'a metrical paraphrase of the treatise *De naturis rerum*, with some considerable additions, and with the omission of most of the stories'.[65] This is true as far as it goes. There is the same underlying

[60] *SD* ii. 827-42: **P**, fol. 227va-vb. Cf. R. Steele, *Opera hactenus inedita Rogeri Baconi*, vi (Oxford, 1926), pp. xix-xx.

[61] Thorndike, ii. 202-3; cf. T. O. Wedel, *The Mediaeval Attitude toward Astrology* (Yale Studies in English, LX, New Haven, 1920), pp. 62-3.

[62] *DNR* i. 7 (pp. 39-40).

[63] *LSD* i. 466-71 (p. 368).

[64] *SD* ii. 1375-8: **P**, fol. 229vb. There is a note on *pigro*: 'piger est particula gradus seruiens Saturno' (fol. 229vb).

[65] Wright, p. lxxv. For Wright's division of *LSD* into ten *distinctiones* rather than seven see Appendix A.

theme that examination of the works of nature leads on to the love of God. Alexander begins and ends with the love and fear of God.[66] But it is more systematic, more scientific in the sense that moralization plays a less important part, and on the whole better proportioned. Subjects which are scarcely opened up in the *De naturis rerum* are treated more fully. In *distinctio* i the stars are enumerated. In *distinctio* iii there is an account of the principal rivers of Europe. *Distinctio* iv is quite new and contains a fuller treatment of various aspects of the theory of the elements than any other of his works. *Distinctio* v is also new. Alexander says he will describe the three parts of the earth: Europe, Libya and Asia. But it is rather a leisurely progress from Rome to England through France with a side-glance at Cologne and Pannonia (v. 429-38). He lists the saints or famous men buried in or connected with each place. In *distinctio* vi the number of precious stones and herbs and trees is much enlarged. In *distinctio* vii the description of the seven liberal arts is shorter and almost independent.

THE *SUPPLETIO DEFECTUUM*

The *Suppletio defectuum* of the *Laus sapientie diuine* has two divisions of 1456 and 1796 lines.[67] The first is called a *capitulum* and the second a *distinctio*. In each of them he defines its relationship to the *Laus sapientie diuine*:

SD i   Laudes namque tuas alio, Sapiencia, scripsi
                   carmine, quod lector huic sociare potest.
               Quosdam defectus illius carminis istud
                   suplebit; summe seruit utrumque Noy.
               Defectus agnosco meos, quos carmine prudens
                   supleo presenti: prodeat istud opus,
               prodeat in lucem, quasi lucis opus: tenebrosas
                   iam didicit liuor Ditis adire fores:
               Inclusus numquam superas euadat ad auras,
                   ne cinice nostrum rodere possit opus.[68]

SD ii   Precinui stellas, mare, fontes, flumina, pisces
                   et prolem capitis, seua Medusa, tui;

[66] *LSD* i. 1–68 (pp. 357–8) and x. 197–278 (pp. 500–2).
[67] **P**, fols. 218va–24rb; 224rb–31va.
[68] *SD* i. 559–68: **P**, fol. 220vb.

urbes descripsi cum gentis moribus, et quas
  prospiciens nobis terra recondit opes.
Quod diuina tibi seruit sapientia carmen
  explicat ista, tamen addere plura libet.
carminis illius suplecio, parue libelle,
  diceris, cuius assecla fidus eris.[69]

The first division mainly covers ground once or twice trodden. The order is different from that of the *Laus sapientie diuine*, which is based on the order of the four elements. After a short introductory section in praise of divine wisdom (1-34) Alexander comments on the habits of birds (35-176). There follow descriptions of various trees (177-260), herbs (261-586), birds (587-928) and animals (929-1456). Each tree or plant has a couplet, occasionally two or three. He repeats or slightly amplifies what he has said before. Thus of the ash—'fraxinus apta | bellis humano laeta cruore madet' becomes 'fraxinus artificis manibus parere parata | quem sitit humano tincta cruore madet'.[70] For the birds and animals the 'facts' are the same, but a new moral is given or one supplied if it was lacking. In the *Laus sapientie diuine* the 'fact' that the eagle exposes its young to the rays of the sun is related without a moral. Here it is moralized:

Solares radios prolem que ferre recusat,
  tanquam degenerem regia spernit auis.
Ne cernas uerum si claudis lumina mentis
  celestis quod agis gratia spernet opus.[71]

There are a few additional birds and animals, including the hoopoe (*SD* i. 819-35), which is followed by the passage in praise of Alexander's mother, the hedgehog (1071-89), the pig (1091-4), the porcupine (1097-1112), the snail and the beetle (1183-8) and some material taken from Bernardus Silvestris (1221-31). All this part is of little interest. The only relief is the fable of the mouse's search for a wife, told in a mock-heroic style (1321-1418). The mouse approaches in turn the sun, the clouds, the wind, the rain,

---

[69] *SD* ii. 1-8: **P**, fol. 224[rb].
[70] *LSD* viii. 53-4 (p. 482); *SD* i. 227-8 (**P**, fol. 219[va]). In the same way Alexander reworks his account of the orach: *LSD* vii. 173-6 (p. 476); cf. *SD* i. 375-8 (**P**, fol. 220[ra]).
[71] *SD* i. 593-6 (**P**, fol. 221[ra]): cf. *LSD* ii. 165-8 (p. 377).

the earth. They all politely refuse and finally earth gives judgement that like should marry like, in accordance with Naso's teaching.

The second part of the *Suppletio defectuum* begins with a short section on the work of creation (ii. 17–76), and then various problems about man are discussed: his faculties, especially the 'spiritus rationalis' (ii. 77), the junction of body and soul in our first parents (247), the immortality and simplicity of the soul (309), original sin (369) and what would have happened if the desire to eat the forbidden fruit had not been indulged—a typical run of questions without answers. Thus:

> Constat quod culpa est letalis praua uoluntas
> et quod debetur pena perhennis ei.
> Esto quod affectus numquam prodiret in actum
> esus illiciti, mens moreretur? Ita.
> Nam mors est anime cum uite uita recedit;
> mens corrupta foret, numquid et ipsa caro?
> Numquid posteritas obnoxia tota maneret
> culpe? Num fieret quam modo culpa minor?
> Quid si stante uiro cecidisset sola uirago?
> Num proles misere digna perire foret?
> Num soboles letum communi iure subiret;
> an legum mortis nescia rite foret?[72]

We pass on immediately to a description of paradise (429–530). Then comes the astronomical section (531–1378), whether the moon was new or full when it was created (531–646), the eclipse of the sun and moon (647–706), various questions on the computus and reckonings of time, in which are incorporated the verses already used in the *De naturis rerum* (i. 11–12, 707–926). Alexander goes on to the planets and their movements, the signs of the Zodiac (927–1141), the equinox (1142–1288) and various questions on the moon (1289–1378). The last section is on theology and the seven liberal arts (1379–1796). It is in the form of an allegory. Unfortunately it is unfinished, breaking off in the middle of Rhetoric. This second part of the *Suppletio defectuum* deserves to be printed.

Great as was Alexander's interest in scientific questions, it was only one among his many interests, and none of his

[72] *SD* ii. 417–28: **P**, fol. 226ra.

works is entirely devoted to them. The *De naturis rerum* is in form an introduction to his *Commentary on Ecclesiastes*.[73] It fills the first two of the five books that make up the commentary. The explanation is given by a passage in the proem to the *Commentary on Proverbs*, itself obscure at first sight:

Considerationi igitur reciproce: qua quis sue conditionis statum attendit, se debet LIBER PARABOLORUM; considerationi uanitatum mundanarum obnoxius est ECCLESIASTES; contemplationi diuine obsequitur LIBER CANTICORUM.

(i) Clamat Idida quia *inicium sapiencie timor domini*; (ii) concionatur Ecclesiastes dicens *uanitas uanitatum uanitas uanitatum et omnia uanitas*; (iii) suspirat ad pacis delicias Salomon inquiens *osculetur me osculo oris sui*.

Idida, id est 'dilectus eris a domino', per humilitatem, que et sui contemptorem esse hominem docet et timorem discretum adducit.

Concionatoris nomen conferent tibi prudentia et spes et temperantia. Prudentia nimirum naturas rerum transitoriarum inuestigans eas esse uanitatibus obnoxias comprehendit. Spes manu desiderii deum ipsum iam tenens omnia preter deum uanitati multiplici subiecta esse prefitetur. Temperantia modicum esse quod nature sat est perpendens rerum amorem temporalium abiciendum esse nouit.

Amor sanctus et deuotio osculo et amplexibus dilecti deliciantur.

Triplici igitur considerationi tria trinomii Salomonis opera sunt obnoxia.[74]

Alexander is referring to the ancient threefold division of knowledge, which was taken up by Origen and applied to the three books of Solomon.[75] Proverbs represents *ethica*, Ecclesiastes *physica* and the Song of Songs *inspectiua*. From Origen it passed to Jerome and from him to Isidore.[76] In the twelfth century it is often found in the divisions of knowledge.[77]

---

[73] Antequam igitur Ecclesiasten aggrediar, libet de nonnullis uanitatum speciebus mentionem facere: *DNR* ii. 173 (p. 307).

[74] *CProv.*, prol.: J, fol. 58va.

[75] Origen, *in Cant. Cant.* prol.: *MPG* xiii. 74AB.

[76] Jerome, *in Eccles.* i. 1 (*MPL* xxiii. 1012C) and *Ep.* 30 (ed. I. Hilberg, [*CSEL* LIV, Vienna, 1910], p. 243); Isidore, *Etymologiae*, ii. 24. 8.

[77] For example Hugh of St Victor, *Homilies on Ecclesiastes*, i (*MPL* clxxv. 116B), and the anonymous introduction to a commentary on the Song of Songs in MS London, BL, Royal 2 C. XII, fol. 3rb. See further B. Bischoff, 'Eine verschollene Einteilung der Wissenschaften', in *Mittelalterliche Studien* (Stuttgart, 1966), i. 273–88, with references.

In the preface to the *De naturis rerum* Alexander is careful
to warn the reader not to expect a philosophical or scientific
treatise on the nature of things. He intends to write a moral
treatise. 'Therefore I leave the golden chain of Homer to others.
I call men to the liberty of which it is said in the gospel,
If the Son shall make you free, ye shall be free indeed.'[78] He
is a canon regular writing primarily for his fellow religious.[79]
He stops himself from touching on things in astronomy
which would not be familiar to everybody. If he did not,
he would seem to be showing off his smattering of scientific
knowledge ('ostentator scientole mee') or breaking the
promise made at the beginning.[80] That he did not always
succeed in restraining himself must be clear from what has
already been said of his sources. Many of his readers would
have been profoundly shocked if they had realized the
implications of his love for Aristotle. But the pill had a sugary
coating, which has misled modern as it must have soothed
medieval readers. It would have been better for his fame if he
had restrained himself less. But then he would not have been
Alexander. For his approach to knowledge ('scientia') was a
moral one; yet in his treatment of it it is the scientist, the
man who investigates the nature of things, whom he has in
mind. The love of knowledge is naturally implanted in the
human mind. Hence it aspires to an understanding of it.
It seeks out the causes of things, and by induction aims at
reducing nature to art.[81] It is the moral rather than the
intellectual dangers that Alexander emphasizes. He is no
anti-dialectician.[82] As our knowledge advances, vainglory so

---

[78] *DNR*, praef. (p. 3); cf. John 8: 36. According to Alexander's interpretation
the golden chain (*Iliad*, viii. 19) is 'philosophica eruditio'. Contrast Macrobius,
In 'Somnium Scipionis' i. 14. 15, ed. J. Willis (Teubner, Leipzig, 1970), p. 58, and
Bernardus Silvester, *De mundi uniuersitate*, II. vii. 1, ed. P. Dronke (Leiden,
1978), p. 134. Nearer to Alexander is Isaac de Stella, *De anima: MPL* cxciv. 1885C.

[79] Nolo scripto commendare quid sit fellare, propter iuniores: *DNR* i. 61
(p. 111 app.); cf. i. 3 (p. 21), i. 5 (p. 36), ii. 36 (pp. 149-50), ii. 154 (p. 240).

[80] *DNR* i. 5 (p. 36); cf. i. 13 (p. 51) and 15 (p. 65).

[81] Amor igitur scientie naturaliter animo humano insitus est, unde ad eius
comprehensionem suspirat. Inquirit ergo rerum causas [*cod.* curas] et per multo-
rum similium inductionem naturam in artem transferre studet: *in Eccles.* iii.
10 (**C**, fol. 106^{ra-rb}).

[82] Absit autem ut subtiles inquisitiones dialecticorum ad electionem ueri et
fugam falsi tendentes reprehendamus. Sed nugas cauillatorias quis maturi pectoris
commendet?: *CCant.* i. 8 (**M**, fol. 13va).

easily creeps in and brings with it a train of vices. The search can only be justified if it is undertaken in the service of God and man. It must be kept within due bounds. There are some questions which it is not proper to ask, as why fire is hot or water cold, earth dry or air damp. The divine wisdom has conferred certain natural properties on things, according to the requirements of the coherence of nature.[83] 'I condemn vain inquiries which waste the flower of youth.'[84] 'There are some sciolists all too ready to give a reason for the most remote causes of hidden things.' His whole attitude is summed up in the phrase 'discretam et humilem inquisitionem circa licita'.[85]

[83] Hec igitur debet esse causa inquisitionis causarum ut uberius nutriatur in nobis amor auctoris rerum et ut scientie thesaurum hilariter proximis distribuamus. Relegetur procul inuidia tabescens, que solare iubar censet detrimentum splendoris incurrere, dum ipsius beneficium pluribus impendit solatium . . . Non est concessum inuidie uel limen domus sapientie tangere, nec cum aliqua uirtutum habet commertium pestis sibi ipsi pernitiosissima: in Eccles. iii. 18 (C, fol. 133vb).

[84] Sed inquisitiones reprehendo superfluas, in quibus flos iuuenilis etatis consumitur: in Eccles. iv. 5 (C, fol. 148va).

[85] In Eccles. iv. 3 (C, fol. 144va); cf. ibid., iii. 12—'O scientia scolarium, molestis empta laboribus, dum quibusdam minutiis et arguta subtilitate rerum fugitiuarum consumitur uirtus ingenii' (C, fol. 113vb).

VII
THE PREACHER

ALEXANDER'S sermons belong with few exceptions to the period when he was teaching at Oxford.[1] Apart from Oxford we do not know the places where he preached. But the headings of a few of the sermons tell us the class of audience he was addressing and in others we can infer it from internal evidence. There are sermons at synods, to monks, including one to the Cistercians, to canons, to 'scolares', to laymen and to mixed audiences of 'scolares' and laymen. They therefore include most of the possible audiences of the day and he must have been a fairly well known preacher. The sermons certainly had some immediate circulation, since there are extracts from them in one of the works of William de Montibus.[2]

The sermon in the twelfth century was for the most part simple in form compared with the elaborate divisions which came into fashion in the thirteenth.[3] The development is certainly parallel to, if it does not derive from, the increasing elaboration of the methods of biblical exegesis. In Alexander's sermons we shall find some of the new devices, but they are used sparingly. In his remarks on preaching style, rhetoric and matter are the main concern. In style he attacks the use of ornament. Some preachers pay too much attention to style and tickle the ears, but they do not speak to the heart.[4] They have succumbed to the desire of showing

---

[1] See Appendix B.

[2] The *Similitudinarius*: Hunt, 'English learning' (n. VI. 41 above), p. 21.

[3] Alexander's sermons are conservative in form, given the increasing use of *distinctiones c.*1200. For later sermon technique see E. Gilson, *Les Idées et les lettres* (Paris, 1932), pp. 93–154; cf. M. M. Davy, *Les Sermons universitaires parisiens de 1230-1* (Paris, 1931). Gascoigne has an interesting passage on the 'modernus modus praedicandi': *Loci e libro Veritatum*, ed. J. E. Thorold Rogers (Oxford, 1881), p. 44.

[4] Predicant nonnulli uerborum eleganti forma circumspectius utentes, sed dum aurium pruritui satisfacere student, non loquuntur ad cor Ierusalem [Is. 40: 2]. Commendabilis est predicatio tenens arcum sacre scripture, dum sagittis

off, and seek to arrange their words in rhythmical order, and under the foliage of the fatuous fig-tree fruit is not found.[5] Those who should be bound to make sermons of exhortation compose rhymes. 'Whenever I hear sermons', he says, 'that strive after eloquence rather than usefulness, I call to mind the saying of Moses in Exodus: *It is not the voice of them that shout for mastery neither is it the voice of them that cry for being overcome, but the noise of them that sing do I hear.* Of what use is preaching if it does not encourage the hearers to flee vice or to fight against the world, the flesh and the powers of the air?'[6] The preacher should stick close to the scriptures and his words should be the sharp arrows of the mighty piercing the heart. But modern audiences will not allow themselves to be berated. They will only listen to things that soothe them. They say: 'Give us the nice things from the Bible, not the doleful ones.'[7] The preacher does not need to use ornament.[8] It must be set down to Alexander's credit that he follows these precepts himself. They are

sententiarum acutis penetrantur auditorum corda et carbonis desolatoriis [Ps. 119: 4] accenduntur ad amorem dilecti: *SMF* (J, fol. 96[va-vb]).

[5] Prodolor degenerat iam nobile predicationis officium ostentationi iam et elationi superciliose deditum, relegata procul utilitate proximis conferenda in uerbis exortationis. Ridmica desideratur uerborum prolatio et sub foliis ficus fatue fructus non repperitur. Vellem uidere predicatorem tenentem manu sinistra lignum ueteris testamenti, dextera flectentem arcus cordam et emittentem sagittas potentis acutas ad occidendum ueterem hominem: *in Eccles.* iii. 16 (C, fol. 123[va-vb]).

[6] O dedecus! Qui sermones exortationis facere tenerentur ridmos componunt; et dum ueritatem supprimunt, non seriis sed ludicris indulgere uidentur. Quotiens sermones audio eloquentie magis obnoxios quam utilitati reduco ad memoriam illud Moysi quod legitur in Exodo [32: 18]: Non est clamor adhortantium ad pugnam neque uociferatio compellentium ad fugam sed uocem cantantium ego audio. Quid confert predicatio nisi auditores inuitet ad fugam uiciorum aut pugnare doceat contra mundum, contra carnem, contra aerias potestates? Eloquia diuina sagitte sunt potentis acute. Vulnerata igitur debent auditorum corda, ut uulneratum se esse telo spiritualis amoris anima protestetur. Salutiferum est huiusmodi uulnus et desiderabile: *in Eccles.* v. 12 (C, fol. 184[rb]).

[7] Quasi dicerent: proponite nobis aliqua dulcia non lugubria de historiis sacre scripture: *GP* 136: 9 (MS Bodley 284, fol. 280[rb]).

[8] Faleris tamen uerborum oracionem uestire predicantis non interest. Arbor enim quandoque ab ubertate fructus destituitur que foliorum multitudine luxurians exterius uirescit. In aliis siquidem facultatibus stilus deseruire gaudet qualitati materie. Humilis materia humilem stilum uendicat. Antilocus [sic] stilus magestati materie sue sponte sese offert. In celesti uero pagina ardua materia humilem stilum non renuit, immo simplici et humili sermone explicari desiderat: Sermon 30 (W, fol. 86[v]).

refreshingly direct and simple in contrast to the overloaded style of many of his other works.

Alexander tells us that he taught in the schools that the preacher should go in and out from the gate of severe judgement to the gate of the infernal prison to strike terror into the hearts of his hearers; and that their hearts might be uplifted the word of the preacher should proceed from faith, which is the gate for those entering the church militant, to the gate of the entrance of celestial paradise.[9] He is a little apologetic in rebuking his own audience. Preaching on Job 10: 9—'Remember, I beseech thee, that thou hast made me as the clay'—he says: 'Brothers, do not be angry with me, do not be indignant, we are surely clay.'[10] In the same strain he says they have hearts of stone.[11] He tells them they should bear the word of God, and lightly and patiently support the upbraiding of prelates and doctors instructing them about faith and morals.[12] The dangers of hell-fire do not obtrude themselves unduly.

It is hard to discover a rigid schema in any of the sermons. They vary considerably according to the audience, subject-matter and the difficulty of the text. Alexander always starts from a scriptural text, a verse or more in length. It is sometimes drawn from the Epistle or Gospel for the day. There follows usually something of an introduction, which may even start from a second text,[13] but it is not like the *prothema*. The introduction is obviously intended as a

---

[9] In scolis uero docuimus predicatoribus eundem esse et redeundum [Exod. 32: 27] a porta districti examinis ad portam ingressus carceris infernalis ad incutiendum timorem auditoribus. Vt autem corda ipsorum erigantur ad superna recurrere debet sermo predicatoris a fide que est porta intrantibus ecclesiam militantem ad portam introitus paradisi celestis: *CCant.* iv. 5 (M, fol. 105vb).

[10] Viri fratres, ne succenseatis michi, nolite indignari. Certe lutum sumus: Sermon 6 (W, fol. 16^v); cf. Sermon (111) (G, fol. 161^v).

[11] Viri fratres, ne sit uobis molestum uerbum quod propositurus sum uobis. Vos et laici, uos et lapidei estis, cor habentes lapideum, adeo ut uerus Moyses, uobis reluctantibus, lacrimas deuocionis, aquam compunctionis a corde uestro lapideo non possit eicere neque elicere, aut propter indignitatem uestram non uelit: Sermon 32 (W, fol. 92).

[12] Portare etiam debetis uerbum domini et sustinere leuiter et cum omni paciencia correpcionem prelatorum et doctorum instruencium uos de fide et bonis moribus. Ardue enim subtilitates rerum inuestigabilium non debent uobis proponi: Sermon 37 (W, fol. 108).

[13] e.g. Sermon 30.

captatio beneuolentiae; and it is skilfully done. We may take some examples from sermons to different audiences, first a synodal sermon:[14]

> Qui solet ante homines ⟨Cicerone⟩ disercior esse,
> facundus minus est cum uenit ante deos.[15]

Vos autem dii estis iuxta illud—*Ego constituam te deum Pharaonis* [Exod. 7: 1] et item—*Ego dixi dii estis et filii excelsi omnes* [Ps. 81: 6]. Impedicioris enim lingue factus sum ab heri et nudius tercius, et ut uerbis prophete utar—*A a a domine deus, puer ego sum et nescio loqui* [Jer. 1: 6]. Vt igitur calculus sumatur cum forcipe de altari quo emundentur labia mea, sunt enim incircumcisa; sed decet, immo oportet me parere, parere et obsequi uoluntati prelati mei et precepto magistri mei. Magna est enim uirtus humilitatis, magna est uirtus obediencie quod elucescit per illud factum Helisei, qui ueniens ad aquas Iordanis pallio Helie aquas percussit et non diuisit eas et secum deliberans prorupit in uocem ammiracionis dicens: Vbi est et nunc deus Helie? Vt enim ait Gregorius: Nominans Heliam confessus est per consequens se discipulum esse Helie et in confessione humilitatis iterato percussit aquas pallio Helie et diuisit eas. Sed quid? Nec Heliseus sum nec pallium habeo Helie. Vt tamen in hoc imitarer Heliseum, ut possem et scirem diuidere, id est subtiliter comminuere et exponere et propinare uobis aquas Iordanis, id est doctrinam sacre scripture, que ducit ad Iordanem, id est ad descensum humilitatis. Vtinam ergo uos a fastidio superbie et fastu discedatis in uallem humilitatis . . .

To monks he confesses his unworthiness:[16]

Spicas licet legere post manus messorum Booz et mel cum summitate uirge Ionathe degustare, summo tamen opere cauendum est ne bos uel asinus in puteum cadat. Claudendum est ergo os putei et obturandum. Bestia enim qui montem tetigerit lapidabitur. Sed quid? Imperfeccionem status mei et statum imperfeccionis mee mecum reuoluens, perturbor quociens uiris claustralibus quorum conuersacio iam in celis est uerbum predicacionis propono. Viri enim religiosi operibus predicant, sed nos scolares uerbo. Illorum predicacio realis est, sed nostra uocalis.

The citizens of Oxford are reminded of their advantages:[17]

Ciues Oxonie, uiri dulcissime conuersacionis, ad longe maiorem morum honestorum obseruantiam tenemini quam ceteri ciues regionis istius.

---

[14] Sermon 12: W, fol. 32.
[15] Hildebert, *Carmina Minora*, 46. 1-2: ed. A. B. Scott (Teubner, Leipzig, 1969), p. 37; cf. *GP* 139: 10 (MS Bodley 284, fol. 286vb).
[16] Sermon 18 (W, fol. 53); cf. Sermon 30 (W, fol. 86).
[17] Sermon 26: W, fol. 74.

Maximum enim temporis spacium euolutum est ex quo iugiter habuistis
uiros litteratissimos qui uos diligenter informarent et pane iocunde
refeccionis spiritualiter sepius reficerent. Fuistis tanquam aree ortorum
irriguis aquarum ductibus sepius irrigate. Non potestis pretendere
excusacionem, quam multi pretendere possunt: *Paruuli pecierunt
panem et non erat qui frangeret eis* [Lam. 4: 4]. Fuerunt siquidem multi
qui uobis panem sacre scripture fregerunt. Sicut ergo Iesus in fractione
panis agnitus est, ita et Christiani in fractione panis agnosci possunt.
Tempore ingruente necessitatis, pauperes Christi semper habetis uobis-
cum. Videte ut eis panem uestrum comminuatis. Si deberetis transitum
facere per siluam in qua latrarent uispiliones, nonnullam partem
pecunie uestre conferretis uiro alicui, qui merces uestras deferret ad
locum munitum et tutum. Tunc ergo et uos eligite locum, regnum
scilicet celorum . . .

Sometimes Alexander starts immediately on the development
of the text, as in this example, which we give in full. *Cantate
domino canticum nouum quia mirabilia fecit.*[18] He begins
with the new song and with newness of life. He next takes
two more passages which emphasize renewal. Then he con-
siders Solomon's 'There's nothing new under the sun', and by
an interpretation which is somewhat forced he brings it into
line with his theme. He contrasts the books studied by
students in liberal arts with those that would lead them to
newness of life. The text is taken up again and the song
referred to spiritual joy; and the old and new song are applied
to age and youth. Finally the text is stated and expounded as
a whole, and two passages from the Psalms are introduced to
illustrate the wonders. This is a fair example of the way in
which the sermon is built up on the text with illustrations
from other passages in the Bible. In this example the text
itself is simple, and does not call for elaborate exposition in
the sense of bringing in technical devices. When the text is
difficult he is ready to use them. The good and bad senses
of a word in the Bible are illustrated.[19] There are a number of
distinctiones, but as in his commentaries they are not used
for their own sake.[20] To put a scene vividly before our eyes he

---

[18] Ps. 97: 1: Sermon 31 (W, fols. 88-90[V]).

[19] Nomen enim deserti et aureis et tetris litteris scribitur in celesti pagina,
tetris ut ibi . . . aureis ut ibi: Sermon 18 (W, fol. 53[V]).

[20] See for example *puluis* (Sermon 6: W, fol. 18); *dies* (Sermon 42: W,
fol. 121[V]); *obliuio* (Sermon 15: W, fol. 46[V]).

has the formula which is used to excess in the commentaries. In the sermons he does not develop it fully, for example:

Dum igitur de mari loquor, dum de Iona loquor, *uideor mihi uidere* cum puero Helie nubeculam ascendentem de mari paruam, quasi uestigium hominis excrescentem, aut in quantitatem hominis.[21]

Apart from the Bible, quotations are used in moderation. There are short sentences from the Fathers and one or two tags from classical or medieval poets in most sermons.

His use of the *exemplum* deserves a word. For though the practice and the word itself are recognized in the *De arte predicatoria* of Alan of Lille,[22] they are rare in sermons of the twelfth century. Alexander thought it was specially appropriate to sermons addressed to laymen. A preacher delivering a sermon and propounding the words of sacred eloquence to laymen should refresh his hearers by various *exempla*.[23] This is in accordance with his practice. There are some twelve *exempla* in seven sermons, and two of them contain three each.[24] One occurs in a sermon to monks[25] and one in a sermon to students.[26] The rest are for the laymen, especially in sermons addressed to mixed audiences. 'You laymen, remember that *exemplum*, which is wont to be put forward for your instruction.'[27] He does not follow Alan's advice and put them at the end. They may be found anywhere. They begin in the traditional manner of telling a story —'Erat enim uir quidam'. The sources are various and I have not succeeded in identifying them all. There are none relating to contemporary events and persons, which make the later collections so valuable. Two are based on stories in the *Vitae patrum*; one is from the Talmud; two have a distinctly oriental flavour; two or three are apparently classical. Twice he gives

[21] Sermon 2 (**W**, fol. 5ᵛ); cf. Sermon 4 (**W**, fol. 13ᵛ)—'Vbi est qui natus est? In presepi. Ponamus presepe ante oculos, contemplemur paruulum nostrum dulcibus pannis dulciter inuolutum, audiamus eum uagientem'. See also Sermons 7 and 28 (**W**, fols. 20ᵛ and 80ᵛ).

[22] In fine uero debet uti exemplis, ad probandum quod intendit, quia familiaris est doctrina exemplaris: *MPL* ccx. 114C.

[23] Sermon (111): **G**, fol. 161. Alexander is addressing 'conuersi'.

[24] Sermons 31 and (97).

[25] Sermon 10: **W**, fol. 26.

[26] Sermon 16: **W**, fol. 50.

[27] Sermon 31: **W**, fol. 89ᵛ.

the story of Midas, but for Midas a 'rusticus' is substituted, perhaps a concession to the audience. One is a fable, and one is an animal story.[28]

The lessons Alexander inculcates are simple ones. If we look at the synodal sermons, which were probably addressed to local synods, we find that no very exalted standard is required. Priests ought to be literate enough at least to expound the literal sense to their flock.[29] They must live clean lives.[30] A special responsibility is on those who handle the body of Christ. It is a privilege not given to angels, only to a male, to a priest.[31] Prelates are criticized. They are compared to jackdaws, who swallow gold if they get a chance.[32] Prelates nowadays like to be addressed in the second person plural, although neither Peter nor any of the Apostles said anything but 'thou' to the Lord. But it is best to humour them for reverence' sake, not out of flattery.[33] Many of the things he has to say need always to be said. 'You lie in your beds, you hug yourselves in your beds. The bell is rung. You pretend

[28] See for example Sermons 9 and 37 (*Vitae Patrum*), 31 (Talmud), 31 and 12 (Midas).

[29] Litteratura pollere debetis, ut saltem litteralem sensum gregi uobis subdito exponatis: Sermon 15 (W, fol. 45).

[30] Viri fratres, *filii hominum* estis, nolite monstra effici, nolite mutari cum sociis Vlixis uel in suem uel in lupum uel in uulpeculam, sed habeatis faciem humanam, faciem euntis in Ierusalem. Sed precipue cauete uobis a monstruosis choitibus in quibus homo hominem exuit et monstrum induit. Nonne legitis quia masculum et feminam creauit eos deus. Viri fratres, filii hominum estis. Nolite ergo imitari bruta animalia: Sermon 12 (W, fol. 33).

[31] O quam mundas debetis habere manus, qui manibus uestris tractatis corpus Iesu Christi. Vobis datum est quod non est datum alicui angelorum, nulli nisi mari, nulli nisi sacerdoti datum est conficere corpus domini. Si ergo mundi debent esse Nazarei qui ferunt uasa domini, o quam mundi debent esse illi qui manibus suis ferunt ipsum dominum: Sermon 12 (W, fols. 33ᵛ-4); cf. Sermon 15 (W, fol. 46).

[32] Prelati ecclesiarum facti sunt monedule que aurum uisum statim degluciunt, si detur eis copia super auro uiso. Nimis uerum est quod Ouidius tanquam fabulosum refert, quendam scilicet optasse ut singula que tangeret aurum efficerentur et tactis cibariis facta sunt cibaria aurum et sic periit. Aurum sitisti, aurum bibe cum Crasso [*Met.* xi. 100-45]: Sermon 12 (W, fol. 35).

[33] Hodie ergo uolunt prelati ecclesiarum ut uobiscetur cum eis, cum numquam cum numquam [*sic*] Petrus uel aliquis discipulorum dixit domino 'Vos'. Ait enim Petrus domino: Tu scis, domine, quia amo te. Non dicit: Vos scitis, domine, quia amo uos. Et tamen quia scriptum est: cui honorem, honorem, satis placet michi ut saltem causa reuerencie dicatur prelato 'uos', non causa adulacionis: Sermon 12 (W, fol. 36).

not to hear.'[34] Or 'We complain and murmur if we have to
go a mile or two to hear divine office, and when we have a
slight desire to go to church, a shower of rain calls us back,
or the heat which, though not great, we pretend to be too
much to be borne.'[35] It is interesting to see what he relies
on for illustration. 'There is not a woman among you who
does not seek to be or to appear beautiful. How each of you
would clap her hands, if she could be as beautiful as Helen!'[36]
We wonder how many of the ladies of Oxford at the end
of the twelfth century knew who Helen was. Again to the
citizens of Oxford he says: 'Narcissus did not recognize himself and so he perished. He saw his shadow, desired it and in
this desire vanished. Each of us is Narcissus.'[37] He tells
students not to give money to minstrels. It is like putting
money in a sack with holes in it. They should make their
gifts to poor students.[38] He disapproves of the wide sleeves of
the *cape* of little boys:

Nolo loqui de manubiis caparum modernarum, quibus pueruli huius
temporis uolare uidentur, dum incedentes uerrunt aera. Absit ut alis
hiis euolant in regionem dissimilitudinis.[39]

To monks he makes the familiar charge of not treating
great and small alike. If a man seeks hospitality in the name

---

[34] Iacetis in lectis uestris, fouetis artus uestros stratis uestris. Pulsatur cam-
pana: dissimulatis uos audire: Sermon 9 (W, fol. 24).

[35] Ecce conquerimur et murmuramus si unum stadium uel duo oportet nos
emetiri ut diuinum audiamus officium; et siquando adest exilis uoluntas [*cod.*
uoluntantis] ecclesiam adeundi, reuocat nos pluuia modica, uel calor, licet modera-
tus, quem fingimus esse immoderatum: Sermon 4 (W, fol. 13).

[36] Non est inter uos mulier aliqua uestrum que non appetat esse uel uideri
formosa. O quanto applaudiret quelibet uestrum si esset eque formosa Helene:
Sermon 8 (W, fol. 23).

[37] Narcisus seipsum non cognouit et ideo periit. Vmbram uidit, desiderauit
et in hoc desiderio euanuit. Quilibet nostrum Narcisus est: Sermon 26 (W,
fol. 75ᵛ).

[38] Qui pecuniam mittit in saccum pertusum uidet ipsam, dum eam mittit in
saccum in saccum [*sic*], sed non uidet eam dum excidit a sacco: sic qui munera
dat histrioni pleno rimarum uidet quod dat, sed non uidet quod perdit. Perdit
quidem quod mittit in saccum pertusum. Saccus enim pertusus histrio est. Date
uos scolares munera pauperibus scolaribus: Sermon 38 (W, fol. 112ʳ⁻ᵛ). Cf. Sermon (120): 'Histrionis egentis nature subuenire nouit caritas, sed non histrio-
natui' (G, fol. 13).

[39] Sermon 38: W, fol. 111. For the phrase 'regio dissimilitudinis' see P.
Courcelle, 'Tradition néo-platonicienne et traditions chrétiennes de la *région de
dissemblance* (Platon, *Politique* 273d)', *AHDLMA* xxxii (1957), 5-33.

of the king's justiciar and mentions the king's name, he is at once made welcome, and the best food is put before him. But if one comes who says he has no lord but Christ, they answer: 'Friend, you have no wedding garment: you profess to be a servant of Christ, go to Christ.' And if he is taken in, it is as if he had not been. It displeases me, Alexander says, that you are so far theologians, saying with Augustine that it is a venial sin to refresh a poor man with plain food.[40]

We have been assuming so far that the sermons, as we have them, are pretty much the sermons as they were preached. They certainly give the impression of some spontaneity. They contain phrases like 'Attendite, uos laici, si placet' or the oft-repeated 'Viri fratres, attenti sitis'. Once he says:

Multa habeo adhuc uobis dicere, sed non potestis portare modo [John 16: 12] quia et fatigati estis prolixitate sermonis et perturbati perplexitate difficultatis, sed sperate et confidite in domino.[41]

But there are grave difficulties in the assumption. The cross-references and the appeals to the reader, which we have already noticed,[42] show that the sermons have undergone some revision. For some of them at least there arises the question of language. The general rule seems to be that only sermons addressed to clerks were delivered in Latin.[43] All others were spoken in the vernacular, even if their written

---

[40] Prohdolor! prohdolor! Si dicat hospes, 'nomine iusticiarii regis hospicium peto', uel eciam si nomen regis semel proferat, dicetur ei clara uoce, 'Bene ueniatis. Suscipite nuncium regis!' Statim uidebis opus ministrancium feruere, lauticiam cibariorum et regalium epularum apponi. Si uero dicat pulsans, 'Non habeo dominum nisi Christum', dicetur ei: 'Amice non habes uestes nupciales [cf. Matt. 22: 12]. Christi te profiteris esse seruum, uade ad Christum.' Prohdolor! Qui fatetur se esse nuncium regis regum, dominatoris dominancium non suscipitur, uel si forte suscipiatur, perinde est ac si non esset susceptus . . . Displicet michi quod adeo theologi estis cum Augustino dicente, ueniale peccatum esse pauperem minus laute reficere. Non rogo ut eos nimis laute reficiatis, sed pro temporis malicia aliquo [thus G. a W] solacio munificencie uestre gaudeant in domino: Sermon 16 (W, fols. 49ᵛ-50; G, fols. 82ᵛ-3ᵛ).

[41] Sermon 34: W, fol. 101ᵛ.

[42] See above, chapter II.

[43] The relation of the written text of a sermon to the mode and language of its actual delivery is not yet [1984] fully understood. For France, where the language gap between Latin and the vernacular was less acute, see M. Zink, La Prédication en langue romane avant 1300 (Paris, 1976); for England see M. Richter, Sprache und Gesellschaft im Mittelalter (Stuttgart, 1979), especially parts ii-iii.

form is Latin. Applied to Alexander's sermons we should be inclined to say that a sermon preached to the 'scolares' at Oxford with its technicalities would be given in Latin, and that one to the citizens would be in English or possibly French. But what are we to say of those to mixed audiences?[44] In one of these at least, the appeal for the building fund of St Frideswide's, he seems to turn from one section of the audience to the other:

Ceterum ut laicis assistentibus condescendamus et morem ieramus stilum mutantes comico sermone utamur.[45]

But usually there is no special section for them, except that the *exemplum* is introduced for their benefit. If we suppose that this section alone was in the vernacular, they will have missed the force of the appeal; and earlier in the sermon he has spoken of the collection 'which you have been accustomed to make on Ascension Day' (fol. 93^v), where the context makes it plain that he is addressing the whole audience. He uses a similar phrase in another sermon to laymen: 'Vtor comico et uulgari sermone quia simplicibus et non litteratis loquor'.[46] He seems to mean nothing more than a homely way of speaking, though the exact significance is hard to catch. We seem to be driven to the conclusion that such sermons must have been delivered in the language understood by the whole audience. What would this language have been? French or English? It is doubtful if the whole audience would know French. But can we say that Alexander knew English well enough? It is probable *a priori*, but the works supply little evidence of it.[47] All his explanations of words are in

---

[44] For instance Sermon 31.   [45] Sermon 33: W, fol. 96^{r-v}.

[46] Sermon 8 (W, fol. 21^v); cf. *GP* 135: 8: 'Sicut dicitur comice "Iste est potestas illius ciuitatis" quia preest illi ciuitati' (MS Bodley 284, fol. 277va); *CP* on 2 Macc. 2: 18: 'Comico etiam sermone dicitur "Iste uenit de ultra paruum pontem". Similiter dicimus "Iste loquitur de Iram pande michi", ut sic pro libro fiat suppositio', and *CP* on John 8: 29: 'Quemadmodum comice dicitur "Aristotiles semper bene disputauit", hoc est quandocumque disputatuit bene disputatuit' (B, fols. 42vb and 66va). See also *CCant.* vi. 12: 'Et ut utar uerbis uulgaribus "Tota uita christiani recte uiuentis crux est et martirium"' (M, fol. 171ra); *GP* 10: 6: 'Sicut uulgo dicitur de eo qui aliquem uult interficere "Infelix tu suspendis te"' (MS Bodley 284, fol. 16ra).

[47] *CP* on 3 Kgs. 22: 26 (B, fol. 29va: Meyer 1896, p. 677) refers to the definite article in English; *LSD* v. 879-80 (p. 461) derives 'Merleburgia' from 'Merlini tumulus'.

French, never, as far as I have noticed, in English. Again, could all the part addressed to 'scolares' be expressed in French or in English? He makes some interesting remarks on the subject of translation, in the course of which he says: 'Who could faithfully express in French the meaning of these words: *instrumentum dicendi non subest sue dictioni*?'[48] There seem to be passages in Sermon 31 which fall under this head, as that on the squaring of the circle.[49] And what are we to say of the quotations from the classical poets? It is a dilemma. If we accepted Mabillon's argument that St Bernard's sermons were given in Latin because of *perpetuus natiuusque uerborum lusus in uocibus latinis* and *eiusdem stili in sermonibus et in aliis eius libris et tractatibus aequalitas*, we could say the same of Alexander's; and perhaps Hauréau was right in saying the rule was too absolutely expressed.[50] But the sermons of Alexander by themselves do not provide enough evidence for us to decide.

---

[48] Hinc est quod dum per aliud idioma fideliter tanquam uerbo ad uerbum interpretari satagimus, nunc ipsa breuitate obscuritas procreatur, nunc intellectum debitum non representat ordo uerborum. Quis enim lingua gallica fideliter exprimeret intellectum horum uerborum: 'instrumentum dicendi non subest sue dictioni'? Hinc est etiam quod non solum propter dignitatem primitie ecclesie sed etiam propter impotentiam fide interpretationis hanc formam uerborum obseruamus: 'Baptizo te'. Nullum enim uerbum in angustia latini idiomatis repperiri potuit, quod ex equo responderet huic uerbo greco 'baptizo'. Si enim dicatur 'intingo' uel 'immergo' non peruenitur ad uirtutem significationis predicti uerbi: *in Eccles*. iii. 8 (C, fol. 101rb).

[49] Quadrare circulum uultis: si sciretis quod alpha est et ω, haberetis quod trigonum equilatrum esset equale circulo, sed omne trigonum est equale quadrato. Si igitur uideatis quonammodo trigonum sit ω, habebitis quadraturam circuli: W, fol. 88^v.

[50] *MPL* clxxxiii. 15 = Mabillon's preface, cap. X.

VIII

THE COMMENTATOR

THE commentaries in bulk are more than half the work of Alexander. This is natural, since the Bible was the fundamental book both in the schools and in the monasteries. In his commentaries we can see the influence of both; and though on analysis it is difficult to say in detail what is the difference between the monastic and scholastic types, there are some general differences, which can be pointed out. The prototype of the monastic commentary is the *Moralia in Job* of Gregory the Great. It contains long excursions on problems not closely connected with the matter in hand. The scholastic type is the running commentary of the teacher with short disquisitions on doctrinal points as they arise.[1] This distinction is valid for the commentaries of Alexander, though, as we have seen, none of them were put into their present form until after he had become a monk. The monastic commentaries are the *Solatium fidelis anime, De naturis rerum et super Ecclesiasten, Super Cantica Canticorum, Super Parabolas Salomonis,* and *Super mulierem fortem.* To the scholastic type belong the *Gloss on the Psalter* and the second part of the *Corrogationes Promethei.* Between the two types there is first of all a formal difference. The scholastic type is continuous: the monastic is divided up rather arbitrarily. The *De naturis rerum et in Ecclesiasten* is in five books, of which the last three contain the commentary proper. Each book is divided into chapters and each chapter deals with one or more verses of the text. The arrangement of the *Commentary on the Song of Songs* is similar. The *Commentary on Proverbs* is a lop-sided fragment in the manuscript, and its plan is not clear.[2] The others are

---

[1] G. Lacombe, *La Vie et les œuvres de Prévostin* (Bibliothèque Thomiste, XI, Le Saulchoir, 1927), pp. 114–17.

[2] The Florilegium includes (G, fol. 77^v) a piece from *CProv.* 1: 4 (= J, fol. 60vb) with the title 'capitulum secundum'.

concerned with shorter passages of special interest. The *Solatium fidelis anime*, on the Hexameron, was probably divided into twenty-two chapters. This is not certain because the manuscript has not been rubricated. The *Super mulierem fortem* is in three main sections, but is otherwise shapeless.

Common to both types is the theory of exegesis.[3] This is never formally set out; and it is difficult to be sure how far he is not merely adjusting his remarks to the passage he is commenting on. He usually refers to the four senses: *historia*, *allegoria*, *tropologia*, *anagoge*. They are typified by the four rivers of Paradise,[4] the four kinds of bread[5] and by the four kinds of wine-jar.[6] But when he is commenting on the threefold cord which is not quickly broken,[7] he only gives *historia*, *allegoria* and *tropologia*. Elsewhere referring to the same passage he says that *anagoge* is included under *allegoria*.[8] While it is true that *anagoge* is not much used, it is not entirely neglected, so that he probably held to the fourfold division. *Historia* or the literal sense is the foundation of the others. Allegory is concerned with the mysteries of faith. Tropology is elicited from allegory and is concerned with

---

[3] G. Paré, A. Brunet and P. Tremblay, *La Renaissance du XIIe siècle: les écoles et l'enseignement* (Paris and Ottawa, 1933), cap 5; and see now H. de Lubac, *Exégèse médiévale: les quatre sens de l'Écriture* (Paris, 1959–64), 2 vols.

[4] *GP*, prol.: MS Bodley 284, fol. iii^{ra–b}. The passage closely resembles the preface to the longer version of Langton's gloss on Peter Comestor, *Historia Scholastica*: see G. Lacombe, 'Studies on the commentaries of Cardinal Stephen Langton', *AHDLMA* v (1930), 5–266, at 42–3.

[5] Sed prodolor! panis cotidianus, historialis uidelicet intellectus paruipenditur, azimus allegorie panis abicitur, subcinericius panis tropologie contempnitur, similagineus anagogice subtilitatis abhorretur: *in Eccles.* v. 5 (C, fol. 174va).

[6] Cella etiam uinaria sacra scriptura dici solet. In hac cella sunt quatuor genera doliorum, que sunt hystoria, allegoria, tropologia, et anagoge. In primo dolio continetur uinum quo simplices potandi sunt. Factis enim antiquorum et exemplis ad honestatis amorem inuitandi sunt. Allegoria continet elucidationem fidei. Tropologie se debet morum compositio. In quarto dolio continetur uinum subtilissime comprehensionis supracelestium: *CCant.* iii. 16 (M, fol. 77va). Cf. *SMF* (J, fol. 119ra).

[7] Subtiliter et artificiose connectit Ecclesiastes historiam allegoriam et tropologiam; et iste est funiculus triplex qui difficile rumpitur, dum eas ueritas indissolubiliter confederat. Adde quod historia fundamentum est allegorie et tropologie et ex allegoria moralis elicitur intellectus: *in Eccles.* iv. 1 (C, fol. 141ra). Cf. Paré *et al.*, (n. 3 above), p. 223 n. 1.

[8] At *GP* 15: 6 (MS Bodley 284, fol. 21rb): a *distinctio* on 'funis' and 'funiculus'—'Est funiculus sacre scripture. Vnde *Funiculus triplex difficile rumpitur*. Tripliciter enim exponitur sacra scriptura, historice allegorice, moraliter siue tropologice, ut sub allegoria comprehenditur anagoge'.

morals. *Anagoge* is concerned with the elucidation of the most subtle mysteries. In practice it is seldom that he uses all four senses in any one passage.[9] He is often content to draw the more general distinction between the *litteralis* or *historialis intellectus* and the *spiritualis*.[10] In the monastic commentaries his special concern is with tropology. In the preface to the *Solatium fidelis anime* he says: 'I intend to give special attention to tropology in this work, reserving anagoge for other tracts.'[11] Again in the prologue to the *De naturis rerum* he says: 'I have decided to toil in works that are tropological before I turn to the heights of the subtleties of *anagoge*.'[12] There is an advance in the *ingressus* to the *Commentary on Proverbs*: 'I intend principally to serve tropology, specially reserving some passages for allegory.' And he goes on: 'Let no rash judge accuse me of prolixity. I do not wish to take only the role of commentator, but also to refresh the minds of monks with consolatory meditations.'[13] This programme is realized most fully in the *Commentary on the Song of Songs*.

SCHOLASTIC COMMENTARY

1. Lectio

In the schools in Alexander's time there were two main exercises: *lectio* and *disputatio*. To take *lectio* first, it is a reading of the text and gloss with comments.[14] It starts not from the text of the Bible alone, but from the text and the gloss on it. Whoever the compilers were, there appears to be a complete set of marginal and interlinear glosses for the whole Bible by about the middle of the

[9] I give two examples of an elaborate series: at *GP* 23:3 (MS Bodley 284, fol. 44$^{\text{ra-rb}}$) 'Ad litteram, preter seriem lectionis, moraliter, anagogice'; at *in Eccles.* iii. 6 (C, fols. 99ra-100rb) 'historialiter, moralitas, subtilior meditatio tropologica, alia meditatio moralis'.

[10] Or 'ad litteram' and 'mistice'.

[11] Anagogen itaque tractatibus aliis reseruans, specialem in hoc opere tropologie daturus sum operam: *SFA* 1 (MS Canterbury Lit. B 6, fol. 2ra).

[12] *DNR*, prol. (p. 2).

[13] Principaliter uero tropologie indulgere proposui, ita ut allegorie loca quedam specialiter reseruentur. Nec me prolixitatis arguat temerarius arbiter; neque enim expositoris officium tantum assumere libet, sed etiam consolatoriis meditationibus recreare claustralium animos: J, fol. 59$^{\text{rb-va}}$.

[14] Cf. *GP* 15: 4 (MS Bodley 284, fol. 20$^{\text{va-vb}}$): sed nos, more nostro, procedamus continuando lectionem nostram de sanctis, sic.

twelfth century.[15] This is what we call the 'Glossa ordinaria'; but in the twelfth century it was simply the *Glosa*, and each separate item is also called *glosa*, often with the addition of *marginalis* or *interlinearis*. This is the Gloss which the master read out with the text and which he commented on. The best representatives of this type of commentary are Peter Comestor[16] and Stephen Langton.[17]

For the Psalter and the Pauline Epistles, the two most important books in the curriculum, the situation is more complicated. Here we are only concerned with the Psalter. There are the ordinary gloss of Anselm of Laon, which was sometimes called the *parua glosatura*, the gloss of Gilbert de la Porrée, which was known as the *media glosatura*, and the gloss of Peter Lombard, which was known as the *magna glosatura*. We do not at present know what was the procedure in the schools in the face of this complicated apparatus. Unfortunately Langton's gloss is still unidentified. In the thirteenth century the gloss of Peter Lombard drove out its rivals.[18] Alexander starts from the text itself, but makes constant reference to the glosses, especially that of Anselm of Laon. We will give some examples of his use of the threefold apparatus.[19]

(a) the ordinary gloss, or 'parua glosatura'

ET ORATIO MEA IN SINU MEO CONVERTETVR [Ps. 34: 13]

Nota marginalem: Orabam, sed non alium quam qui michi personaliter unitus est.[20]

---

[15] B. Smalley, 'Gilbertus Universalis, bishop of London (1128–34), and the problem of the *Glossa Ordinaria*', *Recherches de théologie ancienne et médiévale*, viii (1936), 24–60, especially 34–49.

[16] A. Landgraf, 'Recherches sur les écrits de Pierre le Mangeur', ibid. iii (1931), 341–72, especially 366–72.

[17] G. Lacombe and B. Smalley, 'Studies on the commentaries of Cardinal Stephen Langton', *AHDLMA* v (1929), 5–220, at 52–182.

[18] Peter Lombard's *magna glosatura* is found in twenty-two manuscripts in Oxford, twelve in the Royal collection in the British Library and eight at Lincoln Cathedral; the corresponding figures for the *parua glosatura* are three, one and nil.

[19] Only Peter Lombard's gloss (the *magna glosatura*) is conveniently accessible in print: *MPL* cxci. 55A–1296B. Gilbert de la Porrée's gloss (the *media glosatura*) is unprinted, bar a few excerpts. The *parua glosatura* exists in several recensions, none of which is even tolerably reflected in the printed editions: *MPL* cxiii. 841–1080 or, bettter, *Biblia cum glosis ordinariis* (Venice, 1495). Hence the number of manuscripts cited for the *parua glosatura*.

[20] *GP* 34: 13 (MS Bodley 284, fol. 81[ra]); cf. MSS Bodleian Auct. D. 2. 4, fol. 21[v] (marginal); Bodley 862, fol. 44, and Laud lat. 17, fol. 31 (both interlinear).

PERMANET IN AETERNVM IN CONSPECTV DEI [Ps. 60: 8]

Vnde interlinearis: Si uis in eternum psallere, redde uota in isto die, donec peruenias in illum diem.[21]

MOAB OLLA SPEI MEAE [Ps. 59: 10]

Anselmus: Filia male utens patre genuit Moabitas. Qui male utitur lege generat mala opera, ut qui bene bona. A male autem utentibus lege oritur ecclesie tribulacio.[22]

OMNIA OSSA MEA DICENT QVIS SIMILIS TIBI [Ps. 34: 10]

Omnia ossa mea naturalia et maxime gratuita. Vnde glosa: *Omnia ossa* id est omnis fortitudo mentis *dicent domine* etc. Vide marginalem Anselmi: carnes non habent uerbum, quia infirma apud te penitus silent, sed fortia magnum laudant et tremunt. Hoc sumptum est ex Moralibus Gregorii, cuius tamen uerborum idemptitas hic non obseruatur. Ideo libet et uerba apponere. Ait ergo Gregorius . . .[23]

BEATVS VIR CVI NON IMPVTAVIT DOMINVS PECCATVM
[Ps. 31: 2]

Super hoc nomen ergo *uir* est interlinearis Anselmi hec: Vt Iob et Nathanael quos laudat deus, in quibusdam codicibus, sed corrupti sunt. Super hoc nomen *peccatum* est hec interlinearis Anselmi: Etiamsi aliquod leuius peccatum. Vnde dixi iniquitates maiora crimina enormia, peccata minora mortalia, peccatum ueniale. Sed mirum est quare Glosa Anselmi dicat: Etiamsi aliquod leuius peccatum . . .[24]

There is one reference to the *glosa scolastica* in Alexander's *Gloss on the Psalter*:

SANA ME DOMINE QVONIAM CONTVRBATA SVNT OSSA MEA
[Ps. 6: 3]

Alie rationes assignantur a glosa scolastica—scilicet ut suadeat anime in que mala se precipitauit, et ut anima magis caueat sibi in posterum, et ut ostendatur que pena sit non conuersis, si tanta est difficultas conuersis, quia si uix iustus saluabitur, impius ubi parebit?—Et nota quia difficultatem ingerit glosa marginalis Anselmi que dicit Anselmus: Nondum enim tam perfecte orat ut dicatur ei, Adhuc te loquente, dicam, ecce assum.[25]

It is clear from the *Corrogationes Promethei* that *glosa scolastica* means the ordinary marginal and interlinear gloss,

---

[21] *GP* 60: 8 (MS Bodley 284, fol. 150[va]); cf. MSS Bodleian Auct. D. 2. 4, fol. 40, and Bodley 862, fol. 77[v] (both interlinear).

[22] *GP* 59: 10 (MS Bodley 284, fol. 148[vb]); cf. MSS Bodleian Auct. D. 2. 4, fol. 39[v], and Bodley 862, fol. 76[v] (both marginal).

[23] *GP* 34: 10 (MS Bodley 284, fol. 80[rb]); cf. MSS Bodleian Auct. D. 2. 4, fol. 21[v], and Bodley 862, fol. 43[v], and Laud lat. 17, fol. 30[v] (all marginal).

[24] *GP* 31: 2 (MS Bodley 284, fol. 70[vb]); cf. MSS Bodleian Auct. D. 2. 4, fol. 19, Bodley 862, fol. 39, and Laud lat. 17, fol. 25[v] (all interlinear).

[25] *GP* 6: 3 (MS Bodley 284, fol. 8[vb]); cf. MSS Bodleian Auct. D. 2. 4, fol. 3[v], and Bodley 862, fol. 6 (both marginal).

the *parua glosatura* of Anselm of Laon. In that work it is the usual title given to it:

ET MEDIA INTERCOLVMNIA QVADRATA, NON ROTVNDA
[3 Kgs. 7: 31]

> Media intercolumpnia. Media inter basim scilicet et epistilium. Glosa tamen scolastica legit media intercolumpna, et uocat mediam intercolumpnam tabulam superiorem.[26]

And later in the same text—

PRECOQVAS FICVS DESIDERAVIT ANIMA MEA [Micah 7: 1]

> Precoquas ficus, id est pre aliis feruore solis coctas et prematuras. Glosa tamen scolastica exponit aliter, sic: id est immaturas ficus scilicet grossos.[27]

(*b*) *The gloss of Gilbert de la Porrée, or* 'media glosatura'

The gloss of Gilbert is referred to comparatively seldom. It is usually called 'glosa Gilberti' and only once 'glosatura media':

TIMOR DOMINI SANCTVS PERMANENS IN SAECVLUM SAECVLI
[Ps. 18: 10]

> In ingressu tamen illius psalmi *Beati omnes qui timent dominum* in glosatura media quiddam ponitur quod uidetur huic quod dico contrarium, et uidetur facere cum glosis iam dictis secundum quod sonant in superficie; sed hoc non omittemus suo loco.[28]

(*c*) *The gloss of Peter Lombard, or* 'magna glosatura'

The gloss of Peter Lombard is generally 'Lumbardus', 'glosa Lumbardi' or 'Lumbardus in glosatura sua'. There are some citations of a 'magister' who is apparently the Lombard:

EXVRGE, QVARE OBDORMIS DOMINE [Ps. 43: 23]

> Secundum magistrum sic: Etsi sciunt Christum non dormire et sibi resurrexisse, precantur resurgere sed gentibus que putant mortuum. Si enim et illi crederent surrexisse, credentes in eum non persequerentur, sed et ipsi crederent.[29]

The Lombard is probably used more frequently than appears on the surface. But Alexander does not follow him step by step as Petrus Cantor does.[30]

---

[26] *CP* on 3 Kgs. 7: 31 (**B**, fol. 29[ra]): cf. MS Bodleian Auct. D. 3. 15, fol. 156[v] (marginal).

[27] *CP* on Micah 7: 1 (**B**, fol. 36vb): cf. MS Bodleian Auct. D. 2. 13, fol. 72 (interlinear). [28] *GP* 18: 10: MS Bodley 284, fol. 32[va-b].

[29] *GP* 43: 23: MS Bodley 284, fol. 110va; cf. Peter Lombard ad loc. (*MPL* cxci. 435D–6A).

[30] Petrus Cantor's Psalter-commentary has not been edited: see F. Stegmüller, *Repertorium Biblicum Medii Aevi* (Madrid, 1954) iv, no. 6475.

The method of paying so much attention to the glosses created difficulties where none were.[31] For Alexander Anselm was 'authentic'.[32] Where Alexander differs from Petrus Cantor is in a more extensive display of patristic authorities. The references to Jerome are most frequent, apparently to a commentary on the Psalter. But it is not the genuine commentary, nor the *Breuiarium*, and I have not been able to identify it. The later part of the gloss degenerates into something like a mere conflation of the Gloss and 'Jerome'.

One of the most striking developments in biblical exegesis in the second half of the twelfth century was the systematic introduction of the *distinctio*.[33] In its simplest form it was a method of deciding the meaning of a word in any given passage. For each meaning a text was cited and an 'ut hic' added to the meaning required. There was, of course, nothing new in this. It was used by the Fathers.[34] But it was greatly extended and attached to the doctrine of the four senses, employed in elucidating metaphor and finally applied out of habit. In the space of a few years, it would seem, alphabetical collections of *distinctiones* were made by Petrus Cantor, Alan of Lille, Garnier of Rochefort and William de Montibus, so that a commentator might have them ready-made to hand.[35] It is not clear who started the fashion. There are only occasional *distinctiones* in the Gloss of Peter Lombard. But his disciple Peter of Poitiers made a set of them to supplement the Lombard's Gloss.[36] They are particularly

---

[31] Ecce que iurgia proueniunt ex glosis, cum tamen in textu nulla sit difficultas: *GP* 27: 1 (MS Bodley 284, fol. 58ra).

[32] *GP* 60: 9 (MS Bodley 284, fol. 150va): 'Lectio ista plena est scrupulositatis, et ideo autentice lectioni Anselmi tutum est adherere'; cf. M. -D. Chenu, 'Autentica et magistralia', *Divus Thomas*, xxviii (1925), 257-85, and G. Paré *et al.*, op. cit. (n. 3 above), pp. 147-9.

[33] Lacombe, op. cit. (n. 1 above), pp. 117-20; id., 'The Lombard's commentary on Isaias and other fragments, II', *The New Scholasticism*, v (1931), 137-55, especially 139-40; F. M. Powicke, *The Medieval Books of Merton College* (Oxford, 1931), pp. 254-5.

[34] See for example Jerome, *In Esaiam*, XVII. lxiv. 7: ed. M. Adriaen (*CCSL* LXXIIIA, Turnhout, 1963), pp. 737-8.

[35] See R. H. and M. A. Rouse, 'Biblical distinctions in the thirteenth century', *AHDLMA* xli (1974), 27-37, with bibliography.

[36] P. Glorieux, *Répertoire des maîtres en théologie de Paris au XIIIe siècle* (Paris, 1933), p. 230. The work of Michael de Meaux is apparently similar, to

common in commentaries on the Psalter, though by no means confined to them. Alexander makes considerable use of them in his gloss on the Psalter.[37] Like Petrus Cantor he does not set them out schematically, but weaves them into the text. They are much more common in the first fifty psalms than later. This is probably due to the less elaborate character of the later part of the plan, which we have already noticed. As might be expected, they are less frequent in Alexander's other commentaries. As an illustration we will take one from the commentary on Ecclesiastes:

> Sed ut ea que hic dicuntur dilucidius intelligantur, proponenda est breuiter quedam distinctio, non causa curiositatis sed gratia utilitatis. Quidam ergo sunt auersi, quidam euersi, alii subuersi, alii peruersi. Auersi sunt qui a luce ueritatis et a beneficio eruditionis sese auertunt, quadam insolenti desidia ad hoc ducti. Euersi sunt quorum mens tota rebus terrenis infixa est, similes illis histrionibus mimicis, qui manibus sese sustentant et portant, summitate capitis fere tangente terram.[38]

2. Disputatio

We must now turn to the *disputatio* element in the commentaries. Mandonnet's theory that the *disputatio* grew out of the *lectio* seems to have won acceptance as a working hypothesis.[39] It is supposed that the dispute was first attached to the lesson and gradually became an independent exercise. The two were certainly distinct in Langton's time, and the same is true for Alexander. Once or twice when he finds himself being drawn into a discussion, he checks himself and says he is not exercising the function of one who disputes but of an expositor;[40] and once he breaks off with—'disputationi sunt ista'.[41] But it is generally true that in the Middle Ages the rise of something new did not mean the immediate

judge from MS Oxford, New College, 36: 'Incipiunt distinctiones magistri Michaelis super psalterium' (fol. 1). For Michael see further B. Smalley, 'Robert Bacon and the early Dominican school at Oxford', *TRHS* 4, ser. xxx (1948), 1-19, at 7 and 13.

[37] *GP* 4: 1-10: MS Bodley 284, fols. 5[rb]-7[ra].

[38] *In Eccles.* iii. 10: **C**, fol. 107[rb].

[39] See R. M. Martin, *Œuvres de Robert de Melun*, i (Spicilegium Sacrum Lovaniense, XIII, Louvain, 1932), pp. xxxiv-xlvi.

[40] Sed his supersedeo ad presens, expositoris potius assumens officium ad presens quam disputatoris: *GP* 24: 9 (MS Bodley 284, fol. 48[ra]); cf. *in Eccles.* iii. 18 and iv. 3 (**C**, fols. 133[ra] and 145[ra]).

[41] *GP* 50: 8: MS Bodley 284, fol. 129[va].

abolition of the old. The old and the new continue side by side for a time. So in the commentaries and especially in the *Commentary on the Psalter* there are *questiones* in various stages.[42] We may take two examples of them in embryo:

NEQVE IN IRA TVA CORRIPIAS ME [Ps. 6: 2]
Sed nonne debet quis uelle esse in purgatorio? Nonne scit quod si est in purgatorio saluabitur? Respondeo. Durum est incidere in manus domini [*cf*. Heb. 10: 31].

And later in the same Psalm—

TVRBATVS EST A FVRORE OCVLVS MEVS [Ps. 6: 8]
Sed numquid tenetur quis singula peccata confiteri? Quid si unum tradiderit obliuioni? Respondeo. Illud delebitur in generali contritione; si tamen illud ad memoriam redierit, tenebitur postmodum redire ad sacerdotem, ut illud ei reuelet et etiam circumstantie turpes reuelande sunt sacerdoti.[43]

Most of the questions are on this scale. But there are some more elaborate ones. It seems as if the formulae were kept for introducing a discussion on any particular point in the midst of the exposition. We find phrases like 'Volo tamen hic querere utrum', 'Incidimus in questionem illam qua queritur utrum'.[44] Occasionally in the monastic commentaries there are definite theological digressions.[45]

THE MONASTIC COMMENTARIES

The monastic commentaries vary from tractates on special passages to commentaries on whole books. The one that approaches most nearly to the normal type is the *Commentary on Ecclesiastes*. But it has a long introduction, the *De naturis rerum*. The connection between the two we have explained above. We turn to the four that remain.

The *Commentary on the Song of Songs* is still longer than

---

[42] See for example *CP* on Ps. 4: 9 (**B**, fols. 43vb-4ra). See now J. -P. Torrell, *Théorie de la prophétie et philosophie de la connaissance aux environs de 1230: la contribution de Hugues de Saint-Cher* (Spicilegium Sacrum Lovaniense, XL, Louvain, 1977), pp. xv-xviii.

[43] *GP* 6: 2 and 8: MS Bodley 284, fols. 8va and 9ra.

[44] *GP* 15: 5 and 81: 4: MS Bodley 284, fols. 21ra and 198ra.

[45] Questio autem est scolastica utrum bona propria prosint ad diminutionem pene eterne. Proponantur igitur duo qui eque mali decedant . . .: *in Eccles*. iv. 24 (**C**, fol. 166vb). Again, 'De ordine uero caritatis succincte pauca perstringemus': *CCant*. iii. 15 (**M**, fol. 77rb).

the *Commentary on Ecclesiastes*. The first book is an introduction mainly concerned with the Virgin Mary. Each
chapter begins with a text and is homiletic in form. The
commentary itself is almost entirely allegorical. Though
Alexander does not reject the traditional interpretation of
the Song of Songs as typifying the relations of Christ and the
Church, more space is devoted to explaining it as the story of
Christ and the Virgin. It may turn out to be of some importance in that line of exegesis. There are traces that it was
delivered in the form of addresses.[46]

The *Solatium fidelis anime* is a short moral Hexameron,
in which Alexander had not quite found his characteristic
manner. The work of each day is moralized, then 'the rivers
return to the place from whence they came' and we go back
to the beginning. This time the seven days are interpreted
as the seven gifts of the Holy Ghost. There follow two
chapters (21–2) on the four virtues and the various kinds of
death.

The *Commentary on Proverbs* begins with a long introduction (*ingressus*), of which the theme is stated in the
opening words:

Meditatio humana nunc in ipsum hominem reflectitur, nunc in ceteras
transit creaturas, nunc in auctorem rerum dirigitur.[47]

From the first two movements of thought arise speculations
on the vanity of things or on their utility. The third is higher
and far sweeter. For the one will lead man on to despise the
world and the second to the love of God. The three are
then discussed in greater detail. The vanity of the world is
illustrated by an unusually long list of men in high places,
and the various fates they met.[48] Among the deceased contemporaries are Richard I, William Rufus and the Emperor
Frederick I. The usefulness of things is shown by the care
with which God has ordered the world for man's benefit.
Finally Alexander turns to the Passion and to contemplation.
The three correspond to Ecclesiastes, Proverbs and the Song

[46] Hodierne refectioni, fratres, sufficit fragmen istud mali punici: *CCant.*
iv. 12 (M, fol. 114[va]).

[47] J, fol. 57[ra].

[48] *CProv.*: J, fol. 58[ra]. For the theme *ubi sunt* cf. *DNR* i. 20 (pp. 67–8),
i. 27 (p. 81); *SMF* (J, fol. 95[vb]).

of Songs.[49] The introduction is therefore in a sense an introduction to all three books. The commentary proper begins on a large scale. But already in chapter II it becomes more jejune and continues so until it ends in III. 27. He gives his own comments and then copies out the corresponding section in the commentary of Bede on Proverbs. Each piece from Bede is introduced by 'Beda sic'.

The *Tractatus super mulierem fortem* is a commentary on Proverbs 31: 10–31. It falls into three parts. He expounds the verses first in honour of St Mary Magdalen, then in honour of the Blessed Virgin and finally in honour of the Church. The first two parts have allegorical introductions, which are the most interesting part of the work. Their form is not at all finished. After dilating in flowery language on the washing of the feet of Christ he says:

Iam tunc uisus est michi benignissimus desideriorum mentis interpres [*sc*. Christ] ita se dixisse: Accede mulier pudorata, oculi tui columbarum absque eo quod latet intrinsecus, sicut cortex mali punici sic gene tue absque occultis tuis.[50]

The theme is picked up again after a digression. Mary Magdalen dares not approach the presence of the Lord alone; and while she debates what she shall do, Hope accompanied by Fortitude and Constancy come to her. Hope encourages her and says that Preventive Grace and Piety will sponsor her; Wisdom will be her patron and Pity will befriend her. She approaches and kisses the feet of Christ—'alternis itaque uicibus nunc hunc, nunc illum osculata pedem' (**J**, fol. 79va). Christ speaks to her in the words of the Song of Songs: 'Thine eyes are like the fishpools in Heshbon by the gate of Bathrabbim' (AV). Mary Magdalen is enflamed with new love:

Hec est ergo mulier fortis, dulcis deuotione feruentissima, leni conuersatione mitissima. In commendatione huius mulieris sub admiratione exclamat Salomon, tanquam tuba Spiritus sancti dicens: Mulierem fortem quis inueniet? Procul et de ultimis finibus terre precium eius.[51]

The tract continues in this high-flown style. Mary Magdalen is

---

[49] *Scilicet*: (i) 'in ipsum hominem'—vanity—Ecclesiastes; (ii) 'in ceteras creaturas'—utility—Proverbs; (iii) 'in auctorem rerum'—Passion and contemplation—Song of Songs.

[50] **J**, fol. 79rb.   [51] **J**, fol. 79vb.

addressed in a strain that appears a little extravagant. She is called 'apostola ueritatis' (fol. 81ra), 'euangelizatrix uerissima' (fol. 81va) and 'prima ecclesie magistra' (fol. 81^{va-b}).[52] The introduction to the exposition in honour of the Blessed Virgin turns on the incarnation.[53] It is an extended allegory. Pity appears before the throne of the Highest and says that the world has waited long for its saviour. The chosen virgin has now been born. Justice replies pointing out how much has been done already for the world. The promises made to the Patriarchs will be fulfilled in due course. Let Wisdom be summoned, whom nothing can deceive. Wisdom comes accompanied by Peace, Concord and Counsel and speaks. Wisdom declares that a woman must repair the mischief that woman did and that a strong woman ('mulier fortis') must be chosen. The advice pleases the Creator, who orders that it should be carried out. Wisdom consults with Counsel, who says a strong man should be sent as a messenger to the strong woman. Gabriel (his name means 'strong') leaped forth and said, 'I am ready to obey the divine commands' (fol. 99vb). The allegory then shades off into history.

There remains one special feature of Alexander's monastic commentaries, the 'consolatory meditations'. In the *Commentary on Proverbs*, as we have it, there are none, but in the others there are several, especially in the *Commentary on the Song of Songs*. They are the overflow of his personal devotion. For example in *SMF*, at Proverbs 31: 20—'She stretched out her hand to the poor'—he says:

Sepius autem dum dulcissimam ymaginem Crucifixi corporeis oculis conspicio occurrit memorie mee locus iste: *Aperuit manum suam inopi et palmas suas extendit ad pauperem.* Cerno manus apertas

---

[52] Cf. *SMF* on the meeting with our Lord in the garden: 'Set ad preclariores titulos laudes Magdalene, licet non ueriores stilum transmittit scribentis deuotio. Elegit ergo magister ueritatis, sed et magister ueritas, Magdalenam ad excellentissimum priuilegiate dignitatis fastigium, ut esset uidelicet prima salutis pubblice nuntia, disertissima magistrorum ecclesie magistra, testisque ueritatis, omni exceptione maior et euangelizatrix uerissima . . . Quis christiane religionis professor se discipulum esse apostolorum negare presumat? Quis ergo se discipulum esse apostolorum magistre non profiteatur letabundus? Magdalenam igitur uenerari debet totus fidelium cetus tanquam primam ecclesie magistram' (J, fol. 81^{rb-vb}).

[53] J, fols. 98vb-100ra.

quas saluator extendit, cerno, inquam, oculis interioribus. Intueor illud corpus regium nudatum, latus apertum conspicio, pedes cerno perforatos, aspicio manus extensas clauis confixas. Cernite uiri fratres, cernite oculis fidei . . .[54]

Usually the meditations are more elaborate in form. Alexander uses them as a means of conjuring up scenes from the Bible vividly. The regular opening formula is: 'Videor michi uidere'. They are almost like a regular devotional exercise. Their title is generally *Meditatio*, but these meditations with their detail and heavily laden imagery are unlike the decent and sober ones of St Anselm and his successors, to whom he no doubt owed much.[55] We may take an example:

Constituamus ergo pre oculis mentis[56] matrem dulcedinis et filium dulcedinem sese dulciter amplexantes. Videor quidem michi uidere nunc matrem leticie maternis brachiis leniter filium suum sustentantem, nunc osculum prebere sidereis pueri ocellis, nunc fronti niuee, nunc genis purpureis, nunc collo lacteo, nunc labiis roseis. Quandoque rapit oscula uis amoris materni, quandoque spatioso temporis tractu oscula tenellis labiis imprimit, inexhaustas bibens delicias ex illo ore sanctissimo. Nunc filium quasi e diuersa regione contra faciem suam statuit, ut liberius illius uultum iocundissimum leto sidere oculorum percurrat; nunc pectus admouet pectori, os ori. O quam florido aspectu uirgo mater filium deum respicit, quam leta ipsam leticiam intuetur![57]

---

[54] J, fol. 121va.

[55] Cum ignea loquitur deuotio, fiunt labia cordis sicut uitta coccinea. Augustini lege meditationes fructuosas in scriptum redactas et uulnerabitur cor tuum telo spiritualis amoris . . . Dulcissimas inspice Gregorii meditationes et palato cordis tui [*cf. Wilmart, op. cit. (n. 56 below), p. 583*] dulce sapiet manna dulcedinis eloquentie suauissime. Relege iocundissimas Anselmi Cantuariensis meditationes, in quibus tam flores quam fructus suauitatis legere poteris, uelut in orto quodam deliciarum constitutus: *CCant*. vi. 13 (M, fol. 173vb).

[56] Cf. *DNR* i. 17 (p. 60). Cf. and contrast Stephen of Salley (d. 1252): A. Wilmart, *Auteurs spirituels et textes dévots du moyen âge latin* (Paris, 1932), pp. 345-6.

[57] *CCant*. ii. 8: M, fols. 46rb-7ra. In the margin is 'Dulcis meditatio'. Cf. the Virgin's speech describing her feelings in Egypt: 'Cum uero certis fame indiciis instructa sum super nece paruulorum, in quo nimis ausa est effrenis rabies tirannici furoris, o quam perterrita, o quam gemebunda, o quam crebra suspiria ab intimo cordis traxi. Codicem doloris legere michi uisa sum, noui operis noua commentatrix. Matres paruulorum sparsis crinibus, scissis uestibus, pectora manibus tundentes, eiulantes, me sequentes uidere michi uisa sum, et fecunditate uteri(s) mei se suis orbatas esse paruulis uise sunt protestari' (*CCant*. ii. 18: M, fol. 54vb).

ALEXANDER'S KNOWLEDGE OF HEBREW

There is no reason to believe that Alexander knew any more Greek than the letters of the alphabet.[58] Most of the observations he makes on the language show more ignorance than knowledge. But a prima facie case can be made out for his knowledge of Hebrew.[59] He seems to make real use of it in the commentaries. In a number of passages he refers to the 'hebraica ueritas' or uses phrases like 'Hebreus habet', 'Hebrei dicunt'.[60] Such phrases are part of the stock in trade of the medieval commentator and are usually derived in the last resort from Jerome. Examples of such derivative information can naturally be found in Alexander, and for a source we need not go further than Peter Lombard:

NEQVANDO TACEAS A ME [Ps. 27: 1]
Miror quod glosatores dicunt istud *ne quando taceas a me* non esse de ueritate hebraica, et ideo obelum dicunt esse appondendum, cum tamen et in romano psalterio et in translatione Ieronimi hoc contineatur et in tenore seriei textus modernorum Iudeorum contineatur.[61]

But there are references to the Hebrew text which appear to be independent:

APVD IOAS FILIVM AMELECH [3 Kgs. 22: 26]
Omnes codices quos inspexi, preter hebreos et paucos latinos

---

[58] See for example *CP* I (**B**, fol. 12va) on X̄P̄C̄: 'He ergo figure x, p, c apud Grecos representant elementa, que representant he figure apud nos c, r, s. Sed hec figura x apud Grecos chi dicitur, hec figura p apud Grecos dicitur ros, quod nos dicimus r; hec uero figura c, ut dictum est, apud Grecos representat sima, hoc est s. Si[c] igitur x p c apud Grecos cum apice superposito representarent nomen Christi, ac si[c] c r s cum apice superposito representarent hoc nomen apud nos, si usus adesset sollempnitas.' There are one or two Greek words in the text of *CAth.*: MS London, BL, Harley 3133, fols. 97^v, 98^v.

[59] Landgraf has published an Isagoge of the twelfth century in which considerable knowledge of Hebrew is shown: *Écrits théologiques de l'école d'Abelard* (Spicilegium Sacrum Lovaniense, XIV, Louvain, 1934), pp. 63–285. See further R. Loewe, 'The mediaeval Christian Hebraists of England: Herbert of Bosham and earlier scholars', *Transactions of the Jewish Historical Society of England*, xvii (1951-2), 225–49.

[60] For example *CP* II (**B**, fols. 29rb, 34vb); *GP* 21: 6, 44: 13 and 67: 17 (MS Bodley 284, fols. 37ra, 114va and 164va); *CCant.* ii. 13 and iii. 25 (**M**, fols. 50ra and 88ra); *CProv.* (**J**, fols. 63va, 73va).

[61] *GP* 27: 1 (MS Bodley 284, fol. 57vb); cf. Peter Lombard, *Commentary on the Psalter*, ad loc.: *MPL* cxci. 277D–8C. See also *GP* 39: 5 (MS Bodley 284, fol. 98vb), from Peter Lombard ad loc. (col. 401A).

correctos, sunt hic corrupti et habent *Amalech*, quod quidem est nomen populi cuiusdam.[62]

In various places Alexander discourses on the meaning of Hebrew words. The most elaborate is that in the *De naturis rerum*, where he tries to show that the mystery of the Trinity is contained in the opening words of Genesis in Hebrew.[63] Moses was inspired to choose just those words for 'In the beginning' and he gives a list of other words which mean the same thing. He also mentions the vowel-points. More convincing still are the references to the 'Hebrei moderni':

Falluntur autem Hebrei moderni existimantes pomum citrinum esse fructum arboris pulcherrime. Est enim arbor ista malus ferens poma aurei coloris, unde et mala aurea dicuntur.[64]

The final proof is given in the *Commentary on the Song of Songs*, where he says he has heard the Hebrews expounding[65] and talks of conferring with 'litteratores hebrei':

Sepe cum litteratoribus Hebreis contuli, querens quid ad *dentium* pertineat pulchritudinem quod omnes oues *ascendentes de lauacro fetus gemellos* [Cant. 4: 2] habuisse perhibentur. Repperi quondam disertum in expositione litterali de fetibus hic nullam fieri mentionem asserentem. Hebraica enim ueritas sic habet: *Omnes gemellantes et lesus non est in eis*. Ad ordinatam dentium seriem referendum hoc uidebitur. Decens enim ipsorum ordo in precisinis precipue equalitatem quandam desiderat. Sed in area sacre scripture legant Iudei paleas, dummodo nobis grana relinquant.[66]

He never gives the names of those from whom he learned or with whom he conferred. There are five quotations from Gamaliel, which is normally the title medieval writers give to the Talmud.[67] It will be seen that the quotations are spread

[62] *CP* on 3 Kgs. 22: 26 (**B**, fol. 29[va]: Meyer 1896, p. 667); cf. *CCant*. iii. 25 (**M**, fol. 88[vb]).

[63] *DNR* i. 1 (pp. 7–10).

[64] *CCant*. iii. 12 (**M**, fol. 75[ra]); cf. *GP* 41: 2 and 45: 10 (MS Bodley 284, fols. 104[ra] and 116[va]).

[65] *CCant*. iv. 5 (**M**, fol. 105[vb]): 'Vix quicquam Hebreos audiui commodius exponere transitu isto'.

[66] *CCant*. iv. 10 (**M**, fol. 113[ra]), commenting on Cant. 4: 2. For 'precisinis' cf. 'precisor', an incisor tooth.

[67] *CP* on Prov. 26: 8 (**B**, fol. 38[rb]); *GP* 28: 9 (MS Bodley 284, fol. 61[va]); *DNR* i. 23 (p. 72); *in Eccles*. iii. 10, added chapter (MS London, BL, Royal 12 F. XIV, fol. 134[rb]; *SMF* (**J**, fol. 88[vb]). For an *exemplum* from the Talmud see above, p. 89.

throughout the commentaries. The references are usually respectful: 'Hec legimus in uenerabilibus scripturis uenerandi Gamalielis'.[68] Only once is he really savage[69] when he says that he does not know whether to laugh or cry at their puerile expositions of a passage in the Song of Songs. Their superficial exposition makes one laugh, but the supine and crass ignorance by which their foolish heart is darkened makes one grieve.

[68] *In Eccles.* iii. 10, added chapter: MS London, BL, Royal 12 F. XIV, fol. 134va.

[69] *CCant.* v. 10: M, fol. 144^{ra-rb}.

IX

THE THEOLOGIAN

AT the end of the twelfth and the beginning of the thirteenth century there was no sharp division between philosophy and theology.[1] No hesitation was now felt in applying dialectical methods to theological problems; and it is at this period that such application reaches its peak in the *summae* of men like Peter of Poitiers and Simon of Tournai. The problems of reconciling the two hardly arose, since the effect of the metaphysical writings of Avicenna and Aristotle was scarcely perceptible. We have seen that it was the naturalists who played the most important part in the introduction of the new knowledge; and that as a naturalist Alexander was in the movement. It will be interesting to see how far it is applied in dealing with theological problems.

The chief theological work of Alexander is the *Speculum speculationum*. It is apparently only preserved in one manuscript; and though as far as the text goes it is *optimae notae*, there are several problems raised by it, which could only be solved by the finding of another manuscript for comparison. The work is divided into four books, which was the conventional division. The normal arrangement of matter, following the example set by the *Sentences* of Peter Lombard, was to put the doctrine of God and the Trinity in the first book, the doctrine of creation and of angels in the second, the incarnation and virtues in the third, and the sacraments in the fourth. Alexander's arrangement is much the same as this, but not the division into books. For the whole of the first two books are taken up by the doctrine of God and the Trinity. The third begins with the creation (1-14) and goes on to angels (15-77). Then we return to problems connected with creation (79-82). The book ends with the soul and its faculties (83-94). The fourth book is concerned with grace

---

[1] M.-D. Chenu, 'La théologie comme science au XIIIe siècle', *AHDLMA* ii (1927), 31-71.

and free will (1–15) and with other problems of grace (16–25). This corresponds roughly to the middle of the second book in Peter Lombard. The work certainly is not complete as we have it. The hand changes three pages before the end (fol. 92^r), and the last chapter breaks off in the middle of a sentence. In the fourth book the list of chapters is added in another hand, with initials in red and green ink instead of red and blue as in the rest of the manuscript; and at this point altogether forty-one lines are left blank (fols. 74^v–5). The numbering of the chapters within the text is mysterious. After XIV comes L–LIIII (= iv. 15–19), then no number (= iv. 20), then XXI–XXV. Now L–LIIII and iv. 20 fit in here according to the sense. But it is possible that the manuscript preserves the true numbers for these chapters and that they have been transferred here. There is a parallel to this in the odd arrangement of Book Three, where Alexander turns from creation to angels and then returns to creation. That there was more to come is clear from the preface (fol. 1rb):

Vt autem seriei ordinis quem obseruare decreuimus in tractatu instituendo meditationum nostrarum ordinata dispositio se conformet, a summo bono tamquam a primo principio sumamus exordium, ut a paradiso summe beatitudinis trium personarum seipsis mutuo eternaliter fruentium gaudio ineffabili transeamus, tam ad iocunde felicitatis supernorum ciuium quam ad amenitatis celi empirei paradisum. Cum autem una sit res pubblica[2] ex ecclesia triumphanti et militanti, dirigere meditationes a paradiso iam dicto ad paradisum militantis ecclesie et ad paradisum leticie tranquille consciencie dignum duximus. De benignissima etiam dispensatione misterii incarnationis dominice et efficacissima uirtute sacramentorum ecclesie, de uirtutibus eciam et uiciis nonnulla proponemus in medium, annuente illo sine cuius subsidio nichil bene inchoatur aut feliciter consummatur.

There are several references to a section on virtues. In iii. 95 he says: 'Vtrum autem fides uirtus sit superior scientia uel inferior determinabitur inferius.'[3] There is now no discussion of faith. At the beginning of iv. LIIII (= iv. 19) Alexander says that though he has not yet begun the tractate on virtues yet it will be a suitable opportunity to discuss whether sharp

---

[2] Alexander's regular spelling.
[3] *SS* iii. 95 (**R**, fol. 74va); cf. iii. 44 (**R**, fol. 60ra): 'Sed in uirtutibus precedit naturaliter habitus usum, ut dicetur infra.'

temptation can be resisted with little charity.[4] How far the rest of the subjects referred to were ever finished we cannot tell. In iii. 29 there is a reference to a discussion on the Communion of saints, which would perhaps have come right at the end. A contemporary hand has written in 'pencil' in the margin: 'Memorandum quod inquiratur ubi magister tractauit [?] de communione sanctorum'.[5] The work starts out on such a large scale that it may well have been left unfinished.

No attempt can be made to give any systematic account of Alexander's theology. In the first place it is too difficult and technical a subject for one who has had no theological training, and secondly there is not enough comparative material available.[6] Alexander's method of discussion is to put down side by side all the definitions or views on a subject that he knows. Some are discussed in detail, some not. His own view often only appears incidentally. The difficulty of following him is further increased by his way of conducting an argument in a long series of rhetorical questions. We will take two doctrines in which the views of his contemporaries have been investigated in some detail: free will[7] and synderesis.

After a short introductory section saying that free will has a natural freedom and is under no 'necessity of inevitability or of compulsion'[8] or the influence of the planets or stars, the first definition, that of Boethius, 'liberum de uoluntate iudicium' (cf. *DCPhil.* V, pr. 2), is put forward:

(i) Freedom is from the will, judgement from reason. Therefore sin is from the will, but not from judgement. In discerning a man does not sin, but in choosing evil or repelling good.

(ii) But is not will from reason? Is it not from reason that a man will choose evil? On this view, will never comes from the power of discerning, but will and freedom of the will are

---

[4] *SS* iv. 19 [alias iv. LIIII] (**R**, fol. 86vb).

[5] *SS* iii. 29 (**R**, fol. 58ra).

[6] See A. M. Landgraf, *Introduction à l'histoire de la littérature de la scholastique naissante* (Montréal and Paris, 1973), *passim*; Nequam briefly at p. 178.

[7] O. Lottin, *Psychologie et moral aux XIIe et XIIIe siècles*: i (2nd edn., Gembloux, 1957), pp. 11–63.

[8] This is a current distinction: Lottin, op. cit., p. 147 app., quoting Alexander of Hales. RWH attributed a very similar passage, which I have been unable to find, to Stephen Langton.

regulated according to the power of choosing or repelling. But is it not a sin to deliberate or to wish to deliberate whether Christ should be denied? Does not the will come from and is it not regulated by the power of discerning? Again if free will is judgement, it will only be the power of discerning. But is there not also a judgement that chooses and repels? Is free will then one judgement or more? But free will is in the faculty of desiring and of 'anger'. The movement towards the desire for virtue is in the faculty of desiring. If free will is in all three faculties, what is its moving power? It cannot be will, because that belongs to the reasoning faculty. It cannot be a special power. Since all merit comes from free will, do not the vices also? Pride and the movement towards pride are in the faculty of desiring. Therefore one can win demerit by the faculty of desire; and if so free will is not in the faculty of discerning alone.

The second view is Alexander's own. The faculty of reason contains powers of choosing and discerning or repelling. The power of discerning that concerns theologians here is the power of discerning between things that are good and evil. Therefore the power that concerns discerning—in this sense— and choosing and repelling, especially in the way that these single powers are concerned with good and evil, is free will. It is an aptitude or ability, not substantial like rationality or the power of walking, which have nothing directly to do with free will, but accidental. It is exercised in discerning between good and evil, choosing good or evil or repelling good and evil.

(iii) The third definition is that of Peter Lombard: 'Liberum arbitrium est facultas uoluntatis et rationis qua bonum eligitur gratia assistente uel malum eadem desistente'.[9] This is dismissed in a word. It is followed by a long discussion whether a madman who fornicates or commits murder is acting of his own free will and how far sin can be imputed to him.

(iv) Finally Alexander gives the definition of St Anselm,[10]

---

[9] Peter Lombard, *Sententie*, II, dist. xxiv. 3, edd. PP. Collegii S. Bonauenturae (Grottaferrata, 1971), i. 452–3 (also *MPL* cxcii. 702).

[10] Anselm, *De libertate arbitrii*, 3: ed. F. S. Schmitt, *Anselmi Opera* (Edinburgh, 1946), i. 212.

on which he simply observes that those who say that 'free will is will' finish the matter in a few words.

Closely connected with the doctrine of free will is that of synderesis.[11] Synderesis is a Greek word of uncertain meaning, which is only found in Jerome's *Commentary on Ezekiel.*[12] For Jerome it is the spark of conscience above and outside the three faculties, which in man is never extinguished. On this passage a considerable structure was raised. Alexander begins by saying that almost all men are agreed that it is not extinguished in any man, not even in Cain. There are three different views on its nature. (*a*) Some say it is to discern or choose; if to discern, then the Devil has it; if to choose, the movement by which we wish for good comes from it. That is meritorious, therefore free will embraces it. Again there is free will in bad angels. If synderesis is not part of free will now, it never was or free will has lost something. Do all those who have charity always win merit, because synderesis always moves men to good? Is faith according to synderesis, since it is above the intellect? Do the charitable then win merit by a movement of faith? (*b*) Others say that synderesis is a natural affection to good, of which it has the image in itself. For as men never cease to desire temporal things, so no crime can extinguish the will for the highest good. It is the spark never extinguished. It never disagrees with reason, because it wants that which reason shows to be desirable. Hence it differs from reason, because we do not desire by reason, but decide what is to be desired. But does not desire belong to the faculty of concupiscence? Does anyone win merit by desire? If not, is it not superfluous in the charitable? (*c*) Others again say that it is the higher part of reason, by which a man, however bad he may be, comes back to himself. For reason has other functions besides discerning good from evil. By this part of reason there is a natural kindliness extinct in the Devil and in the damned after judgement. This seems to be the view Alexander favours.

---

[11] O. Renz, *Die Synteresis nach dem hl. Thomas von Aquin* (*BGPM* X. 1-2, Münster-i.-W., 1911), pp. 238-40; cf. O. Lottin, op. cit. (n. 7 above), pp. 58-62.

[12] Jerome, *In Hiezechielem*, I. i. 6/8 (the four living creatures): ed. F. Gloria (*CCSL* LXXV, Turnhout, 1964), p. 12 and app.

The first person to point out the connection between free will and synderesis was Stephen Langton.[13] But the search for a relationship between Langton and Alexander is disappointing. In the discussion on free will there are some things which are reminiscent of Langton. There is the use of the example from 'the ability to walk' ('gressibilitas'), and there is a similar use of the gloss on the three measures of meal. But the doctrine itself is not very close to that of Langton. In the discussion on synderesis there are some important divergences, especially in its relations to reason. Such agreement as there is between the two men is probably due to the common material. This is made certain by the contrast in their handling of the definition of faith in Hebrews. Langton's exposition is a notable step forward. Alexander's is still in the common rut.[14]

It is by his interest in psychology that Alexander stands out. In his article on the identity of the soul and its faculties Dom Lottin says that the question was not broached until about 1220: 'The hour of psychological questions had not yet struck'.[15] But Alexander does touch on the problem in the chapters 'De uiribus anime'.[16] He is conscious that he is an innovator. At the end of the discussion on the faculties he says:

De uiribus ergo rationalis anime compendiosum iam instituimus tractatum ex parte, nouo usi distinctionis modo, utinam competenti. Communis autem opinio diuidit animam rationalem quasi in tres partes, quarum inferiorem dicunt uim concupiscibilem mediam irascibilem, suppremam rationabilem, quam quidam in duas partes, quidam in tres subdiuidunt, dicentes tres esse rationes.[17]

[13] O. Lottin, op. cit. (n. 7 above), pp. 361-2. Lottin there treats MS Paris, BN, lat. 14556, as distinct from Langton. It is now generally agreed to be his work.

[14] G. Englhardt, *Die Entwicklung der dogmatischen Glaubenspsychologie in der mittelalterlichen Scholastik* (*BGPM* XXX. 4-6, Münster-i.-W., 1933), pp. 63, 115-23. See *CAth.* (MS London, BL, Harley 3133, fol. 92^{r-v}): 'Est enim fides argumentum, id est probatio non apparentium. Fides enim sibi ipsi fidem facit. In logicis dicitur quod argumentum est ratio rei dubie faciens fidem. Sed in theologicis dicitur quod quia ut dicit apostolus, "que uidentur temporalia sunt, que non uidentur eterna" [2 Cor. 4: 18]'; cf. Englhardt, pp. 34-5 (Hervé of Bourg-Dieu).

[15] O. Lottin, 'L'identité de l'âme et de ses facultés pendant la première moitié du XIIIe siècle', *Revue néoscholastique de philosophie*, xxxvi (1934), 191-210, at p. 192.

[16] *SS* iii. 90-2: **R**, fols. 72ra-4ra.   [17] *SS* iii. 90: **R**, fol. 73va.

But a little later he almost abandons it:

Ne autem uidear uelle abrogare doctrinam maiorum sustineatur plures esse uires anime.[18]

The reason for his interest in these problems is that he has read the *De anima* of Avicenna, as is demonstrated in a passage in Book III. 95:

In brutis quidem animalibus est *estimatio ordinata in media concaui-tate cerebri* ad discernendum rem sensui subiectam uel ymaginationi . . . *Diiudicat* enim estimatiua et indicat *oui quod* ei expediat *fugere lupum.* Sed numquam uersatur estimatio circa *compositionem et diuisionem?* Numquid *diiudicat ouis* secundum estimatiuam, *quod lupus sit fugien-dus?* Numquid diiudicat ueritatem uel falsitatem? Absit. Ouis enim lupum iudicat esse fugiendum sed non attendit compositionem.[19]

No indirect source has been found and the borrowing is probably direct.

The only doctrine by which Alexander was remembered was his advocacy of the Immaculate conception. William of Ware says: 'Alexander Nequam in ultimo uitae suae exposuit illud Canticorum: *Tota pulchra es, amica mea et macula non est in te* neque actualis neque originalis de beata uirgine.'[20] William of Nottingham mentions his advocacy 'in fine uite sue'.[21] In an anonymous sermon preached at the Council of Basel he is put forward as a defender of the view: 'Primo Alexander Nequam doctor Oxoniensis in sermone incipiente Fiat lux'.[22] But when we examine what he really said himself, we find that he was not so decided as these extracts would have us believe. The upshot of the discussion in the *Commentary on the Song of Songs* is that he allows the doctrine in such a limited form that in effect he denies it.[23]

[18] *SS* iii. 92: R, fol. 74[ra].

[19] R, fol. 74[va]: cf. Avicenna, *De anima*, I. v, ed. S. van Riet (*Avicenna Latinus*, Louvain and Leiden, 1972), p. 89, verbal agreement underlined.

[20] William of Ware, OFM, *Quaestio utrum beata Virgo concepta fuerit in originali peccato* (*Bibliotheca Franciscana Scholastica Medii Aevi*, III, Quarrachi, 1904), pp. 6-7. William of Ware taught in Oxford in the late thirteenth century; Duns Scotus is said to have been among his pupils; cf. Emden, *BRUO* 1986.

[21] William of Nottingham, *in Sententias*, iii: MS Cambridge, Gonville and Caius College, 300 (514), fol. 173va. This is William of Nottingham II (*fl.* early s. xiv): Emden, *BRUO* 1377-8, with references.

[22] MS Oxford, Balliol College, 165A, p. 588, citing Sermon 23 (W, fols. 66-7[v]).

[23] See X. Le Bachelet, 'Immaculée Conception', in *Dictionnaire de théologie catholique*, vii (Paris, 1921-2), 845-1218, at 1037-42; and further A. Wilmart, 'Les homélies attribuées à S. Anselme', *AHDLMA* ii (1927), 5-29, at 25-6.

X

THE SURVIVAL OF
ALEXANDER'S WORKS

THE purpose of this chapter is to put together a few facts about the use of Alexander's writings after his death; and it seeks to avoid any suggestion of 'influence'. No attempt has been made to search systematically for traces of this survival, nor indeed to record all those that have been found. To do so would have been pointless. It seemed better to pick out those which were significant.

We will begin with the chief local monument to him, the *Florilegium* extracted from his works, to which so much reference has been made: MS Cambridge, University Library, Gg. 6. 42 (**G**). The compiler put a verse epistle at the beginning and end of the first book and perhaps at the end of the second.[1] He tells us that his name is Galfridus and that he is a monk. He is submitting his work for correction to someone whom in the first epistle he calls the sun of Malmesbury and the moonlight of monks and a *pius pastor*—by which he presumably means the abbot. In the second he gives the name of this paragon—Gaufridus; and there was an abbot of Malmesbury called Geoffrey who ruled from 1246 to 1260. Unfortunately we have no sure clue to the monastery of the compiler of the *Florilegium*. From the way he addresses Abbot Geoffrey we may infer that he was not a monk of Malmesbury. The script of **G**, the insertion of the slip at fol. 70 and the inserted leaf at fol. 92 and its general correctness make it probable that in this manuscript we have one of the original fair copies. But the book has no early *ex libris*, and its connection with Cirencester is late and obscure. The familiarity of the compiler with Alexander's works and the fact that he had access to such good manuscripts of so many

---

[1] G, fol. 3 (Walther 18380); fol. 71ᵛ (*inc.* 'Pagina dulce putat cum te mea sponte salutat . . .'); fol. 212ᵛ (*inc.* 'Nunc pater et domine tu uideris hic liber omne . . .').

of them tempt one to say that he must have been a canon of Cirencester. But it is no more than a guess.

The work of Alexander which had the most immediate success was certainly the *Corrogationes Promethei*. More manuscripts of it have survived than of any other work and there are far more references to it in library catalogues. We have already mentioned the enthusiastic letter in praise of it by the prior of Malmesbury.[2] But it will be observed that the manuscripts with few exceptions are hardly later than the end of the thirteenth century. It was only a manual and it had its day. But the manuals which succeeded it did not fail to incorporate the parts which were most practical, that is to say the explanations of biblical words. It might have had a more lasting success if it had been arranged alphabetically;[3] but when Alexander wrote alphabetical arrangement had only just spread from glossaries to collections of *distinctiones*, and there were no concordances. Probably the first person to use the *Corrogationes Promethei* for a biblical word-book was Willelmus Brito, a Franciscan at Lyons, who wrote about the middle of the century.[4] He follows Alexander closely in his choice of words to be explained and often incorporates his notice, using various other sources in addition. When he quotes Alexander by name it is nearly always the versification to which he refers. It was this Franciscan work which roused Roger Bacon's anger and contempt and led him to formulate his famous judgement of Brito, erring 'cum suo Alexandro Necquam'.[5] The Dominican Simon of Hinton, a contemporary of William Brito, used the *Corrogationes Promethei* on at least four occasions in his *Commentary on the Twelve Minor Prophets*. Of the plumb-line (Amos 7: 7, AV) he writes '*Trulla* sicut dicit Alexander Nequam est instrumentum ad congregandos cineres uel ad uerrendum pauimentum'; and there are three similar

---

[2] See p. 12 above.

[3] An alphabetical version does exist in MS Cambridge, Corpus Christi College, 460, fols. 37^V–68 (s. xiii–xiv: ? East Anglia); title, 'Explicit compendium super promatheum Alexandri Nequam' (fol. 68).

[4] *Expositiones uocabulorum Biblie*, edd. L. W. and B. A. Daly, 2 vols. (Thesaurus Mundi, 15–16, Padua, 1975).

[5] Roger Bacon, *Compendium Studii Philosophiae*, vii, ed. J. S. Brewer, *Fr. Rogeri Bacon Opera* (RS, London, 1859), p. 457.

passages in his exposition of Amos.[6] The most elaborate of the imitations is the *Liber de expositionibus uocabulorum biblie* of Rogerus Compotista, a monk at Bury, who is said to have flourished about 1360.[7] In his preface he says he is indebted to the help of Reginald of Walsingham, also a monk of Bury. He wrote for the benefit of novices and collected his material 'ex multis et diuersis glosariis',[8] which he does not name particularly. It is arranged in the same way as Part II of the *Corrogationes Promethei*,[9] but Roger also takes in the Prologues to each book. He used the *Corrogationes Promethei* extensively and occasionally quotes the *De naturis rerum*.[10] He glosses words in French. The grammatical part of the *Corrogationes Promethei* also had some vogue. There is a quotation from it in the gloss *Admirantes* (which was the work of an Englishman) on the *Doctrinale*,[11] and in another gloss on the same work.[12] There is an extract in Whethamstede's *Collectanea*,[13] and there are other pieces here and there.[14]

The most solid foundation of Alexander's reputation was the *De naturis rerum et super Ecclesiasten* and the *Commentary on the Song of Songs*. There is evidence of the

[6] MS Oxford, Bodleian, e mus. 29 (*SC* 3505), fol. 312[V] (Amos 7: 7); cf. fol. 310 (Amos 6: 7). For Simon himself see B. Smalley, *The Study of the Bible in the Middle Ages* (2nd edn., Oxford, 1952), pp. 273, 318-23; cf. id. 'Two biblical commentaries of Simon of Hinton', *Recherches de théologie ancienne et médiévale*, xiii (1946), 56-85.

[7] See MSS Bodley 238 (*SC* 2050), fols. 200[Va]-62ra; Bodleian Laud Misc. 176, fols. 32-163[V] (*expl.* . . . Argentarius/[Acts 19:24]; Oxford, Magdalen College, 112, fols. 172ra-211vb; Worcester, Cathedral Library, F. 61, fols. 1ra-63va (entitled 'promotheus' in a later hand: fol. 1[rb]): cf. T. Tanner, *Biblioteca Britannico-Hibernica* (London, 1748), p. 194.

[8] MS Bodley 238, fol. 213[Va].

[9] Roger gives a general index of words treated: ibid., fols. 200[Va]-213[Va].

[10] See for example MS Bodley 238, fol. 248ra (electrum).

[11] *Doctrinale*, 611-12 (ed. cit., p. 48 above): 'mas aut commune', glossed 'propter hanc dictionem *merges* ponamus hec uerba magistri Alexandri Nequam, *Cum utrumque et pro aue et pro gerba debeat dici* (MS Orléans, Bibl. Mun., 299 [252], fol. 12): C. Thurot, op. cit. (n. III. 28, p. 515).

[12] *Doctrinale*, 2106-7: 'saphirum iunge papyro | appellans lapidem', glossed 'Porticus est Rome, qua dum spaciando fero me, | res querendo nouas inueni de saphiro uas: *Alexander Nequam*' (MS Stuttgart, Württembergische Landesbibliothek, Q. 58, ad loc., cited by Reichling, p. 141 app.).

[13] MS Cambridge, Gonville and Caius College, 230 (116), p. 88, quoting *CP* I. i: B, fol. 2ra.

[14] *CP* I is quoted in the margin of William of Conches, *Dragmaticon* (MS Cambridge, Corpus Christi College, 385, p. 122); and in a gloss on Ps. -Ovid, *De mirabilibus mundi* (MS Oxford, Bodleian, Digby 100, fol. 169[V]).

continuous use of the former by theologians, commentators and chroniclers. There are quotations in Thomas Docking,[15] Henry of Harclay,[16] Robert Holcot[17] and in the *Moralitates super Ysaiam* of his school.[18] Finally a decade later another Dominican, William D'Eyncourt, borrowed extensively from Nequam for his Commentary on Ecclesiastes.[19] The De naturis rerum is quoted in Higden's *Polychronicon*[20] and by John Brompton.[21] An apparent citation in the Chronicle of Geoffrey le Baker[22] was to be taken up by Drayton in his account of Lundy Island—

> This Lundy is a Nymph to idle toyes inclin'd
> And, all on pleasure set, doth whollie give her mind
> To see upon her shores her Fowle and Conies fed
> And wantonlie to hatch the Birds of Ganimed.[23]

Many of the stories in the *De naturis rerum* were absorbed in collections of *exempla*.[24] A copy of the book was solemnly

[15] Thomas Docking, *Commentary on Deuteronomy*, 15: 19 and 32: 33 (MS London, BL, Royal 3 B. XII, fols. 79ra and 174rb). Docking was regent of the Oxford Franciscans 1260-5: see Emden, *BRUO* 580.

[16] Henry of Harclay, *questio* 'Vtrum astrologi uel quicumque calculatores possint probare secundum aduentum Christi': MS Worcester, Cathedral Library, F. 3, fols. 181^v-7^v, at 186^v. Harclay was a secular and a theologian, who died in 1317: Emden, *BRUO* 874-5.

[17] See for example Holcot's exposition of Wisdom 7: 24, 16: 22-4, 18: 5-8: *M. Roberti Holcoth . . . in librum sapientiae regis Salomonis praelectiones CXIII* (? Basel, 1586), pp. 322, 607, 653-4. For Holcot himself see B. Smalley, *The English Friars and Antiquity* (Oxford, 1960), cap VII, and Emden, *BRUO* 946-7.

[18] MS London, BL, Royal 7 C. I, fol. 243vb: on Isaiah 6: 5.

[19] Smalley, *English Friars* (n. 17 above), pp. 204-8, at 206 n. 1. See for example MS Balliol 27, fol. 339va (Eccles. 3: 7).

[20] Higden, *Polychronicon*, III. xxiv and xliv: ed. J. R. Lumby (RS, London, 1871-2), iii. 358-68, iv. 242-4; cf. *DNR* ii. 189 and 174 (pp. 337-8 and 309-10).

[21] R. Twysden, *Historiae Anglicanae Scriptores* x (London, 1652), col. 814-15, citing *DNR* ii. 21 (p. 141).

[22] Lunday est insula in flumine Sabrina . . . habundans pascuis et auenis, cuniculos producit copiose, columbis, eciam strucionibus, quos uocat Alexander Necham Ganimedis aues . . .: *Chronicon Galfridi le Baker de Swynebroke*, ed. E. M. Thompson (Oxford, 1889), p. 22; cf. *DNR* i. 46 (p. 97), misread.

[23] *Poly-Olbion*, iv. 11-14: ed. J. W. Hebel, *The Works of Michael Drayton* (Oxford, 1961), iv. 69. Selden corrects to 'the birds of Palamede' (cranes), citing *DNR* i. 46 (p. 97): ibid., p. 82. For the identification of the birds of Ganymede see now R. Sharpe, 'Geoffrey le Baker's *aves Ganymedis*, Lundy Island and Alexander Nequam', *Notes and Queries* (1984).

[24] Notably MS London, BL, Harley 7322: see Herbert, *Cat. Rom.* iii. 166-79; cf. J. -T. Welter, *L'Exemplum dans la littérature religieuse et didactique du moyen âge* (Paris and Toulouse, 1927, pp. 368-9.

presented to the University Library at Oxford in 1452,[25] and there were copies in the libraries of half a dozen colleges at Oxford and Cambridge. The *Commentary on the Song of Songs* is not cited to the same extent. But it remained in use and was consulted by later commentators as in the anonymous commentaries in MSS Balliol College 19 and Exeter College 13. It too was well represented in the college libraries at Oxford and Cambridge.

In the re-edition of the *Tabula septem custodiarum*, which is contained in Peterhouse 169,[26] many additional references come from Alexander's *Commentary on the Song of Songs* and some from his *De naturis rerum*. We will give the references to the book of Ruth as a specimen:[27]

In diebus unius iudicis quando iudices preerant facta est fames in terra (1: 1): Ambrosius allegorice usque ad finem capituli li. 3 super Lucam super illud 'Qui fuit Booz' exponit hec.

Abiit Neomi [rectius '*homo*'] *in regionem Moabitidem* usque *uacuam reduxit me dominus* (1: 1–21): Alexander super Cantica li. 4 c. 7b, Neomi est anima.

Ne uocetis me Neomi id est pulchram (1: 20): Alexander li. 2 Canticorum 21c, Videbitur alicui.

Ruth collegit spicas post terga metentium (2: 3): Hugo de claustro anime c. 8, In agro uero.

Extende pallium tuum super famulam tuam (3: 9): Alexander super Cantica li. 3 c. 3g, Sensus non litera ad probationem pertinet.

Extende pallium tuum quo operiris et tene utraque manu (3: 15): Augustinus moraliter super cano. Io. Debemus enim Omelia 4e, Sicut enim uelimus implere.

Tolle calciamentum (4: 8): Ambrosius li. 3 de Fide de par. 4, Et ille quid(em).

---

[25] See the letter of thanks to master J. Somerseth (Emden, *BRUO* 1727-8): *Epistolae Academicae Oxon.*, no. 218, ed. H. Anstey (*OHS* XXXV, Oxford, 1898), pp. 309-10.

[26] MSS Cambridge, Peterhouse, 169, fols. 1ra-54rb; 81ra-181va [New Testament] (s. xv$^{in.}$: English), and—its direct copy—London, BL, Royal 3 D. I, fols. 1ra-105vb, 113ra-232^{v} (a. 1452: Cambridge). The ordinary version of the *Tabula septem custodiarum* is in MS Bodley 685 (*SC* 2499), fols. 1ra-235va, text quoted at fol. 30rb (a. 1339: English), and other manuscripts. See R. H. and M. A. Rouse, *The 'Registrum Anglie'* (*CBMLC* I: forthcoming).

[27] MS Cambridge, Peterhouse, 169, fol. 13^{ra-rb}: *CCant.* ii. 21 (M, fol. 58vb), iii. 3 (M, fol. 65ra), iii. 7 (M, fol. 70rb) and iv. 7 (M, fol. 108va); cf. MS Bodley 685 (*SC* 2499), fol. 30rb, lacking the references to Alexander.

Dixerunt mulieres ad Neomi Benedictus dominus usque *Obed* (4: 14–17): Alexander super Cantica li. 3 ca. 7, Tipica ista Neomi.

Explicit tabula super Ruth. Deo gracias. Amen.

Far the most important of the later users of Alexander is Ringstead in his *Postills on Proverbs*, to which we had occasion to refer in the discussion on the verse. The author was probably the Dominican who was bishop of Bangor from 1357–1366.[28] It is of the type of Holcot's *Commentary on Wisdom*, that is to say it is crammed full of quotations from classical and medieval authors. How far they are taken at first hand only a detailed investigation could show. Those from Alexander certainly appear to be. Ringstead quotes from six works, which in order of frequency are: the *Laus sapientie diuine* and its *Suppletio defectuum*, the *Gloss on the Psalter*, the *Corrogationes noui Promethei*, the *De nuptiis Mercurii* and[29] the *Commentary on Proverbs*. The prominence of the *Laus sapientie diuine* is interesting. For its manuscript tradition is different from that of other works. Only the Paris manuscript is of the thirteenth century. The three English manuscripts are all of the fifteenth century. There are other slight indications of the later interest in the poem in the shape of extracts in a notebook in the Bodleian,[30] and in a rudimentary chronicle based on the *Polychronicon*.[31]

As Manitius observes, the manuscript tradition of Alexander's works points early and late almost exclusively to England.[32] Apart from the *Corrogationes Promethei* and

[28] Smalley, op. cit. (n. 17 above), pp. 211–20. Manuscripts of the *Postills on Proverbs*: Cambridge, Peterhouse, 125; London, Lambeth Palace, 33; Oxford, Bodley 829; Oxford, Balliol College, 34; Oxford, Lincoln College, lat. 86; Oxford, Trinity College, 35; Vatican, Bibl. Apost., Ottobon. lat. 72.

[29] Once only, concerning quicksilver: MS Balliol 34, fol. 8^V.

[30] MS Bodley 487 (*SC* 2067), the commonplace book of John Curteys (d. 1510), contains excerpts from *LSD* vi, with the rubric 'Vnde Alexander Nequam de naturis rerum de istis 7 lapidibus' (fol. 51): see Emden, *BRUO* 529.

[31] MS Bodleian Digby 82, fols. 7 and 17$^{r–v}$, a fifteenth-century paper manuscript written in England, quotes passages from *LSD* iii and v: see J. Taylor, *The Universal Chronicle of Ranulf Higden* (Oxford, 1966), p. 159.

[32] Manitius, iii. 792. Leland talks of Alexander being known 'to the French, the Italians and indeed to the whole world': *Commentarius in cygneam cantionem* (London, 1545), c iii. But to judge from Sabbadini the learned Italian encyclopaedists of the fourteenth century made no use of him: *Le scoperte dei codici latini e greci nec secolo xiv e xv* (Florence, 1967), pp. 199–261.

two early works there is almost nothing outside England. But there are a few small pieces of evidence pointing to a knowledge of the *De naturis rerum* and the *Commentary on the Song of Songs*, which may be put down in the hope that the connection may be elucidated some time. Raimund de Beziers (*fl. c.*1300) cites the *De naturis rerum*.[33] There is a German commentary on the Song of Songs compiled by a frater Andreas, in which Alexander's commentary is used to some extent.[34] There are quotations of Necam and Nequam in the sermons of the Franciscan Marquart von Lindau (d. 1392), one of which seems to come from the commentary.[35] The same text is quoted repeatedly by the Basel Franciscan Otto von Passau in his *Vierundzwanzig Alten*.[36] Alexander Nekam is named in the Prologue among the sources of the German Passion of yet another Franciscan, Johannes von Zazenhausen, which was written between 1362 and 1371.[37]

---

[33] Raimund de Biterris, *Liber Kalile et Dimne*, iv *ad fin.*: ed. L. Hervieux, *Les Fabulistes latins: Jean de Capoue et ses dérivés* (Paris, 1899), p. 503.

[34] MS Munich, Bayer. Staatsbibl., Clm 8827, fols. 15^V-65^V (s. xv: Munich Franciscans).

[35] P. Strauch, 'Die deutschen Predigten des Marquart von Lindau', *Beiträge z. Geschichte d. deutschen Sprache u. Literatur*, liv (1930), 161-201, at 183. See now the facsimile, ed. J. W. van Maren, *Marquard von Lindau: 'Die zehe Gebot' (Strassburg, 1516 and 1520): Ein Katechesicher Traktat* (Quellen u. Forschungen z. Erbauungsliteratur des späten Mittelalters u. der frühen Neuzeit, XIV, Amsterdam, 1980), p. 24.

[36] See *Lexikon f. Theologie u. Kirche* (2nd edn., Freiburg, 1962), vii. 1309.

[37] L. Oliger, 'Die deutsche Passion des Johannes von Zazenhausen O.F.M. Weihbischofs von Trier (†c.1380)', *Franziskanische Studien*, xv (1928), 245-51: 'Alexandri Nekam', one in a list of expositors of the Passion (p. 246). Oliger's manuscript (Würzburg I. 93) was destroyed in 1945. See now W. Baier, *Untersuchungen zu den Passionsbetrachtungen in der 'Vita Christi' des Ludolf von Sachsen* (Analecta Cartusiana, 44, Salzburg, 1977), iii. 411.

APPENDIX A
NEQUAM'S WORKS

NEQUAM appears in the two great surveys of English libraries that were drawn up in the fourteenth century: no. 42 in the Franciscan *Registrum Anglie* (s. xiv¹) and no. 4 in the *Catalogus* of Henry of Kirkestede (s. xiv²). Both these texts are being prepared by R. H. and M. A. Rouse for publication as *Corpus of British Medieval Library Catalogues*, I-II (British Academy and British Library joint publication); I give the revised date of the *Registrum Anglie*. Meanwhile see MS Oxford, Bodleian Library, Tanner 165, fol. 117 (*Registrum*: OPERA ALEXANDRI NEQVAM), and T. Tanner, *Bibliotheca Britannico-Hibernica* (London, 1748), p. xxvib (*Catalogus*: ALEXANDER NEQVAM). Further evidence of the same kind is provided in the mid-sixteenth century by John Leland in his *De rebus britannicis collectanea*, and by Bishop Bale's census of British authors: see p. xi above. The provenance both of surviving manuscripts and of others now lost is known principally from the *Registrum* and *Catalogus* and from the medieval catalogues of individual libraries; full references to the latter are given in Ker, *MLGB* ad loc. The census that follows owes much to Esposito, pp. 460-71.

I. AUTHENTIC WRITINGS

Although Nequam's writings can seldom be precisely dated, they may be arranged in the approximate chronological groups that have been proposed in Chapter II.

(i) EARLY WRITINGS, *c*.1177-*c*.1190

    c.1177+   *De nominibus utensilium*, Commentary on Martianus Capella, *Nouus Auianus, Nouus Esopus*

(ii) OXFORD PERIOD, *c*.1190-*c*.1197

    c.1190+   Commentary on the Athanasian Creed, *Questiones*, Sermons

(iii) CANON OF CIRENCESTER, *c*.1197-1213

    c.1197+   *Laus beatissime uirginis, Solatium fidelis anime, Corrogationes Promethei, Corrogationes Promethei* versified, Gloss on the Psalter

    pre-1205   *De naturis rerum et in Ecclesiasten*

    1199-1210 *Sacerdos ad altare*

    pre-1213   Commentary on Proverbs, Commentary on the Song of Songs; *Speculum speculationum*

    c.1213   *Laus sapientie diuine*

(iv) ABBOT OF CIRENCESTER, 1213-1217

1213+   *Corrogationes noui Promethei, Super mulierem fortem*
1216-17   *Suppletio defectuum*

(v) *Undated*

De commendatione uini, hymns, minor verses, *Meditatio de Magda-*
lena, Exhortatio ad religiosos

(vi) *Undated and lost*

De nuptiis Mercurii, Epistola ad discipulum, Passio sancti Albani.

(vii) *Excerpts*

Florilegium

De nominibus utensilium [*DNV*]

inc.   Qui bene uult disponere familie sue et rebus suis . . .
expl.   . . . nisi quisque fideliter firmiterque crediderit saluus esse non
poterit. Explicit.

Manuscripts

BERLIN (W.), Staatsbibl. Preussisch. Kulturbesitz, lat. fol. 607 (*olim*
Phillipps 13835), fol. 1^(ra)-9^(rc) (s. xiv¹), heavily glossed.
BESANÇON, Bibl. Mun., 534, fo. 35^v (s.xiv²); glossed.
BRUGES, Bibl. Publ., 536, fols. 80-9^v (s. xiii/xiv); glossed.
— Bibl. Publ., 546, fol. 1^(r-v) (s. xiii); *expl.*: . . . sali mixta/(Scheler,
p. 61, line 14).
CAMBRAI, Bibl. Mun., 969 (867) (s. xiv); *title*: Dictionarius magistri
Iohannis de Gallandia; *gloss*: In principio huius uoluminis plura
incurrunt inquirenda . . .
CAMBRIDGE, Gonville and Caius College, 136 (76), pp. 1-20 (s. xiii²);
glossed.
— Gonville and Caius College, 385 (605), pp. 341-4 (s. xiii); text
much abbreviated.
— Trinity College, O. 7. 9 (1337), fols. 122-35 (s. xiii); *title, in gloss*:
partes magistri Alexandri; *gloss*: Cognitioni uniuscuiusque causati . . .
CANTERBURY, Cathedral Library, Add. 129/1 (s. xiv²).
COPENHAGEN, Kongelige Bibliotek, Fabricius 92 (iv) 8°, fols. 25^v-
42 (a. 1308); *title*: Dictionarius magistri Alexandri nequam; *gloss*:
materia libri scriptoris sunt utensilia . . .
DUBLIN, Trinity College, 270 (D. 4. 9), fols. 26 and 157 (s. xiii);
glossed; two copies of the text.
EDINBURGH, National Library of Scotland, Advoc. 18. 4. 13, fols iii-
iv^v (s. xiv); heavily glossed; outer bifolium of quire, containing
beginning and end of text only.
ERFURT, Wissenschaftl. Bibl., Amplon. O. 12, fols. 12^v-22^v (s. xiii/
xiv); *title, in gloss*: partes magistri Alexandri Nequam; *gloss*: Materia
huius libri sunt utensilia . . .
KIEL, Universitätsbibl., KB 38, fols. 6-25^v (s. xiv); *expl.*: sic inutile a
me sepe accepisti; heavily glossed; *title, in gloss*: auctor . . . magister

Alexander Nequam; *gloss*; In principio huius libri ista sunt scienda et notanda . . .
LINCOLN, Cathedral Library, 132 (C. 5. 8), fols. 37-51 (s. xiii).
gloss: Nota quod hec diccio . . .
LONDON, BL, Add. 8092, fols. 1-5^v (s. xiii[1]); *expl*.: prosequutus sum/ (Scheler, p. 163, line 4); *title, in gloss*: Incipiunt epistole magistri Alexandri Nequam de utensilibus domorum; *gloss*: Materia huius libelli sunt utensilia . . .
— BL, Cotton Titus D XX, fols. 3-66^v (s. xiv), *gloss*: In principio huius libri sunt ista inquirenda. scilicet quid sit titulus, quis sit auctor, que materia . . . secundum magistrum Alexandrum . . .
— BL, Harley 683, (*a*) fols. 12-19 (s. xiii); glossed; (*b*) fols. 36^{r-v} (s. xiii), continuous commentary with lemmata on beginning of *DNV*, (*c*) fols. 38-54^v (s. xiii); *gloss*: In principio huius libri uidendum est quod auctor dicitur magister Alexander . . .
— Wellcome Institute for the History of Medicine 801A, fols. 104ra-18rb (s. xiii[in.]: Bury St Edmunds; *olim* Bury cathedral 4); glossed.
MILAN, Bibl. Ambros., I 246 inf., fols. 10-24 (s. xiv).
OXFORD, Bodleian Library, Digby 37, fols. 121-33^v (s. xiii); *expl*.: et depingendum/ (Scheler, p. 171, line 7); *title, in gloss*: Hic incipiunt partes magistri Alexandri Nequam; *gloss*: Intentio autoris est nomina utensilium colligere . . .; owned by Elias of Trykyngham: see Emden, *BRUO* 1905-6; Ker, *MLGB*, p. 292.
— Bodleian Library, lat. misc. b. 13, fol. 49 (s. xiii), fragment; *inc*.: /tate emergente . . . (Scheler, p. 165, line 3); *expl*.: . . . et nunc superioretur/ (Scheler, p. 166, line 22).
— Bodleian Library, Laud misc. 497, fols. 300-3^v (s. xiii[1]), fragment; *inc*.: /penula taxea . . . (Scheler, p. 63, lines 23-4); *expl*.: . . . cererem terre/ (Scheler, p. 162, line 11); *gloss*: [specimen printed by Meyer (1868), p. 298].
— Bodleian Library, Rawl. G 96 (*SC* 15567), pp. 177^a-96^b (s. xiii); *gloss*: Virorum (*recte* cum rerum) noticia . . .
— Bodleian Library, Rawl. G. 99 (*SC* 15462), fols. 138-49^v (s. xiii); *title, in gloss*: libellus magistri Alexandri Nequam de utensilibus; *gloss*: [incipit illegibile].
— St John's College, 178, fols. 402-11 (s. xiii); *expl*.: . . . scribi debet/ (Scheler, p. 169, line 20); a few glosses.
PARIS, BN, lat. 7679, fols. 5^v-23^v (s. xv); *title*: Incipit de utensilibus Alexandri; *gloss*: Hec dictio *qui* quandoque est relatiuum . . .
— BN, lat. 15171, fols. 176ra-95ra (s. xiii[2]); *expl*.: . . . nomina uel uocabula/ (Scheler, p. 173, line 13); *title, in gloss* (fol. 194va):Explicit libellus magistri Alexandri Nequam; *gloss*: Sicut dicit Tullius in principio siue prologo sue retorice, Eloquentia sine sapientia nocet . . .
— Bibl. Ste-Geneviève, 1210, fols. 70-3^v (s. xii$^{ex.}$); *expl*.: [imperf.].
SAINTE-CLAUDE (Jura), Bibl. Mun., 6, pp. 123-46 (s. xiii).
VIENNA, Nationalbibl., 12535, fols. 1-8 (s. xiii); glossed.
WOLFENBÜTTEL, Herzog-August-Bibl., 13. 10 Aug. 4° (3035), fols. 190-7 (s. xiii), fragment (Scheler, pp. 63-74, 155-6); see *Egidii*

Corboliensis Viaticus, De signis, ed. V. Rose (Teubner, Leipzig, 1907), p. xvii app.

WORCESTER, Cathedral Library, Q. 50, fols. 5-18^V (s. xiii[1]); *gloss*: In principio huius libri hec inquirenda sunt, Quis auctor . . .

Manuscripts are recorded at: Cambridge, Peterhouse (James, MS 215: pp. 25, 257-8); Canterbury, St Augustine's (James, *ALCD*, p. 319: no. 1117); Durham (*Cat. Vett.*, p. 33); Eton (Bale, p. 23); Norwich (Bale, p. 23); St Benet's, Hulme (Leland, iv. 29); Syon (Bateson, p. 4: A. 17); Titchfield (Wilson, pp. 256-7, 265: M XIII, XV, N XVIII); Witham (Thompson, p. 318: no. 15); York, Austin Friars (James, *Fasciculus*, p. 72: 502).

Editions

T. Wright, *A Volume of Vocabularies* (privately printed, 1857), pp. 96-119.

A. Scheler, 'Trois traités de lexicographie latine du XIIe et du XIIIe siècle', *Jahrbuch für romanische und englische Literatur*, vii (1866), 58-74, 155-73.

Commentary on Martianus Capella I-II [*CMC*]

inc. Marciani Minei Felicis Capelle de nuptiis Philologie et Mercurii fabula incipit. Titulus iste demonstrat . . .

expl. . . . 'Habes electorum'. Quasi diceret, scis quid scriptum et quid scribendum sit.

Manuscripts

CAMBRIDGE, Trinity College, R. 14. 9 (884), fols. 38-63 (s. xiv); *title*: Allexander Nequam super Marcianum de nupciis Mercurii et philologie.

OXFORD, Bodleian Library, Digby 221, fols. 34vb-88ra (s. xiv); *title*: Alexander Nequam super Marcianum de nupciis Mercurii et Philologie.

Manuscripts are recorded at: Reading, Franciscans (Leland, iv. 57); and in Bale's own library (Bale [1559], ii. 167).

Edition

Miss Katherine Emerson, of the Pontifical Institute of Mediaeval Studies in Toronto, is preparing an edition.

Nouus Auianus [*NA*], six fables

inc. Vincere quod lenis nequit exhortatio uincit . . .

expl. . . . Si conferre potes omnibus ergo tibi.

Manuscripts

CAMBRIDGE, University Library, Gg. 6. 42, fols. 232^V-4^V (s. xiii$^{med.}$), nos. 1-6 (= G).

MADRID, Biblioteca de Palacio, II. 468, fol. 24^V-7 (s. xiv), nos 1-6.

PARIS, BN, lat. 11867, fols. 217va-18ra (s. xiii[2]), nos. 1-6 (= P).

Bale owned a manuscript (Bale, p. 26).

Editions

E. du Méril, *Poésies inédites du moyen âge* (Paris, 1854), pp. 260-7.

L. Hervieux, *Les Fabulistes latins*, iii. *Avianus et ses anciens imitateurs* (Paris, 1894), pp. 222-34, 462-7.

Nouus Esopus [*NE*], forty-two fables

inc.   Ingluuie cogente lupus dum deuorat ossa . . .
expl.   . . . Qui nostre causas utilitatis habent.

Manuscripts

BASEL, Universitätsbibl., F. IV. 50, fols. 174^V-81 (s. xv^2), nos. 1, 3, 4, 22, 24, 25, 29 (imperf.), 30-3, 36, 39, 42.

BERLIN, (E.), Deutsche Staatsbibl., Santen B. 4, fols. 38va-42va (a. 1449: France), nos. 1-11, 13, 12, 15-17, 14, 18-30, Walther 583, 31-42.

EDINBURGH, National Library of Scotland, Advoc. 18. 4. 9, fols. 57vb-9vb (s. xiv), nos. 31, 32, 34, 38, 39, 41, 42, 19, (43), 8, 6, 1, 2, 9, 10, 13-16, 20-5. No. (43) is unpublished: *inc.* Arboris in patula mel reperit ursa cauerna (fol. 58vb)—the fable of the bear and its cubs.

LONDON, BL, Cotton Vespasian B. XXIII, fols. 110^V-18^V (s. xiv), nos. 1-42.

MADRID, Biblioteca de Palacio, II. 468, fols. 11-24^V (s. xiv), nos. 1-11, 13, 12, 14-42.

PARIS, BN, lat. 2904, pp. 153-4 (s. xii$^{ex.}$), nos. 1-6 and title only of 7.

— lat. 8471, (*a*) fols. 1-15^V (s. xiii^1), nos. 1-42; (*b*) fols. 16-17^V, summary.

Bale owned a manuscript (Bale, p. 26).

Editions

E. du Méril, *Poésies inédites du moyen âge* (Paris, 1854), pp. 169-212.

L. Hervieux, *Les Fabulistes latins: Phèdre et ses anciens imitateurs* (2nd ed., Paris, 1893-4), i. 668-84, ii. 392-416.

Commentary on the Athanasian Creed [*CAth.*]

incl. prol.   Capud aquile uisum ab Ezechiele eminentius erat tribus ceteris capitibus suppositis . . .
expl. prol.   . . . et eradicare intendit Athanasius in hoc simbolo dicens.
inc. text   'Hec est enim uictoria que uincit mundum' . . .
expl. text.   . . . ut eueniret unam et eandem personam esse hominem et esse deum, cui persone honor et gloria in sempiterna secula AMEN

Manuscripts

CAMBRAI, Bibl. Mun., 977 (875), fols. 172-84 (s. xiii$^{in.}$); *title*: Tractatus magistri Alexandri Nequam super Quicumque uult.

LONDON, BL, Harley 3133, fols. 92-100 (s. xiii^1); *title*: Explicit fides catholica Anthanasii episcopi exposita a magistro Alexandro de sancto Albano.

OXFORD, Bodleian Library, Auct. D. 2. 9 (*SC* 2330), fols. 184va-8^{rc} (s. xiii); *title*: Expositio fidei catholice a magistro Alexandro edita.
— Bodleian Library, Bodley 284 (*SC* 2339), (*a*) fols. 297-306 (s. xiii[1]: Cirencester); (*b*) fols. 306-7, another short exposition, anonymous; *inc.*: Caput aquile . . .; *expl.*: . . . sicut inquam hoc est ita etc./
— Bodleian Library, Rawl. C. 67 (*SC* 15517), fols. 86-92 (s. xiii: ?Hereford); *title*: Expositio simboli Athanasii episcopi secundum Mag(istrum) Alex(andrum) Nequam; a variant recension.

Manuscripts are recorded at: Bury St Edmunds (*Catalogus*); Canterbury, Christ Church (James, *ALCD*, p. 110: no. 1256); Hexham (*Catalogus*); Peterborough (James, *Peterborough*, '*matricularium*': nos. 157, 160); Ramsey (*Catalogus*); St Albans (*Registrum*).

[*Edition*]

None; but see G. D. W. Ommanney, *A Critical Dissertation on the Athanasian Creed* (Oxford, 1897), pp. 241-8.

Questiones

inc.   Queritur utrum Abraam alio modo posset saluari . . .
expl.   . . . perfecta suadentur.

Manuscript

LONDON, Lambeth Palace Library, 421, fols. 124va-7ra (s. xiii$^{in.}$), twenty-eight short questions; *title*: Incipiunt questiones secundum magistrum Alexandrum de sancto Albano.

Manuscripts are recorded at Ramsey (*Catalogus*) and Witham (*Registrum*).

No edition

Sermons

See Appendix B.

Laus Beatissime Virginis [*LBV*]

No manuscript survives, but there are extensive excerpts in the *Florilegium* (G).

Manuscripts are recorded at: Cirencester (Leland, iv. 158); and as known to Bale (Bale [1548], fol. 99^v; Bale [1559], i. 272).

No edition

Solatium fidelis anime [*SFA*]

incl. prol.   Rerum subtilium fugas uenari presentis renuit pagine simplicitas . . .
expl. prol.   . . . quem constituere debemus finem laborum nostrorum.
inc. text   Deus totius origo boni quem non externe pepulerunt . . .
expl. text   . . . malum uero inobedientie detestemur. Quod nobis prestare dignetur qui uiuit et regnat deus per infinita secula seculorum. Amen.

Manuscript

CANTERBURY, Cathedral Library, Lit. B. 6, fols. 2ra-29vb (s. xiii^{in}.:
St Augustine's, Canterbury), *title*: tractatus Moralium super Genesim
qui dicitur Solatium fidelis anime (fol. 1^v).

Extensive excerpts in the *Florilegium*.

The only other record of the *SFA* is a seventeenth-century annotation
to *CCant*. (London, BL, Royal 4 D. XI, fol. 32): 'Neckami liber inscrip-
tus Solatium fidelis animae'. Damon's 'Liber supplicationum' (p. 139
below) is not *SFA* but *SD*.

Corrogationes Promethei [*CP*]

incl. prol.		Ferrum situ rubiginem ducit et uittis non putata in labrus-cam siluescit . . .
expl. prol.		. . . si non circa uilem patulumque morabimur orbem.
inc.	I	Excellentissimo philosopho Platoni uisum est grammati-cam non esse censendam nomine artis . . .
expl.	I	. . . et senex dicitur delirus. Horatius in fine uersus deliret acumen [*Epp.* I. xii. 20] .
inc.	II	Post hec de singulis libris bibliothece aliquas dictiones proferre libet in medium . . .
expl.	II	. . . iam humanam naturam excellentiorem esse angelica.

Manuscripts

BERN, Burgerbibl., B 45, fols. 1-103^v (s. xiv); *expl.*: [beginning of
John] ; fol. 104^v, index.

CAMBRIDGE, University Library, Kk. 5. 10, fols. 323ra-68vb (s. xiii:
Durham, s. xv, from Thomas Swalwell; see Emden, *BRUO* 1828,
Ker, *MLGB*, p. 258), Part II only; *expl.*: . . . mandata eius/ [1 John
5: 2] , *title*: Incipit summa magistri A. Nequam.

— Corpus Christi College, 217, fols. 318-62^v (s. xiii: Worcester).

— Gonville and Caius College, 236 (122), pp. 1^a-309^a (s. xiii^{ex}.:
? Ramsey or St Ives), Part II only (expanded).

— Pembroke College, 103, fols. 85ra-125va (s. xiii^1); *title*: Incipiunt
Corrogaciones Promethei. Prologus magistri Alexandri Nequam.

— Pembroke College, 112, fols. 53-70 (s. xiii^1), Part I only.

— Pembroke College, 275, fols. 15ra-24rb (s. xiii: Reading), Part II
only; *expl.*: . . . de cordibus hominum. De (?) canniate/ [Job] .

DUBLIN, Trinity College, 256, fols. 1-113 (s. xiii^1); *inc.*: /minis ut cum
paricida.

— Trinity College, 257, fols. 1-85^v (s. xiii^1).

> [For MSS 256-7 see M. C. Colker, *A Descriptive Catalogue of the Medieval
> and Renaissance Manuscripts in the Library of Trinity College Dublin*
> (forthcoming).]

ÉVREUX, Bibl. Mun., 72, (*a*) fols. 2-109 (s. xiii: Lyre); *title*: Correc-
tiones Promethei; (*b*) fol. 1^v, letter from S., prior of Malmesbury to
Walter Melidie (see p. 12 above).

LONDON, BL, Egerton 2261, fols. 111rb-74va (s. xiii), Part II only; *title*: Expliciunt excerpta super singulos libros bibliothece edita a magistro Alexandro nequam dicto per contrarium (fol. 174va).

— BL, Harley 6, fols. 150ra-96ra (s. xiii: Chichester); *title*: Corrogationes Promethei.

— BL, Harley 1687, fols. 128ra-39rb (s. xiii), Part I only.

— BL, Royal 2 D. VIII, (*a*) fols. 16-145^{v} (s. xiii$^{ex.}$); *expl.*: . . . Set quid. Nonne/ (1 Thess. 4: 15); (*b*) fols. 1-11vb, text preceded (fols. 1-10) by an alphabetical list of words dealt with in Part II and (fols. 10va-11vb) by the capitula of I-II, headed 'Incipiunt capitula super Ysagogas Magistri Alexandri Nequam'.

— BL, Royal 5 C. V, (*a*) fols. 2ra-57rb (s. xiii-xiv: Sempringham); *title*: Corrogationes Premothei; fols. 57^{rb-vb}, the letter from S., prior of Malmesbury, to Walter Melidie (see p. 12 above).

— BL, Royal 8 A. XXI, fols. 170-83^{v} (s. xiii), Part II only; Exodus to Maccabees.

— BL, Royal 15 B. IV, fols. 16-23vb (s. xiii), Part I only; *expl.*: . . . an ordaceus/.

— Lambeth Palace 162, fols. 67-121^{v} (s. xv), Part II only; *expl.*: . . . ad tactum fimbrie domini sanata est emorissa a profluuio/ [Mark 5: 25 ff.] ; *title*: Ferrum super genesim.

OXFORD, Bodleian Library, Auct. F. 5. 23 (*SC* 2674), fols. 7ra-86rb (s. xiii$^{ex.}$: Coventry); *title*: Libellus iste dicitur ferrum quem exposuit magister Alexander Necham (fol. 85^{v}: s. xiv); Expliciunt exposiciones parcium biblie secundum magistrum Alexandrum Necham (fol. 86: s. xiv).

— Bodleian Library, Bodley 57 (*SC* 2004), fols. 20^{v}, 81-3^{v}, 53^{r-v} (s. xiii-xiv: ? Leicester Can. Reg.), Part II only, excerpts (see P. Meyer, 'Notice du MS Bodley 57', *Romania* xxxv 1906, pp. 576-7; and C. Brown, 'Mulier est hominis confusio', *Modern Language Notes*, xxxv [1920] , 479-82, at 480: *re* fol. 20^{v}).

— Bodleian Library, Bodley 550 (*SC* 2300), fols. 1ra-100rb (s. xiii^{1}: Reading) (= B), *title*: Incipiunt corrogationes promethei (fol. 1ra).

— Bodleian Library, Bodley 760 (*SC* 2673), fols. 99ra-171va (s. xiii$^{ex.}$: Reading), *title*: Explicit liber magistri Alexander Nequam Abbatis (fol. 171vb).

— Bodleian Library, Hatton 44 (*SC* 4094), fols. 3ra-143vb (s. xiii); *title*: ⟨In⟩cipit ysago⟨gi⟩ cum magis⟨tri⟩ Alexandri (fol. 3ra).

— Bodleian Library, Laud Misc. 112, fols. 9ra-42va (s. xiii: Ely); *title*: Incipiunt Corrogaciones promethei. Prologus (fol. 9ra); *in list of contents*: Summa que uocatur Promotheus (fol. 1vb).

— Bodleian Library, Rawl. C. 67, fols. 95-161^{v} (s. xiii: ? Hereford), Part II precedes Part I; *title*: Explicit summa magistri A. Nequam super Bibliam. Sequitur summa de cognicione locutionum figuraturarum [*sic*] ab eodem compilata (fol. 145^{v}); Explicit expositio litteralis diccionum difficilium in totam bibliam (fol. 161^{v}).

— Balliol College, 234, fol. 1 (s. xiii), Part I (fragment).

OXFORD, Merton College, 254, entire manuscript, not foliated (s. xiii[1]);
title; Incipit ysagogicum magistri Alexandri Nequam (fol. 1).

— St John's College, 178, fols. 105-39 (s. xiii[ex]: Westminster), Part I
only; *title*: Prologus magistri Alexandri Nequam.

PARIS, Bibl. Ste-Geneviève, 1211, fols. 277-306 (s. xiii-xiv), Part II
only; see Meyer 1896, pp. 676 n. 1 and 680 n. 4.

TROYES, Bibl. Mun., 1048, item 11 (s. xiii: Clairvaux; see A. Vernet,
La Bibliothèque de l'Abbaye de Clairvaux du XIIe au XVIIIe siècle,
I [Centre Nationale de la Recherche Scientifique, Paris, 1979],
p. 72), Part II only, Ecclus. Sap.; *title*; Glosule magistri A N super
Ecclesiasticum, Job, Parabolos, Ecclesiastem, Cantica Canticorum
et Librum Sapientie.

TURIN, Bibl. Naz., D. V. 29, fols. 1ra-46 (s. xiii: English, later in
Vercelli), Part II only, damaged; *title*: Hic incipiunt expositiones
uerborum bibliothece secundum magistrum Alexandrum Nequam.
Photograph of fol. 1 in *Facsimiles . . . l'École des Chartes*, nouveau
fonds, 380: cf. *Notices des héliogravures de l'École des Chartes*
(Nogent-le-Rotrou, 1894), no. 380.

WORCESTER, Cathedral Library, F. 1, fols. 168ra-234rb (s. xiii:
Worcester).

Manuscripts are recorded at: Bury St Edmunds (*Catalogus*); Cambridge,
King's College (Bale, p. 24); Canterbury, Christ Church (James, *ALCD*,
pp. 68, 73, 77, 79, 109, 117: nos. 561, 650, 710, 727, 1249, 1371,
and—Part II only—pp. 108, 115: nos. 1235, 1355); Canterbury, St
Augustine's (James, *ALCD*, p. 218: nos. 307-9); Dover (James, *ALCD*,
494: no. 439, entitled 'Visio Platonis de grammatica'); Durham (*Cat.
Vett.*, p. 49); Eton (Bale, p. 23); Evesham (*Chronicon*, p. 268); Exeter
(Oliver, p. 374); Gloucester (*Registrum*); Lanthony (Omont, pp. 216,
222: nos. 258, 472); Meaux (*Chronicon*, III, p. xcv); ?Muchelney (MS
London, BL, Royal 7 A. II, fol. 1[v]: 'Memoriale de Mucheln' propter
Ysagogicum magistri Alexandri Nequam'); Norwich, Carmelites
(Leland, iv, 28; cf. Bale, p. 23); Oxford, Exeter College (Bale, p. 26:
Part II only); Peterborough (James, *Peterborough*, 'Abbots', 70; '*matri-
cularium*', 112, 239); Ramsey (*Chronicon*, pp. 356, 362, 364, 365;
Bale, p. 24); Syon (Bateson, pp. 48, 120: nos. E 46, N 14); Titchfield
(Wilson, p. 159: C III); Waltham (Leland, iv. 161: Part II only); York,
Austin Friars (James, *Fasciculus*, pp. 21 and 33: 31, 142); private
owner: Robert Raynhull, vicar of St Cross, Canterbury (1417: *Regis-
trum Henrici Chichele* II, ed. E. F. Jacob [Canterbury and York Society,
XLII, 1937], 119).

Edition

Extensive and useful excerpts in Meyer 1896, pp. 641-82.

Corrogationes Promethei versified [*CPV*]

inc.   Excipit a bissus et ab hoc generatur abissus . . .
expl.   . . . Fluxus adest. exta languentibus exscoriantur.

Manuscripts

LONDON, BL, Royal 9 A. XIV, fols. 141–56 (s. xiii).

OXFORD, Bodleian Library, Digby 56, fols. 101–30 (s. xiii); *title*: Incipiunt expositiones bibliothece (fol. 101); see *Ker Essays*, p. 311.

— St John's College, 119, fols. 121–49^v (s. xiii); *expl.*: . . . Dirigit ut cursus nauis nec promouet ipsam/ [Acts] —i.e., lacks final five lines.

Manuscripts are recorded at: Peterborough (James, *Peterborough*, '*matricularium*': no. 239); Syon (Bateson, p. 48: no. E 46); and Titchfield (Wilson, pp. 253, 256: nos. M III, M XII).

No edition

Gloss on the Psalter [*GP*]

inc. prol.   De ortu deliciarum paradysi . . .
expl. prol.   . . . que per regnum Salomonis designata est.
inc. text   'Beatus uir' . . . Licet psalmus iste exponatur . . .
expl. text   . . . quia idem est deus ueteris et noui testamenti [Ps. 145: 10].

Manuscripts

LONDON, BL, Royal 2 C. XI, fols. 1ra–206va (s. xiii: Ramsey); *title*: Psalterium magistri Alexandri Nequam (s. xiv).

— Lambeth Palace, 61, fol. 1ra–115vb (s. xiii^1: ?Lanthony), text lacks Pss. 30:8–33:2, 56:4–67:10; *expl.*: . . . uisum est quid ideo specialiter/ [Ps. 89: 1]; *title*; Psalterium magistri Alexandri (fol. 1).

OXFORD, Bodleian Library, Bodley 284 (*SC* 2339), fols. iii–295va (s. xiii^1: Cirencester); *title*: Alexander Necham super psalmos (fol. iii: Leland's hand).

—Jesus College, 94, fols. 1ra–56vb (s. xiii^in.: Cirencester), text lacks Pss. 37:2–90:16; *expl.*: . . . uiuifica me iuxta uerbum tuum'/ [Ps. 118: 107].

Manuscripts are recorded at: Bury St Edmunds (*Catalogus*); Canterbury, Christ Church (James, *ALCD*, p. 109: no. 1249); Kelso (*Registrum*); Lantony (Omont, p. 210: no. 55); Leicester, Can. Reg. (James, p. 399: no. 262); London, Royal Library (Bale, p. 27); Peterborough (James, *Peterborough*, '*matricularium*': no. 92); St Albans (*Registrum*).

Excerpts in the *Florilegium*.

No Edition

De Naturis Rerum [*DNR*]

inc. lib.   I   Forma decens admiratione dignis nature munifice dotata deliciis . . .
expl. lib.   II   . . . ut uariatis calicibus uarientur et uina.
inc. lib.   III   [= *in Eccles.*] Superfluo detinerer labore. . .
expl. lib.   V   [= *in Eccles.*] . . . bonorum largitori cui honor et gloria per infinita secula seculorum amen.

Manuscripts

CAMBRIDGE, University Library, Kk. 4. 5, fols. 146ra-239rb (s. xiv^2 : Norwich); *title*: Magister Alexander de naturis rerum.

— Trinity College, R. 16. 3 (951), fols. 1ra-153rb (s. $xiii^{1/4}$). The additional chapter 'De preuaricatione Salomonis et eius penitentia capitulum X' is here a page from another manuscript now slotted into fol. 88. The capitula of lib. i were 'Scripta et laborata per manus fratris Iohannis Tempill. Anno domini $M^oCCCC^oXXX^oIX^o$' (fol. i^{vc}).

— Trinity College, R. 16. 4 (952), fols. 1ra-237rb (s. $xii^{ex.}$: Osney s. xv); *title*: Incipit opus magistri Alexandri de sancto Albano de naturis rerum; capitula of lib. i-v (fols. i^{ra}-iii^{vb}); subject-headings in the margin throughout.

— Trinity College, O. 4.1 (1232), fols. 1ra-168rb (s. xiii: Barnwell); *title*: Incipit opus magistri Alexandri de sancto Albano de naturis rerum.

DURHAM, Cathedral Library, Hunter 58, (*a*) fols. 30–54 (s. $xiv^{med.}$), excerpts; (*b*) fols. 1–3^v alphabetical index by Oliver de Wakefeld.

— University Library, Routh I b 16, pastedown (s. $xiv^{in.}$: formerly at Magdalen College), *DNR* ii. 14-19 (= verso); see N. R. Ker, *Fragments of Medieval Manuscripts used as Pastedowns in Oxford Bindings* (Oxford Bibliographical Society, Oxford 1954), no. 279.

LONDON, BL, Cotton Tiberius A. XII, fols. 46ra-94vb (s. xiii: Eynsham), lib. iii-v only, badly burnt; see Watson, *Savile*, p. 24, no. 29.

— BL, Harley 3737, fols. 2ra-255rb (s. xii/xiii: St Albans; cf. Thomson, *St Albans*, no. 24); *title*: Incipit opus magistri Alexandri de sancto Albano de naturis rerum.

— BL, Royal 12 F. XIV, fols. 3ra-134rb (s. xiii); *title*: De naturis rerum. Incipit opus magistri Alexandri de sancto Albano. Text includes the additional chapter 'De preuaricatione et penitentia Salomonis' (fol. 134^{rb-vb}), with a reference to it at iii. 10 (fol. 74rb).

— BL, Royal 12 G. XI, (*a*) fols. 4ra-208rb (s. xv); *expl.*: . . . per ignem. Est et/(v. 12); (*b*) fols. 1-3, index.

OXFORD, Corpus Christi College, 45, fols. 4ra-185vb (s. xiii^1 : Reading) (= C); *title*: Explicit tractatus magistri Alexandri Necham super ecclesiasten de naturis rerum (fol. 185vb).

— Corpus Christi College, 245, fols. 1ra-94vb (s. xv: Syon, later to John Dee, whose cypher is on fol. 1); see A. G. Watson and R. J. Roberts, *John Dee's Library Catalogue* (Bibliographical Society, London, forthcoming), no. OM149; *expl.*: . . . potest gratiam/[v. 5] .

— Magdalen College, 139, fols. 1ra-135vb (s. xiii); *expl.*: . . . latus cui preest/[v. 2] .

—St John's College, 51, fols. 1ra-170va (s. xiii: later belonged to Henry Savile; see Watson, *Savile*, p. 18, no. 9).

WINDSOR, St George's Chapel, Jackson Collection 32 (s. xiii^1), fragment; see J. Stratford, *Catalogue of the Jackson Collection, Windsor* (London, 1981), p. 99.

Excerpts in the *Florilegium*.

Manuscripts are recorded at: Bordesley (*Registrum*); Bridlington (Leland, iv. 35); Buildwas (*Registrum*); Bury St Edmunds (*Catalogus*); Cambridge, King's College (Bale, p. 24); Cambridge, Queens' College (Bale, p. 23); Canterbury, Christ Church (James, *ALCD*, pp. 77, 80: nos. 708, 738); Canterbury, St Augustine's (James, *ALCD*, p. 289: no. 866); Gloucester (*Registrum*); Leicester (James, p. 398: no. 260); Leominster (*Registrum*); London, Carmelites (Leland, iv. 53); London, Franciscans (Leland, iv. 50); London, Royal Library (Bale, p. 27); Oxford, Canterbury College (Pantin, p. 46: no. 34); Oxford, Merton College (Bale, p. 26); Oxford, New College (list of Wykeham's books, ed. Leach: Oxford Historical Society, *Collectanea*, iii, [1896], p. 224, no. 134); Oxford University (Anstey: see above, p. 122 n.); Reading (*Registrum*); Syon (Bateson, pp. 23, 121: C 22, N 16); Westminster (Robinson and James, p. 32: no. 115); Witham (*Registrum*); York, Austin Friars (James, *Fasciculus*, p. 51: no. 334). Leland had a copy (Bale, p. 27).

Edition

T. Wright, *Alexandri Neckam de naturis rerum* (RS, London, 1863), lib. i–ii only; *in Eccles* (= iii–v) is unprinted.

Sacerdos ad altare [*SA*]

inc.	Sacerdos ad altare accessurus . . .
expl.	. . . clausus puscula muniatur.
inc. gloss	Sacerdos ut dicit Priscianus est nomen compositum . . .
expl. gloss	. . . ad ipsum finaliter tendere debemus.

Manuscript

CAMBRIDGE, Gonville and Caius College, 385 (605), pp. 7–61 (s. xiii).

Edition

Part edition of text in Haskins, pp. 372–6, and (text and gloss) Kantorowicz, pp. 31–7: see above, p. 34 n.

Commentary on Proverbs [*CProv.*]

inc. prol.	Meditatio humana nunc in ipsum hominem reflectitur . . .
expl. prol.	. . . destitui ceperit. mellificare desinit.
inc. text	Parabole Salomonis . . . Vereor ne dum liber parabolarum . . .
expl. text	. . . qui introibant prohibuistis.

Manuscript

OXFORD, Jesus College, 94, fols. 57ra–74rb (s. xiii$^{in.}$) (= J; *expl.*: . . . prohibuistis/[Prov. 3: 27]; *title* Incipit tractatus magistri Alexandri abbatis cyrenc' super parabolas salomonis.

Numerous excerpts in the *Florilegium* and a brief passage in MS Oxford, Bodleian Library, Hatton 102 (*SC* 4051), fol. 200^v.

Manuscripts are recorded at: Lincoln, Dominicans (MS London, BL, Royal App. 69, fol. 3 [= Leland's notes]) and by Bale (Bale [1559], i, 272: *inc.* In primo opere Salomonis).

No edition

Commentary on the Song of Songs [*CCant.*]

inc. prol.   Humilitas uera gloriam excellencie et dignitatis feliciter . . .

expl. prol.   . . . Conferat nobis omnium subsidium dominus noster Iesus noster qui est benedictus in secula. Amen.

inc. text   Ortus deliciarum paradisi celestis scripture amena iocunda . . .

expl. text. . . . ut pro me misero misericordie mater intercedas ad dominum nostrum Iesum Christum filium tuum, cui laus et honor et imperium per infinita secula seculorum. Amen.

Manuscripts

CAMBRIDGE, University Library, Ii. 2. 31, fols. 132ra-254va (s. xiv); *title*: Prohemium Alex. Nequam super cantica.

LONDON, BL, Royal 4 D. XI, fols. 1ra-205vb (s. xiii^1); *title*: Alex. Nequam super cantica (fol. 1: s. xv).

— Lambeth Palace, 23, fols. 1ra-143vb (s. xiv/xv: Durham).

OXFORD, Bodleian Library, Bodley 356 (*SC* 2716), fols. 7ra-257vb (s. xiii: Bury St Edmunds); *inc.*: /hominis deuotis . . . (i. 4); *title*: Alexander Nequam super ⟨cantica⟩ (on spine: s. xiii).

— Balliol College, 39, fols. 2-133 (lib. i-iii), and 40, fols. 1-118 (lib. iv. 4-v) (s. xiii: Buildwas, O. Cist.; s. xv, William Gray, bishop of Ely). Text lacks iv. 1-3.

— Magdalen College, 149, fols. 1ra-194ra (s. xiii; s. xv, John Mower: Emden, *BRUO* 1326-7).

— New College, 43, fols. 3-235^v (s. xvi$^{in.}$: Archbishop Wareham).

Manuscripts are recorded at: Buildwas (*Registrum*); Bury St Edmunds (*Catalogus*); Canterbury, Christ Church (James, *ALCD*, p. 154: no. 42); Canterbury, St Augustine's (James, *ALCD*, p. 281: no. 807); Gloucester (*Registrum*); Leicester (James, p. 397: no. 259); London, Franciscans (Leland, iv. 50); Oxford, Balliol College (Bale, p. 26); Reading (*Registrum*); St Albans (*Registrum*); St Neot's (*Registrum*); Syon (Bateson, p. 60: no. G 16); private owner, Richard Grafton (Bale, p. 26).

No edition

Speculum speculationum [*SS*]

inc. prol.   Paradisum uoluptatis subdiuidit . . .

expl. prol.   . . . sub breui uerborum forma perstringantur.

inc. text   Si duo essent prima rerum principia . . .

expl. text   . . . libertati liberi arbitrii enucleande.

Manuscript

LONDON, BL, Royal 7 F. I, fols. 1ra-94ra (s. xiii^1); *title*: Incipit speculum speculationum magistri Alexandri canonici Cirecestrie (fol. 1ra).

Excerpts in the *Florilegium*: fols. 70, 143^v.

Manuscripts are recorded at Cirencester (Leland, iv. 158) and by Bale (Bale [1559], i. 272).

Edition

Edition forthcoming by R. M. Thomson in *Auctores Britannici Medii Aevi*.

Laus Sapiente Divine [LSD]

inc.   Gloria maiestas deitas sapientia uirtus . . .
expl.   . . . Cum sis ingenii gloria magna mei.

Manuscripts

CAMBRIDGE, Gonville and Caius College, 372 (621), fols. 66–140^v (s. xv); *title*: Incipit liber magistri Alexandri de laude diuine sapientie; text lacks iii. 593–734 (fol. 92^v); *expl.*: . . . origo fuit/[x. 322].
— Trinity College, R. 3. 1 (580), fols. 1ra–30^v (s. xv$^{in.}$); *title*: Incipit liber magistri Alexandri abbatis Cirencestrie qui inscribitur Laus sapientie diuine; *expl.*: . . . placere uiro/[x. 286].
LONDON, BL, Royal 8 E. IX, fols. 1–88^v (s. xv$^{in.}$: Merton priory). Wright's manuscript
MADRID, Biblioteca de Palacio, II, 468 fol. 30–179^v; 189–203^v (s. xiv).
PARIS, BN, lat. 11866, fols. 40–87^v (s. xvii), *expl.* [ii. 868].
— BN, lat. 11867, fols. 189vb–214va (s. xiii^2) (= P); *title*: Incipit liber magistri Alexandri canonici cyrencestrie qui inscribitur laus sapiencie diuine.

Excerpts in the *Florilegium*: fols. 69–71^v.

Manuscripts are recorded at: Hyde abbey (Leland, iv. 148); Peterborough (James, *Peterborough*, 'matricularium': no. 299); Reading (MS London, BL, Harley 979, fol. 1*^{v}); and as owned by Bale (Bale, p. 26).

Edition

T. Wright, *Alexandri Neckam de naturis rerum . . . with . . . De laudibus diuinae sapientiae* (RS, London, 1863). [Following MS London, BL, Royal 8 E. IX, Wright wrongly divided the *LSD* into ten *distinctiones* instead of seven. No. iii should run from iii. 1 to iii. 964; no. iv from iii. 965 to the end of iv; no. v = v; no. vi = vi–viii; no. vii = ix–x.]

Corrogationes Noui Promethei [CNP]

inc.   Induet abbatem qui plus optabit amari . . .
expl.   . . . Que candore caro lilia uincit erit.

Manuscript

PARIS, BN, lat. 11867, (*a*) fol. 216^{ra-va}, lines 1-127; (*b*) fols. 231va-8ra, lines 1-1622 (s. xiii^2) (= P; *title*: Incipiunt metrice corrogaciones [fol. 231^v prorogaciones] noui Promothei (fol. 216ra).

One excerpt in the *Florilegium* (fol. 70*bis*$^{r-v}$) = lines 318-28. Further excerpts in prose: fols. 72^v-3, 147^v-8. Five further verse passages, not otherwise extant, are quoted by Holcot in his commentary on Proverbs: see Damon (below), who, however, equates *CNP* with *CPV*.

No manuscripts are recorded elsewhere.

Editions

M. Esposito, 'On some unpublished poems attributed to Alexander Neckam', *EHR* xxx (1915), 457-9 [= lines 1-127].

H. Walther, 'Eine moral-asketische Dichtung des xiii. Jahrhunderts: *Prorogationes Noui Promethei* des Alexander Neckam', *Medium Aevum*, xxxi (1962), 33-42 [= lines 128-204, 379-448, 1177-1242, 1569-1622]. For Walther's lines 1623-36 cf. *DCV* ii. 737-42.

See also P. W. Damon, 'A note on the Neckham canon', *Speculum*, xxxii (1957), 99-102.

Super Mulierem Fortem [*SMF*]

inc.   'Mulierem fortem quis inueniet?' . . . Splendor radii solaris in iaspide . . .

expl.   . . . Et ecce iam opus consummauimus in laudem domini nostri cui honor et gloria per infinita secula seculorum. Amen.

Manuscripts

OXFORD, Bodleian Library, Bodley 528 (*SC* 2221), fols. 1-53^v (s. xiii: Reading). Inscription and list of contents now a flyleaf (fol. i) in Bodleian, Auct. D 4. 18 (*SC* 2094).

— Jesus College, 94, fols. 79ra-125ra (s. xiii$^{in.}$: Cirencester) (= J).

Excerpts in the *Florilegium* and in Oxford, Bodleian Library, Hatton 102 (*SC* 4051), fols. 200^v-1.

Manuscripts are recorded at: Bury St Edmunds (*Catalogus*); ?Dover (James, *ALCD*, p. 463: no. 198); Reading (*Registrum*); Witham (*Registrum*).

No Edition

Suppletio Defectuum [*SF*]

inc.   Ornatu uario mundus depingitur artis . . .

expl.   . . . Compositus finem principiumque tenet.

Manuscript

PARIS, BN, lat. 11867, fol. 218va-31va (s. xiii^2) (= P); *title*: Incipit

suplecio defectuum operis magistri Alexandri quod deseruit laudi
sapiencie diuine.

Excerpt in the *Florilegium* (fol. 70^v = ii. 547–8); two quotations by
Holcot: see Damon, op. cit. (p. 139 above), pp. 101–2.

No manuscripts are recorded elsewhere.

No edition

De commendatione uini [*DCV*]

inc. lib. I   Cum corpus curas studeas subducere curas . . .
expl. lib. I   . . . Hoc mihi solamen numquam desit precor. Amen.
inc. lib. II   Rursus Bache tuas laudes describo libenter . . .
expl. lib. II   . . . cordi lingua meo dissona semper erit.
inc. lib. III   Nobilis est potus me iudice nobile uinum . . .
expl. lib. III   . . . Ipse deus perpes gloria uera quies.

Manuscripts

CAMBRIDGE, University Library, Gg. 6. 42, fols. 224^v-32 (s. xiii$^{med.}$)
(= G); *title*: Versus magistri Alexandri Nequam de uino.

MADRID, Biblioteca de Palacio, II. 468 fols. 179^v-88^v (s. xiv).

PARIS, BN, lat. 11867, fols. 214va-15vb, 216va-17rb (s. xiii^2) (= P).

Excerpts in Oxford, Bodleian Library, Digby 157, fol. 101 (s. xv:
?Battle).

Bale owned a manuscript (Bale, p. 26).

Editions

M. Esposito, 'On some unpublished poems attributed to Alexander
   Neckam', *EHR* xxx (1915), 452–6 [excerpts from lib. i].
Walther, 'Neckham', pp. 112–21 [lib. ii–iii].

Hymns and Minor Verses

The hymns and minor verses survive mainly in **P**, a collection of rhetorical and devotional texts in which only about fifty folios relate to
Nequam. Within these fifty folios (189vb-240vb) the sequence is so
disordered as to suggest that **P** is at this point a fair copy of loose
schedulae arranged at random. **P** is an English manuscript of the later
thirteenth century, which had reached St-Germain-des-Prés by the
seventeenth. It contains:[1]

fol. 1–165^v Thomas of Capua, *Summa dictaminis* and cog-
                  nate material

[1] The diverse items all belong to the one volume, as the quiring shows: i–viii^{12}
ix^{8}x–xvi^{12}xvii^{14}xviii^{12}xix^{14}xx^{8}xxi–xxii^4. The devotional verses run into quire xvi,
followed by the *Disciplina Clericalis*; the Nequam material runs from the middle
of xvi to the end of xxi. The presence of S., prior of Malmesbury (fol. 240^{va-vb}:
see below), and the script of fols. 189vb-240rb suggest that the manuscript was
written in England. See further Esposito, pp. 450 ff.

fols. 166–83^v	devotional material in prose and verse
184ra–9vb	Petrus Alphonsi, *Disciplina clericalis*, in a cursive hand
189vb–240vb	NEQVAM, in a new text hand
240vb–3vb	*Ars manualis de uita et morte* etc.
243vb–4vb	Donation of Constantine, in a new cursive hand

The Nequam section contains:[2]

fols. 189vb–214va	*LSD*
214va–5vb	*DCV* i–ii
215vb–6ra	verses: nos. 1–5 below
216ra–va	*CNP* 1–127
216va–7rb	*DCV* iii
217rb–8va	verses: nos. 6–37 below
218va–31va	*SD* (the unique manuscript)
231va–8ra	*CNP* 1–1624
238ra	*DCV* fragment; verses 38–41 below
238ra–rb	three hymns: nos. 275–7 above
238rb–va	'Versus magistri Willelmi aurelianensis et magistri Alexandri Nequam': Walther 3561; 15382 (nos. 42–3 below)
238va–9rb	verses: nos. 44–7 below; hymns 278–9, 284–7 above; four others not by Alexander
239rb	mnemonic religious verses, glossed; *Disputatio cordis et oculi*
239rb–40ra	excerpts from St Bernard; miscellaneous verses
240ra	Nequam's verse epistle to Thomas, abbot of Gloucester (Walther 11488): cf. G, fol. 224, and MS Madrid, Biblioteca de Palacio, II. 468, fol. 27^v.
240ra–va	hymns 280–3.
240va–vb	letter of S., prior of Malmesbury to Walter Melidie, canon of Cirencester

P is the sole manuscript of eleven (nos. 275–81, 284–7) of the thirteen hymns discussed in Chapter V; all thirteen are edited in *AH* xlviii, nos. 275–87.

The minor verses in P are to some extent corroborated and augmented in G, fols. 71^v, 223–4: see p. 147 below. They are given here in the order of P, with additions from G at the end:

1. Dulce Verolamium linquo recessurus (4 lines)
    P, fol. 215vb
    Walther 4774; Esposito, p. 456
2. Delirat et desipit quippe iam senescit (18 lines)
    P, fol. 215vb

---

[2] The Nequam section measures: page 353 × 245 mm.; text 286 × 175 mm.; col. 286 × 70 mm.; 63 lines.

Walther 4239; Esposito, p. 456; Walther, 'Neckam', p. 116.
3. Langueo sed pereo (7 lines)
   P, fol. 216ra
   Walther 10104; Esposito, p. 456; Walther, 'Neckam', pp. 116–17
4. Inopes diuitias (6 lines)
   P, fol. 216ra
   Walther 9363; Esposito, p. 456; Walther, 'Neckam', p. 117
5. Qualiter Anglorum possem describere gentem (20 lines)
   P, fol. 216ra
   Walther 15120; Esposito, p. 456; see above, pp. 62–3
6. *De laterna*
   Lucida laterne facies est grata lucerne (2 lines)
   P, fol. 217rb; G, fol. 236
   Walther, *Sprichwörter*, 13985b; Walther, 'Neckam', p. 122
6a. Sic 'rego' dat reges, dat 'duco' duces, 'lege' leges (1 line)
   P, fol. 217rb
7. *De uase aureo in quo continetur eukaristia*
   Non manus artificis non auri gloria dignum (14 lines)
   P, fol. 217rb; G, fol. 235^{r-v}
   Walther 12092; Walther, 'Neckam', p. 122
8. Gaudeo legatus niueum mihi misit olorem (2 lines)
   P, fol. 217rb; G, fol. 236
   Walther, 'Neckam', p. 122
9. *Diuisio huius nominis LABORAVI*
   Casu labor aui, uisu subito laboraui (2 lines)
   P, fol. 217rb; G, fol. 236
   Walther, *Sprichwörter*, 2475; Walther, 'Neckam', p. 122
10. *Diuisio huius nominis ROME*
    En dabit absque mora Celsus Rome tibi mora (25 lines)
    P, fol. 217^{rb-va}; G, fol. 235
    Walther 5373; Walther, 'Neckam', p. 122–3
— Est mihi crede mithos filum sed fabula mithos (4 lines)
    P, fol. 217va
    Walther, 5749
— Vincere quos lenis ne quid exortacio uincit [= *NA* i-vi]
    P, fols. 217va–18ra
    Walther 20349
11. Dulcessit crebro fructus radicis amare (10 lines)
    P, fol. 218ra; G, fol. 235^{v}; MS Madrid, Biblioteca de Palacio, II.
    468, fol. 27^{r-v} (s. xiv).
    Walther 4776; Walther, 'Neckam', p. 123
12. *De prouerbio Anglie*
    Maturum medium cingit utrimque uiror (2 lines: Latin and French)
    P, fol. 218ra (Latin only); G, fol. 235^{v}; also quoted in *in Eccles.*
    (C, fol. 100ra)
    Walther, *Sprichwörter*, 14492a
13. Oppressere diu populos communis egestas (10 lines)
    P, fol. 218ra

Walther 13385; Walther, 'Neckam', p. 124

14. Prata uirent flores fructus spondere uidentur (6 lines)
P, fol. 218ra
Walther 14506; Walther, 'Neckam', p. 124

15. Tempore tristicie communis nos decet esse (8 lines)
P, fol. 218ra
Walther, *Sprichwörter* 31251b; Walther, 'Neckam', p. 124

16. Vi ualeo tota marcas d'or, subtrahe iota (2 lines: Latin and French)
P, fol. 218ra (Latin only); G, fol. 236
Walther, *Sprichwörter*, 33283a; Walther, 'Neckam', p. 125

17. Forma decens oris expugnat castra pudoris (5 lines)
P, fol. 218^{ra-rb}; G, fol. 236
Walther, *Sprichwörter*, 9743a; Walther, 'Neckam', p. 125

18. Iussus uix potui geminos componere uersus (8 lines)
P, fol. 218rb
Walther, 9995; Walther, 'Neckam', p. 125

19. Mente uir annis es puer istud censeo mirum (8 lines, playing on 'Robertus')
P, fol. 218rb
Walther, *Sprichwörter*, 14766a; Walther, 'Neckam', p. 125, cf. p. 56 above.

20. Non color immo colo, non colo sed in mala color (2 lines)
P, fol. 218rb
Walther, *Sprichwörter*, 17388a

21. *Diuisio huius nominis VIRES*
Redde mihi uires, sum debilis et sine ui res (2 lines)
P, fol. 218rb (omitting title); G, fol. 236; also found in MS Cambridge, Trinity College, O. 2. 45.
Walther, *Sprichwörter*, 26430a; Walther, 'Neckam', p. 126

22. Tanti aliis liceas quanti tu te ipse liceris (2 lines)
P, fol. 218rb
Walther, *Sprichwörter*, 31045a; Walther, 'Neckam', p. 126

23. Hospita sit sospes. non hospes ut hospita sospes (3 lines)
P, fol. 218rb
Walther 8470; Walther, 'Neckam', p. 126

24. Si soli detur presentis prima diei (18 lines)
P, fol. 218rb
Walther, 'Neckam', p. 126

25. *Quare prima hora quarte diei cesserit Mercurio cum pocius se soli ut uidetur concessisse debuisset*
Ornatum stellis orbem lux quarta fatetur (28 lines)
P, fol. 218^{rb-va}
Walther, 'Neckam', pp. 126-7

26. Salue festa dies toto uenerabilis euo (3 lines)
P, fol. 218va
cf. Walther 17100a

27. Prima triangula sit tripedem prepone rotunde (2 lines)

P, fol. 218va

Walther, *Sprichwörter*, 22376; Walther, 'Neckam', p. 127

28. ADAM
Nominis esto tui memor ut stet prima secundam (2 lines)
P, fol. 218va
Walther, 'Neckam', p. 127

29. AMA
Arent assiduo tenuata labella labore (2 lines)
P, fol. 218va
Walther, *Sprichwörter*, 1320a; Walther, 'Neckam', p. 127

30. Aspectu leni ueniens pectus michi leni (2 lines)
P, fol. 218va
Walther, *Sprichwörter*, 1542a; Walther, 'Neckam', p. 127

31. Tu michi leso les. uulnus geminitur soles (2 lines)
P, fol. 218va
Walther, *Sprichwörter*, 31663a; Walther, 'Neckam', p. 128

32. Que dicis de me dic si bona si mala de me (2 lines)
P, fol. 218va
Walther, *Sprichwörter*, 22973b; Walther, 'Neckam', p. 128

33. Infaustus locus est, locus est infaustus abito (2 lines)
P, fol. 218va
Walther, *Sprichwörter*, 12296a; Walther, 'Neckam', p. 128.

34. Post pira presbiterum quare uel addere merum (1 line)
P, fol. 218va; G, fol. 236
Walther, *Sprichwörter*, 22042; Walther, 'Neckam', p. 128

35. Ha! quid a quid ama, dic quid quid amare (2 lines)
P, fol. 218va
Walther, 'Neckam', p. 128

36. Vsus mundo sed abusus ne dum ludo sim delusus (6 lines)
P, fol. 218va
Walther, 'Neckam', p. 128

37. Pauper Alexander cum paupere sit Iuliano (1 line)
P, fol. 218va
Walther, *Sprichwörter*, 20892a; Walther, 'Neckam', p. 128

37a. Non morum redimit cumulata scientia damnum (1 line)
P, fol. 218va
Walther, 'Neckam', p. 128

38. Quicquid contraxit carnis peculancia sordis (2 lines)
P, fol. 238ra
Walther, *Sprichwörter*, 25269c

39. Nunc ueterem sectam nunc mentis pone senectam (2 lines)
P, fol. 238ra
Walther, *Sprichwörter*, 19373c

40. Compositus gressus sermo grauis actus honestus (2 lines)
P, fol. 238ra
Walther, *Sprichwörter*, 3022b

41. Pasce gulam parce gula que gula uult nimis arce (2 lines)
P, fol. 238ra

Sprichwörter, 20799a
42. Cum breue quid tibi quis dederit non concedantem (30 lines)
43. Quem tibi transmitto doctor Radulfe nepotem (18 lines)
    P, fol. 238^{rb-va}
    Walther 15382
44. Dulcedo rara dulcescere cogit amara (2 lines)
    P, fol. 238va
    Walther, *Sprichwörter*, 36432
45. Vnica maturat geminum matura uirorem (1 line)
    P, fol. 238va [= no. 49, line 6]
    Walther, *Sprichwörter*, 32196c
46. Non liquet ad liquidum liquido quod cera liquescit (2 lines)
    P, fol. 238va
47. Emmundata liquor, dicat Ceres algidi liquor (3 lines)
    P, fol. 238va

[*Note*: Nos. 48-54 are found in G, but not in P.]

48. *Ridmus de curia*
    In curia|regnat cum iniuria|incuria (40 lines: Latin and French)
    G, fol. 69^{r-v}
49. *Entre dous uerces. lacerce meure*
    Gratior est inter iuuenes matura senectus (7 lines)
    G, fol. 235^{v}; cf. no. 45 above
    Walther, *Sprichwörter*, 10438b
50. *Contra auarum*
    Cur homo qui cinis es per auaritiam sepelis es? (4 lines)
    G, fols. 235^{v}-6
    Walther 3925
51. Multa deus de te dicunt per signa prophete (3 lines)
    G, fol. 236
    Walther, *Sprichwörter*, 15378a
52. *Versus retrogradi*
    Vrbe licet mesta faciunt turbe sibi festa (2 lines)
    G, fol. 236 (MS retrogredi)
    Walther, *Sprichwörter*, 32251a
53. *De ABSCONSA compendiose*
    Lumine pretendor ne ledat lumina splendor (2 lines)
    G, fol. 236 (MS compendioso)
    Walther, *Sprichwörter*, 14098a
53a. *Subcincte*
    Sum ne lux lumen ledat nec cera uolumen (1 line)
    G, fol. 236
54. O stupor! anguillas martyr mutauit in hillas (1 line)
    G, fol. 236
    Walther, *Sprichwörter*, 19585b

Editions

Most of the first thirty-seven items are edited in Walther, 'Neckam',
pp. 116-28. [But essentially this is ephemera, which cannot usefully

be separated from many similar verses by contemporaries: see Walther ad loc.—MG]

Meditatio de Magdalena

inc. 'Osculetur me osculo oris sui'. Ad mensam spiritualis refectionis recumbente Sapientia uenerabili uirtutum cetu stipata . . .

expl. . . . in terris agens leticie nuntia fuisti.

Manuscript

HEREFORD, Cathedral Library, O. i. 2, fols. 131ra-42rb (s. xiii$^{in.}$: Gloucester, 'Liber Thome de Bredone abbatis Gloucestrie' [1223-8]); *title*: Meditatio magistri Alexandri de Magdalena.

Excerpts in the *Florilegium*: fols. 98^v-100.

Manuscripts are recorded at: Bury St Edmunds (*Catalogus*); and by Bale (Bale, p. 25).

No Edition

Exhortatio ad religiosos

inc. Tedia nulla chori tibi sint assiste labori . . .

expl. . . . Vt stes inuictus benedicat rex benedictus.

Manuscript

MADRID, Biblioteca de Palacio, II. 468 fols. 8-9^v (s. xiv).

Bale owned a copy (Bale, p. 27).

De nuptiis Mercurii (*lost*)

inc. [not known]

expl. [not known]

No manuscript

The work is quoted on four occasions by Thomas Ringstead, in his *Postilla on Proverbs*: see above, p. 123 app. Three of the passages he quotes are in prose and one is in verse. Two are taken from a description of the *Domus Fortune*; in one Alexander is said to be describing the manners of the rich; in another—said to come from Book IV—he is speaking in the person of a noble man. The work would appear to have been some sort of an allegory. It has nothing to do with the *Commentary on Martianus Capella*.

Epistola Magistri Alexandri ad quemdam discipulum (*lost*)

inc. Sibi predilecto quondam discipulo . . .

expl. [not known]

Manuscript

OXFORD, Magdalen College, 168, fol. 51, no. 28: see below, p.153.

PLATE I

MS Cambridge, Gonville and Caius College, 385 (605), p. 7, the unique manuscript of
the *Sacerdos ad altare*, showing capitula, text and (second column) gloss

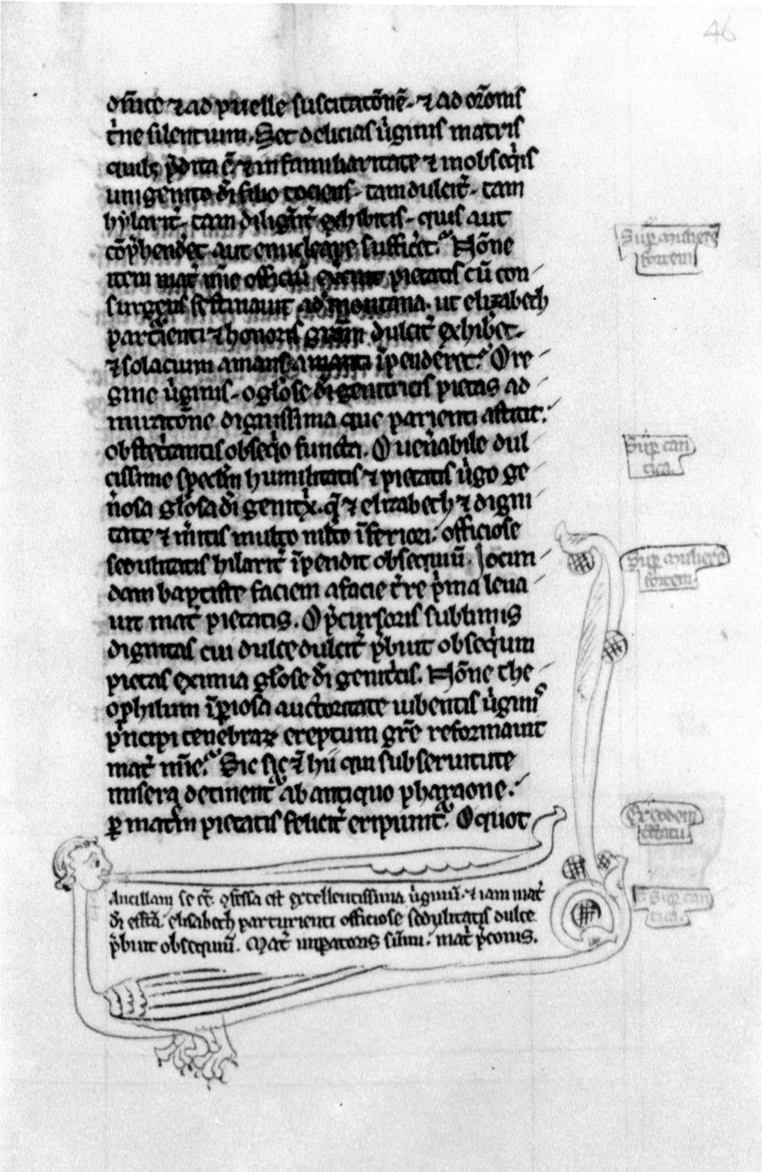

46

cm.

PLATE II

MS Cambridge, University Library, Gg. 6. 42, fol. 46, the *Florilegium*, showing excerpts from *SMF* (:/ 'Nonne', line 6), and *CCant*. (∴ 'uenerabile', line 13), etc. The grotesque surrounds a passage omitted from *CCant*. (after 'obsequium', line 17)

Passio Sancti Albani (*lost*)

All that survives is one couplet in the *Distinctiones Monastice*: see p. 28 above.

Florilegium (*See* Plate II).

MS Cambridge, University Library, Gg. 6. 42 (G) is a mid-thirteenth-century collection, quite possibly from Cirencester itself. It is in three parts:

A	fols. 3–212ᵛ	*Florilegium*
B	fols. 213ᵛ–22	Letter of Geoffrey of Monmouth to Alexander, bishop of Lincoln (= *Historia Regum*, VII. ii)
C	fols. 223–7ᵛᵇ	Minor verses, mostly by Nequam. These include *DCV* (fols. 224ᵛ–32): see p. 140 above

A measures: page 212 × 135 mm.; text 125 × 75 mm.; 26 lines per page. Parts *AB* have line-drawn grotesques in the same hand; *B* has another and superior illuminator (fol. 214ᵛ only). The script of *C* is close to *A*, but the rubrication is slightly different. A leaf has been inserted in *A* with much more sophisticated drawings recto and verso (fol. 5).

The *Florilegium* is a catena of excerpts from Nequam's works, each new passage identified by a title in the margin (red with a blue frame) and by a reference-sign, e.g. a triangle of dots or a dot and diagonal (./). Thus, in Plate II the excerpt from *SMF* is marked by the first framed title and by the sign :/ just perceptible over 'Nonne' in the text opposite. The passage that follows from *CCant.* breaks off too soon: so the scribe has marked 'obsequium' with a *signe de renvoie* ⸿ directing us to the note 'Ancillam se esse . . .' inside the grotesque at the foot of the page. The *Florilegium* continues with the passage from *SMF* that begins (. .) 'Iocundam . . .'. This careful system continues throughout the *Florilegium*.

At the same time the *Florilegium* has no explanatory prologue, and no apparent design in the sequence of excerpts. It is as though some pious hand has transcribed without any clear purpose some of the notes and excerpts in Nequam's *Nachlässe* at Cirencester.

II. DUBIA ET SPURIA

RWH listed twenty-eight texts, that had at one time or another been attributed to Nequam. Some are certainly not his; several are grammatical works, plausibly ascribed to the successful author of the *DNV* and the *CP*. Many are attested only by Leland or Bale. I have included only those that are not demonstrably by other authors; and which either survive in extant manuscripts or are attested before the sixteenth century. Again see Esposito, pp. 464–71. [MG]

Cur filius incarnatur (*lost*)

inc.   Operis immensi quoniam deus . . .

expl.   [not known]

No manuscript

The work is recorded in the *Catalogus* and again by Bale (Bale, p. 25; cf. Bale [1559], i, 273).

De fide spe et caritate (*lost*)

inc.   [not known]
expl.   [not known]

No manuscript

A manuscript is recorded at Reading (*Registrum* and *Catalogus*) and thence by Bale (Bale, p. 25).

De professione monachorum (*lost*)

inc.   [not known]
expl.   [not known]

No manuscript

A manuscript is recorded at Glastonbury (s. xiv): see J. P. Carley and J. F. R. Coughlan, 'An edition of the list of ninety-nine books acquired at Glastonbury abbey during the abbacy of Walter de Monington', *MS* xliii (1981), 502.

Dictionarius metricus *or* Duodecim decades

inc.   Olla patella tripes coclear lanx fuscina cratis . . .
expl.   . . . Allux articulus calx tallus tibia poples.

MS Metz, Bibl. Mun., 169 (s. xv: now destroyed) had the colophon 'Explicit Alexander Nequam'. For further manuscripts and a discussion of the authorship (probably John of Garland) see L. J. Paetow, *'Morale scolarium' of John of Garland* (Memoirs of the University of California IV. ii, Berkeley, 1927), pp. 132-3.

Mythographus Tertius

inc.   Fuit uir in Egypto nomine Sirophanes . . .
expl.   . . . proinde pingitur semihomo semiequus.

MS Cambridge, Trinity College, R 14 9 (884), fol. 21, has the ascription 'Incipiunt mithologie Allexandri Nequam et alio nomine scintillarium appellatur'; Holcot quotes the work as 'Alexander Nequam in scintillario poetarum' (Amsterdam [1586], p. 540). MS Oxford, Bodleian Library, Digby 221, fol. 1rb, has 'Albericus' over an erasure. For a discussion of the authorship (probably Alberic of London) see C. Burnett, 'A note on the origins of the Third Vatican Mythographer', *JWCI* xliv (1981), 160-3, with references.

Regule in theologiam

inc. [unknown]
expl. [unknown]

No manuscript

Manuscripts are recorded at: Buildwas (*Registrum*); Merevale (*Registrum*); Much Wenlock (*Registrum*); Ramsey (*Catalogus*). Probably the *Regule* of Alan of Lille: *MPL* ccx. 621–84. Cf. *Sixth Report of the Royal Commission on Historical Manuscripts: Appendix* (London, 1877), p. 356, col. 2.

Super aue maris stella

inc. prol. Petisti amice in Christo michi dilecte ...
expl. prol. ... et laudantibus iocunda.
inc. text. 'Aue maris stella'. In hoc uersu continetur laus uirginis quadripartita ...
expl. text. ... et sic uidentes semper colletemur.

Six sermons: see Schneyer, *Repertorium*, i. 276–7 (= nos. 81-6 in Appendix B below). The series is attributed to Nequam in MS Durham, Cathedral Library, B IV 30, fols. 1-12 (s. xiv²); title (fol. 1): 'Sermones VI siue tractatus Alexandri Necham super Aue maris stella'. None of the five other known manuscripts has this ascription; notably MS Cambridge, Peterhouse, 255 (s. xiii¹), the only witness to the prologue, is anonymous. MS London, BL, Royal 8 A. X, fols. 36-53ᵛ (*c.*1300), an expanded text, is attributed to Stephen Langton.

No edition

See G. Lacombe and B. Smalley, 'Incipits of Langton's works', *AHDLMA* v (1930), 185.

APPENDIX B
NEQUAM'S SERMONS

J.-B. SCHNEYER (*Repertorium*, i. 271-7) has ascribed ninety-five sermons to Nequam. Not all these attributions stand; and forty-four further sermons can be recovered, wholly or in part. Schneyer's numbering 1-95 is here augmented by the additional items (96)-(139).

1-53	(W)	Oxford, Bodleian Library, Wood empt. 13 (*SC* 8601), fols. 1-144^v (s. xiii^1). RWH doubted the authenticity of nos. 43-55. Nos. 43-4 are also found in MS Oxford, University College, 15, fols. 4^v-8^v, where no. 43 is entitled 'Sermo magistri Iohannis leodii' (fol. 4^v).[1]
54-56	(W)	Ibid., fols. 145^{r-v}. The first three of a long series of sermon-notes, which form the next section in W (fols. 145-56^v). RWH rightly rejected them.
57-58		London, BL, Harley 325, fols. 1-6, 34-7^v, 174-9^v, 203-8 (s. xiii^1). No. 57 = no. 21 (W, fols. 59^v-64); no. 58 (fol. 34^{r-v}) is new. MS Harley 325 also contains nos. 7, 15, 24, 27, 36, 60, (99).
59-60	(J)	Oxford, Jesus College, 94, fols. 74va-7vb (s. xiii$^{in.}$); Despite the formal attribution to 'Alexander, abbot of Cirencester' (p. 22 above) RWH rejected nos 59-69: see pp. 22-3 above.
61-71		Cambridge, University Library, Ii. 1. 24, fols. 123ra-7va, 140rb-2vb. RWH rejected all these: see p. 22 above. The manuscript also contains no. 28: fols. 141-2vb.
72-73		Peter Comestor, nos. 153 and 97 (Schneyer).
74-80		These repeat nos. 61-7.
81-86		Durham, Cathedral Library, B IV 30, fols. 1-12 (s. xiv^2): six sermons on *Ave maris stella*. Probably spurious: see p. 149 above.
87-88		Ibid., fols. 12-20: two sermons on the Crucifixion. To be rejected.
89-94		Worcester, Cathedral Library, Q. 6, fols. 94-101

---

[1] *c.*1200: Holme Cultran (O. Cist.). See further R. W. Hunt, 'A manuscript containing extracts from the *Distinctiones Monasticae*', *Medium Aevum*, xliv (1975), 238-41.

(s. xiii). It is not clear why this material was ever associated with Nequam.

95 Worcester, Cathedral Library, Q. 46 fol. 71ᵛ (s. xiiiᵉˣ·): see A. G. Little and F. Pelster, *Oxford Theology and Theologians c. A.D. 1281-1302* (*OHS* XCVI, Oxford, 1934), pp. 151 ff. To be rejected.

RWH noted eight further manuscripts, which brought further sermons to light, here numbered in brackets (96)-(104):

(96) Cambridge, Corpus Christi College, 217, fols. 119-47ᵛ (s. xiii: Worcester). Contains nos. 1-2, 4-18, 21-2, 26-7, 29, 32-3, 35-6, 41-2, (96). Two further sermons are rejected: *Cum immundus spiritus* (fols. 134ᵛ-5) and *Veni sancte spiritus* (fol. 120).

(97) Cambridge, Peterhouse, 255, fol. 30ᵛᵇ-1ʳᵇ, 32ʳᵇ⁻ᵛᵇ, 42ʳᵃ-3ᵛᵃ, 44ᵛᵃ-6ᵛᵇ (s. xiii¹). Contains nos. 2, 4, 8, 18, 37, (97). The manuscript also contains nos. 81-6.

(98) Hereford, Cathedral Library, O. i. 2, fols. 147ᵛ-9 (s. xiii: Gloucester). Contains no. (98) only. See also p. 146 above.

— London, Lambeth Palace, 481, fols. 88-91 (s. xiii). Contains nos. 31-3.

(99)-(101) Oxford, Bodleian Library, Hatton 102 (*SC* 4051), fols. 135ʳ⁻ᵛ, 201ʳ⁻ᵛ (s. xiii²: Hereford, Franciscans). Contains excerpts from nos. 8, (99)-(101).

— Oxford, Bodleian Library, Lyell 8, fol. 119ᵛᵃ⁻ᵛᵇ (s. xiii: Fountains, O. Cist.). Contains no. 16.

(102) W, fol. 41 (now missing). Contained no. (102), as may be inferred from Clement Canterbury's list of contents (fol. xviʳᵃ).

(103)-(104) Oxford, Merton Coll., 180, fols. 159ʳᵇ-62ᵛᵇ (s. xiii). Contains nos. 2, 11, 13, (103)-(104).

— Canterbury, Cathedral Library, lit. B. 13, fols. 47ʳᵃ-71ʳᵇ (s. xiii: Christ Church, Canterbury). Contains nos. 1-3, 7, 18, 24, 27, 39, (103), (104) and a letter from Walter de Melidie, canon of Cirencester, to R., the archbishop's chaplain, sending him the end of no. 2 (fol. 67ᵃ).

Thus RWH cast doubt on some items in Schneyer's list, and proposed nine new sermons. His additamenta to Schneyer are:

(96) *Ductus est Iesus in desertum* (Matt. 4: 1)
Aurum in igne sepe decoquitur . . .
Cambridge, Corpus Christi College, 217, fol. 132ʳ⁻ᵛ

(97) *Operamini opus uestrum* (Eccles. 51: 38)
Vtinam sciretis et intelligeretis . . .
Cambridge, Peterhouse, 255, fols. 147ᵛᵃ-3ʳᵃ

(98)   *Verno tempore solent reges* (1 Chron. 20: 1)
           Ver ad litteram caput exeruit ...
           Hereford, Cathedral Library, O. 1. 2, fols. 147va–9ra
(99)   *Hec est dies quam fecit deus* (Ps. 117: 24)
           Gloriosa resurrectio capitis per spem ...
           London, BL, Harley 325, fols. 34^v–5^v; Oxford, Bodleian
           Library, Hatton 102, fol. 201^v
(100)   *Scio quod redemptor meus uiuit* (Job 19: 25)
           [excerpt]
           Oxford, Bodleian Library, Hatton 102, fol. 201^{r–v}
(101)   *Dixit deus: fiat lux* (Gen. 1: 3)
           [excerpt]
           Oxford, Bodleian Library, Hatton 102, fol. 201^v
(102)   *Egressus Iesus secessit in purtes Tiri* (Matt. 15: 21)
           [First part (fol. 41^{r–v}) missing]
           W, fols. (41^{r–v}), 42–4^v
(103)   *Dominus ipse ueniet et saluabit me* (Is. 35:4)
           In natiuitate auctoris leticie nasci debet ...
           Oxford, Merton College, 180, fols. 159rb–60ra; Canterbury,
           Cathedral Library, lit. B. 13, fols. 56rb–8va
(104)   *Dixit Iesus Petro. sequere me* (John 21:19)
           Dominus Iesus saluator noster sapientia patris ...
           Oxford, Merton College, 180, fols. 160ra–1ra; Canterbury,
           Cathedral Library, lit. B. 13, fols. 58va–60vb

In addition, the *Florilegium* (G) includes extensive passages from
Nequam's sermons. Some help to validate sermons already known;
but no fewer than thirty-three are unique to G. As these are excerpts,
having neither the incipit nor the explicit of the full sermon, they are
listed here according to their scriptural text, by which they are introduced in G:[2]

(105)	Gen. 16: 8	Agar ancilla Saray
(106)	18: 3	Domine si inueni gratiam
(107)	2 Kgs. 22: 10	Inclinauit celos
(108)	Job 20: 3	Spiritus intelligentie
(109)	39: 27	Numquid ad preceptum tuum
(110)	Ps. 16: 3	Probasti cor meum
(111)	24: 1	Ad te domine leuaui animam
(112)	46:6	Ascendit deus in iubilo
(113)	117:13	Inpulsus euersus sum
(114)	Sap. 3: 6	Tanquam aurum in fornace
(115)	—	Memento homo
(116)	Is. 2: 10	Ingredere petram
(117)	55: 2	Quare appenditis argentum
(118)	Matt. 2: 11	Apertis thesauris suis
(119)	5: 3	Beati pauperes spiritu

(120)	Matt. 6: 17	Tu autem cum ieiunias
(121)	11: 3	Tu es qui uenturus es
(122)	11: 10	Ecce ego mitto angelum meum
(123)	16: 24	Si quis uult uenire post me
(124)	Mark 13: 33	Videte uigilate et orate
(125)	Luke 21: 35	Erunt signa in sole et luna
(126)	24: 29	Mane nobiscum domine
(127)	John 2: 1	Nuptie facte sunt
(128)	21: 18	Cum esses iunior
(129)	—	Tu es pastor ouium
(130)	Acts 12: 1	Misit Herodes manus
(131)	—	Egressus Petrus de carcere
(132)	1 Cor. 5: 7	Pascha nostrum
(133)	Heb. 13: 13	Exeamus extra castra
(134)	Rev. 21: 4	Absterget deus
(135)	21: 5	Ecce ego omnia facio noua
(136)	—	Grata est serenitas
(137)	—	Hodierna die noster dominus

Two lost sermons are noted in MS Oxford, Magdalen College, 168 (s. xiii):

| (138) | — | Quasi modo geniti infantes (in octauis pasche) |
| (139) | Ps. 18: 6 | In sole posuit tabernaculum suum (in natali domini). |

They are numbered 29 and 30 in the list of contents (fols. 50ᵛ–1ᵛ) to a collection of seventy-eight 'sermones modernorum magistrorum'.[2] The text of sermons 1–19 and 31–8 follows: nos. 29–30 are among those missing. Masters named in the contents-list include Archbishop Stephen Langton, master John of Abbeville and master Nicholas of Tournai.

The transmission of the sermons is in some manuscripts associated with the sermons of Peter Comestor, for whom see J. Longère, *Œuvres oratoires des maîtres parisiens au XIIᵉ siècle* (Études Augustiniennes, Paris, 1975), i. 20, with references. Otherwise the text presents few real difficulties: W is the base manuscript, usefully corroborated by Cambridge, Corpus Christi College, 217. The sermons circulated freely for half a century—the Canterbury manuscript offers a glimpse of how they were collected—and then they ceased to command attention.

---

[2] For an account of the manuscript see F. M. Powicke, *Stephen Langton* (Oxford, 1929), pp. 170–6.

INDEX OF MANUSCRIPTS

Aberdeen, University Library
  137: 15 n.

Basel, Universitätsbibl.
  F. IV. 50: 129
Berlin (E.), Deutsche Staatsbibl.
  Santen B. 4: 129
Berlin (W.), Staatsbibl. Preuss. Kultur-
  besitz
  lat. fol. 607: 126
Bern, Burgerbibl.
  B 45: 131
Besançon, Bibl. Mun.
  543: 126

Cambrai, Bibl. Mun.
  969 (867): 126
  976 (874): 20 n.
  977 (875): 129
Cambridge, Corpus Christi College
  217: 22, 37 n., 131, 151, 153
  385: 120 n.
  460: 119 n.
— Gonville and Caius College
  136 (76): 20 n., 126
  230 (116): 120 n.
  236 (122): 131
  300 (514): 117 n.
  372 (621): 138
  385 (605): Plate I; 28, 126, 136
— Pembroke College
  103: 131
  112: 131
  275: 131
— Peterhouse
  125: 123 n.
  169: 122
  255: 151
— Sidney Sussex College
  95 (Δ 5 10): 15 n.
— Trinity College
  R. 3. 1 (580): 71 n., 138
  R. 14. 9 (884): 128, 148
  R. 16. 3 (951): 135
  R. 16. 4 (952): 135

O. 2. 50 (1154): 72 n.
O. 4. 1 (1232): 135
O. 7. 9 (1337): 126
— University Library
  Add. 710: 55
  Gg. 6. 42 (= G): Plate II, 19 n.,
    25 nn., 46 nn., 47 n., 54, 56 n.,
    62 n., 65 nn., 86 n., 89 n., 91 n.,
    92 n., 95 n., 118, 128, 140, 145,
    147, 152-3
  Ii. 1. 24: 22, 150
  Ii. 2. 31: 137
  Kk. 4. 5: 135
  Kk. 5. 10: 131
Canterbury, Cathedral Library
  Add. 129/1: 126
  Lit. B. 6: 25 nn., 45 n., 46 nn., 47 n.,
    97 n., 131
  Lit. B. 13: 151, 152
Copenhagen, Royal Library
  Fabricius 92 (iv) 8°: 126

Donaueschingen, Hofbibliothek
  910: 9 n.
Dublin, Trinity College
  256: 131
  257: 131
  270: 126
Durham, Cathedral Library
  B. IV. 30: 150
  Hunter 58: 135
— University Library
  Routh 1b 16: 135

Edinburgh, National Library of Scot-
  land
  Advoc. 18. 4. 9: 129
  Advoc. 18. 4. 13: 126
Erfurt, Wissenschaftl. Bibl.
  Amplon. O. 12: 126
Évreux, Bibl. Mun.
  72: 131

Hereford, Cathedral Library
  O. i 2: 7 n., 24, 146, 151, 152

Kiel, Universitätsbibl.
KB 38: 126

Lincoln, Cathedral Library
132 (C. 5. 8): 127
London, British Library
Add. 8082: 20 n., 33 n., 127
Cotton Claudius E. IV: 18 n.
Nero D. I: 3 nn.
Tiberius A. XII: 135
Titus D. XX: 126
Vespasian B. XXIII: 129
Egerton 2261: 132
Harley 6: 132
325: 150, 152
495: 15 n.
683: 127
1687: 132
3133: 21 n., 45 n., 108 n.,
116 n., 129
3737: 135
Royal 2 C. XI: 134
2 C. XII: 81 n.
2 D. VIII: 132
3 B. XII: 121 n.
3 D. I: 122 n.
4 D. XI: 131, 137
5 C. V: 132
7 C. I: 121 n.
7 F. I. (= R): 7 n., 16 n., 27,
45 n., 56 n., 68 nn., 69 n.,
70 nn., 72 n., 76 n., 112,
113 nn., 116 nn., 117 n.,
137
8 A. XXI: 132
8 E. IX: 66 n., 138
9 A. XIV: 26, 134
12 F. XIV: 109 n., 110 n.,
135
12 G. XI: 135
15 B. IV: 132
— College of Arms
Arundel 6: 1 n.
— Lambeth Palace Library
23: 18, 137
33: 123 n.
61: 134
122: 37 n.
162: 132
199: 37 n.
421: 130
481: 151

— Wellcome Institute for the History
of Medicine
801A: 127

Madrid, Bibl. Palacio
II. 468: 54, 128-9, 138, 140-2
Milan, Bibl. Ambros.
I. 246 inf.: 127
Munich, Bayer. Staatsbibl.
Clm. 8827: 124 n.

Orléans, Bibl. Mun.
299 (252): 120 n.
Oxford, Balliol College
19: 122
27: 121 n.
34: 123 nn.
39: 66 n., 137
— Bodleian Library
Auct. D. 2. 4: 98 n., 99 nn.
D. 2. 9: 130
D. 2. 13: 100 n.
D. 3. 15: 100 n.
D. 4. 18: 139
F. 5. 23: 132
Bodley 57: 132
238: 120 nn.
284: 7 n., 10 n., 26 n.,
27 nn., 45 nn., 46 nn.,
47 n., 48 n., 51 n.,
76 n., 85 n., 87 n., 93 n.,
96 nn., 97 n., 98 n.,
99 nn., 100 nn., 101 nn.,
102 nn., 103 nn., 108 nn.,
109 n., 130, 134
356: 66, 137
528: 139
550 (= B): 7 n., 25 n., 29 n.,
36 nn., 37 nn., 38-9,
41 nn., 46 n., 47 n.,
48 n., 50 n., 51 n., 70 n.,
93 nn., 100 nn., 103 n.,
108 nn., 109 nn., 120 n.,
132
685: 122 n.
760: 132
829: 123 n.
862: 98 n., 99 nn.
Digby 2: 56
37: 127
56: 12 n., 26, 134
82: 123 n.

100: 120 n.
157: 140
221: 6 n., 48 n., 69 n., 128
e mus. 29: 120 n.
Hatton 44: 132
102: 136, 139, 151, 152
lat. misc. b. 13: 127
Laud lat. 17: 13 n., 98 n., 99 nn.
67: 38-9
Laud misc. 112: 6 n., 132
497: 33 n., 127
Lyell 8: 151
Rawl. C. 22: 37 n., 57 n.,
C. 67: 130, 132
G. 96: 127
G. 99: 127
Wood empt. 13 (= W): 7 nn., 21-2,
23, 24 n., 41 n., 43-4 n., 46 nn.,
70 n., 85 n., 86 nn., 87 nn.,
88 nn., 89 nn., 90 nn., 92 n.,
93, 94 n., 117 n., 150, 151,
152, 153
— Corpus Christi College
45 (= C): 9 n., 11 n., 26 nn.,
46 nn., 48 n., 49 n., 64, 68 n.,
82 n., 83 nn., 85 nn., 94 n.,
96 n., 97 n., 102 nn., 103 n.,
135
59: 57 n.
245: 66, 135
— Exeter College
13: 122
— Jesus College
94 (= J): frontispiece; 17 n., 22-3,
24 n., 27 n., 31, 41 n., 46 n.,
50 n., 51 n., 65, 70 n., 81 n.,
85 n., 95 n., 96 n., 97 n.,
104 nn., 105-6, 107 n., 108 n.,
109 n., 134, 139, 150
— Lincoln College
lat. 86: 123 n.
— Magdalen College
139: 135
149 (= M): 8 nn., 9 n., 44 n., 46 nn.,
47 nn., 49 n., 53 n., 64, 65 nn.,
67 n., 82 n., 86 n., 93 n., 96 n.,
103 n., 104 n., 107 nn., 108 n.,
109 nn., 110 n., 122 n., 137
168: 146, 153
— Merton College
180: 23, 24, 151, 152
254: 133

— New College
43: 137
171: 72 n
— St John's College
51: 135
119: 26, 134
178: 127, 132
— Trinity College
35: 123 n.
— University College
15: 150

Paris, Bibliothèque Nationale
latin 2904: 129
7679: 127
11866: 138
11867 (= P): 1 n., 4 n., 5 n.,
6 n., 12 n., 16 n., 17 n.,
20 n., 27 n., 28, 46 n.,
47 nn., 48 nn., 49 n., 55-6,
58-61, 62 n., 68 n., 75 n.,
76 n., 77 nn., 78 nn.,
79 nn., 80 n., 127, 138,
139, 140-4
14556: 116 n.
15171: 69 n., 128
18499: 72 n.
— Bibl. Ste-Geneviève
1210: 127
1211: 132

Sainte-Claude (Jura), Bibl. Mun.
6: 127
Stuttgart, Württembergische Landes-
bibliothek
Q. 58: 120 n.

Troyes, Bibl. Mun.
1048, item 11: 133
Turin, Bibl. Naz.
D. v. 29: 133

Vatican, Bibl. Apost., Ottobon.
lat. 72: 123 n.

Vienna, Nationalbibl.
12535: 127

Windsor, St George's Chapel
Jackson Collection 32: 135

Wolfenbüttel, Herzog-August-Bibl.
13. 10. Aug. 4º (3035): 127

Worcester, Cathedral Library
F. 1: 133
F. 3: 121 n.
Q. 6: 7 n., 150
Q. 46: 151
Q. 50: 128

GENERAL INDEX

Achilleis (Statius) 48
Adam de Parvo Ponte 5-6, 20, 33, 34-5
Adelard of Bath 73-4
'Ademar', fabulist 42
Admirantes (gloss on the *Doctrinale*)
    120
Aeneid (Virgil) 41, 48, 53 n.
Ailred of Rievaulx 11
Alan of Lille 55, 89, 101
Alan of Tewkesbury 8
Alban, St 57
Alberic of London 21, 148
Alexander, legends of 52
Alexander III, pope 30
Alexander de Villa Dei 30, 40, 48 n.
Alexander of Hales OFM 113 n.
ALEXANDER NEQUAM (1157-1217):
  Life:
    birth and parentage 1-2
    early schooling 2
    periods of study and teaching at
        Dunstable, St Albans, and
        Paris 3-7
    at Oxford 7-10
    canon of Cirencester 10-12
    activities outside cloister 13
    abbot of Cirencester 14-15
    dies 14-15
    character 15-16
    name 3-4, 17-18
    reputation 12, 15, 19, 33, 67,
        117, 119-24
  Characteristics, attitudes, etc.:
    literary style 29, 56-66
    revision of own works 30-1, 92
    knowledge of English 93
    interest in psychology 116-17
    devotion to Virgin Mary 106-7
    attitude to doctrine of Immacu-
        late Conception 117
    attitude to problem of free will
        113-14
  Learning:
    grammatical doctrine 32-41
    rhetoric 41-2

knowledge of classical authors
    43-53
knowledge of Greek 108
knowledge of Hebrew 108-10
scientific knowledge 67-83
  Works:
    Apostropha ad urbem Romam
        59 (see *Laus Sapientie divine*)
    *Commentary on the Athanasian
        Creed* 17, 21, 45, 125, 129-
        30
    Commentary on Ecclesiastes (=
        DNR iii-v) 9 n., 48 n., 49 n.,
        56, 64, 68, 81, 83 nn., 85 nn.,
        94 n., 96 nn., 102-4, 109 n.,
        110 n., 125, 134-7
    Commentary on Proverbs 27, 31,
        50 n., 81, 95, 97, 104-6,
        108 n., 123, 125, 136-7
    *Commentary on the Song of
        Songs* 8, 9 n., 27, 46, 48-9,
        64, 66, 67 n., 82 n., 86 n.,
        93 n., 95, 96 n., 97, 103-4,
        104 n., 106, 107 nn., 109,
        110 n., 117, 120, 122, 124,
        125, 137
    *Commentary on Martianus Ca-
        pella* 19, 20, 21, 69, 125,
        128
    Corrogationes Noui Promethei
        28, 48, 54, 58-61, 123, 126,
        138-9
    Corrogationes Promethei 6, 12,
        18, 21, 24, 25-6, 29-30, 34,
        35-6, 37-9, 50-1, 60, 70 n.,
        93 nn., 95, 99-100, 103 n.,
        108 nn., 109 n., 119, 120,
        123, 125, 131-3
    Corrogationes Promethei versi-
        fied 12, 125, 133-4
    De commendatione uini 16, 54,
        55, 62, 126, 140
    De naturis rerum 6, 17, 20, 24,
        26, 27, 29, 30, 35 n., 36, 41,
        49, 51 nn., 52, 60-1, 63 n.,

ALEXANDER NEQUAM (*cont.*):
  Works (*cont.*):
    De naturis rerum (*cont.*):
      64, 65, 66, 67, 68 n., 69,
      70 n., 71, 72-7, 78, 80,
      81, 82, 95, 97, 103, 107 n.,
      109, 120, 121, 124, 125,
      134-6
    De nominibus utensilium 6, 19,
      20, 29, 32, 33, 34, 44-5,
      48 n., 69, 124, 126-8
    Exhortatio ad religiosos 54, 126,
      146
    Gloss on the Psalter 7, 8 n., 9-
      10 n., 26-7, 31, 45, 47, 50,
      76, 85 n., 93 n., 95, 98 n.,
      99, 100 nn., 101 nn., 103 nn.,
      108 n., 123, 125, 134
    Laus beatissime uirginis 125,
      130
    Laus sapientie divine 1, 5, 12,
      13-14, 17, 27, 51 nn., 52,
      53, 54, 56, 58, 60, 67, 68 n.,
      69 n., 71, 72 n., 75 n., 77-8,
      79, 93 n., 123, 125, 138
    Novus Avianus 41-2, 54, 125,
      128-9
    Novus Esopus 41-2, 54, 125, 129
    Questiones 17, 21, 130
    Sacerdos ad altare 6, 21, 28-30,
      33-5, 40, 43, 48, 50, 68, 76,
      125, 136
    Solatium fidelis anime 25, 47,
      56, 65, 95-7, 104, 125,
      130-1
    Speculum speculationum 17, 27,
      45, 56, 68-9, 70 nn., 72,
      111-17, 125, 137-8
    Super mulierem fortem 17, 31,
      41, 65, 70 n., 84-5 n., 95-6,
      105-7, 109 n., 126, 139
    Suppletio defectuum 1, 5, 14,
      16-17, 27, 49-50, 54, 60,
      67, 68 n., 75 n., 76, 77, 78-
      80, 123, 126, 139-40
    Extracts: *Florilegium* 19, 21, 22,
      23, 24, 25, 28, 60, 95 n.,
      118, 126, 147
    Hymns 55-6, 63, 140-5
    Minor verses 56-7, 140-5; *Ridmus de curia* 54, 63, 145
    Sermons 7 n., 21-4, 64, 65,

    70 n., 84-94 *passim*, 150-3
  Lost Works: *De Nuptiis Mercurii*
    (lost) 123, 126, 146; *Epistola
    Magistri Alexandri ad quemdam discipulum* (lost) 126,
    146; *Passio sancti Albani*
    (lost) 28, 126, 147
  Dubious and spurious works:
    Cur filius incarnatur (lost)
    147-8; *De fide spe et caritate* (lost) 148; *De professione monachorum* (lost)
    148; *Duodecim decades (De
    utensilibus domi)* 20, 148;
    Mythographus tertius 21,
    148; *Regule in theologiam*
    149; *Super Ave maris stella*
    149
Alexandreis (Baudri de Bourgeuil)
  54
Alfraganus 76
Alfred of Sareshel 12, 18
Amphitrio 58
Analecta Hymnica 55-6
Andreas (German commentator on
  Song of Songs) 124
Annales (Trivet) 1
Anselm, St 66, 107, 114-15
Anselm of Laon 98-9, 100-1
Antichrist 52
Aphorismi (Urso) 71
Apollonius of Tyana 53
Appendix Vergiliana 49, 50
Apuleius 74-5
Arabic language 67
Arator 45, 50
Aristotle 51-2, 67-71, 82, 111
Ars amatoria (Ovid) 48
Ars disserendi (Adam de Parvo Ponte)
  6
Ars minor (Donatus) 37
Ars Poetica (Horace) 48
Articella (medical texts) 71 n., 72 n.
Asia, AN's description of 78
astrology, AN's view of 77
astronomy, AN's knowledge of 75-7
Augustine, St, of Hippo, 10 n., 92
Augustinian houses and canons 10
Aurora (Petrus Riga) 61
Avianus 41
Avicenna 111, 117
Aymon, AN's story of 51

Bale, John, bp Ossory 18, 23, 54, 125, 128, 129, 130, 137, 140, 146, 148

Baldwin, archbishop of Canterbury 73

Baldwin II, king of Jerusalem 2 n.

Bangor (N. Wales) 123

Barbarismus (Donatus) 37, 38

Barnwell, O.S.A. (Cambs.) 60

Basel, council of 117

Bath (Somerset) 12

Baudri de Bourgeuil, poet 54

Bede 37, 105

Benedictines 10

Bernard, St 64 n., 94

Bernardus Silvestris 60, 79

Bertran (French epic poet) 51

Bestiary, The 75

Birkenmajer, A. 67 n., 70, 72

Birria 58

Blaye, Roland's burial place 51

Boethius 46, 47, 60, 113

Breuiarium (on the Psalter) 101

Brompton, John (chronicler) 121

Bury St Edmunds (Suffolk) 120

Caesarius of Heisterbach 15, 18

Cambridge 122

Camden, W. 63

Campus Martius 51

Canons (Ptolemy) 76

Canterbury 25

Cassiodorus 74

Catalogus (by Henry of Kirkestede) 23, 125

Cato 35

Celestine III, pope 11, 17

Chalcidius 67, 69

Charlemagne 51, 52

Chaucer, Geoffrey 43

Chippenham 2

Chronicle (Geoffrey le Baker) 121

Cicero, 11, 52, 69 n., 87

Cirencester 4, 10, 11, 12, 13, 14, 17, 19, 22, 25, 27, 31, 118-19

Ciris (attrib. Virgil) 33

Cistercians 32, 57, 84

Claudian 45, 47, 49, 64, 69 n.

Cologne 78

Collectanea (Whethamstede) 120

Combe, O.Cist. (Warwicks.) 11

Commentary on Ecclesiastes (William d'Eyncourt) 121

Commentary on Ezekiel (Jerome) 115

Commentary on Isaiah (Jerome) 45

Commentary on the Psalter (Peter Lombard) 98-100, 103, 108 n.

Commentary on the 'Timaeus' (Chalcidius) 67

Commentary on the twelve minor prophets (Simon of Hinton) 119-20

Commentary on Wisdom (Holcot) 123

compass, earliest reference to 32

Compilatio tertia (canon law) 30

Constantinus Africanus 72

Copa (attrib. Virgil) 50

Cordova 53

Cornificius 6 n.

Culex (attrib. Virgil) 49-50

Curteys, John 123 n.

Daniel of Morley 45

De amicitia (Cicero) 11

De amicitia (Peter of Blois) 11-12

De anima (Aristotle) 68, 69

De anima (Avicenna) 117

De anima (Isaac de Stella) 82 n.

De arte predicatoria (Alan of Lille) 89

De celo et mundo (Aristotle) 69

De commixtionibus elementorum (Urso) 71-2

De consolatione philosophiae (Boethius) 113

De deo Socratis (Apuleius) 74

De dietis uniuersalibus (Isaac Israeli) 72

De generatione animalium (Aristotle) 69

De generatione et corruptione (Aristotle) 68

De libertate arbitrii (St Anselm) 114 n.

De medicamine faciei (Ovid) 48

De mirabilibus mundi (Solinus) 50

De motu cordis (Alfred of Sareshel) 12, 18

De natura deorum (Cicero) 69 n.

De raptu Proserpinae (Claudian) 47

De rosis (attrib. Virgil) 50

De schematibus et tropis (Bede) 37

Dictionarius (John of Garland) 32

Disticha Catonis 47

Distinctiones monasticae 28, 57

Doctrinale (Alexander de Villa Dei), 30, 40, 120

Doctrinale Novum, see *Doctrinale*
Dominicans 119, 121, 123
Donatus 35, 37, 38
Dover 14
Dragmaticon (William of Conches) 45
Drayton, Michael 121
Dreves, G. M. 55, 56
Du Boulay, C. E. 3
Dunstable 3-4, 7

Eberhard of Bethune 40
Eclogue (Theodolus) 35
Eclogues (Virgil) 35, 41, 48
Egypt, AN's discussion of 52
Elegies (Maximian) 47
Ellis, Robinson 33
England, AN's descriptions of 51, 78
English language 93-4
Entheticus (John of Salisbury) 35
Epistles (Horace) 48
Epodes (Horace) 48
Est et non (attrib. Virgil) 50
Ethics (Aristotle) 69
Ethion (master at Petit Pont) 5
Etymologiae (Isidore) 33, 34, 74
Europe, AN's descriptions of 78
Exchequer, AN's opinion of 9

Fabianus (monk of St Albans) 3
Fables (Avianus) 41
Fasti (Ovid) 48
Fourth Lateran Council, AN's preparations for 14
France, 41
  AN's descriptions of 78
Franciscans 119, 121, 124
Frederick I (Barbarossa), King of Germany and Emperor 104
free will, doctrine of 112, 113-15
French language 93-4

Gabriel, archangel 106
Galen 72
Galfridus (compiler of *Florilegium*) 118, 119
Galfridus Anglicus 42 n.
Gamaliel (*see* Talmud)
'Ganymedes Chrysopolita' 47
Garinus (abbot of St Albans) 3, 4
Garinus of Sopwell (master at St Albans, succeeded AN) 3

Gaufridus (*see* Geoffrey, abbot of Malmesbury)
Gautier de Châtillon, poet 54
Geoffrey, abbot of Malmesbury 118
Geoffrey, abbot of St Albans 4 n.
Geoffrey Brito, AN's nephew 13 n.
Geoffrey, sub-prior of Ste-Barbe-en-Auge 10 n.
Geoffrey de Vinsauf 42
Geoffrey le Baker, chronicler 121
Geoffrey of Monmouth 51
Georgics (Virgil) 41, 48, 49
Gerard of Cremona, translator of Aristotle 70
Gerbert (Pope Silvester II) 51
Gesta abbatum (Matthew Paris) 3, 4 n., 18
Gesta regum (William of Malmesbury) 51
Geta (Vitalis of Blois) 58-9
Gigantomachia (Claudian) 45
Gilbert de la Porreé 98, 100
Giles de Corbeil 71 n.
Giraldus Cambrensis 30, 45 n., 73-4, 75
Girart de Vienne (Bertran) 51
'Glossa Ordinaria' 98-102
grace, doctrine of 111-12
Graecismus (Eberhard of Bethune) 40
Greece, AN's discussion of 52
Greek language 67, 108
Gregory the Great, pope 87, 95
Gualo of Caen, monk and versifier 6 n.
'Gualo sophista' 6 n.

Haskins, C. H. 3 n., 28, 29, 30, 31 n., 33 n., 34 n., 35 n., 68 n.
Hauréau, B. 34, 69, 94
Hebrew, language 108-10
Helen of Troy 91
Henricus de Alemannia, king's messenger 13
Henry of Harclay, theologian 121
Henry of Kirkestede (author of *Catalogus*) 4, 23
Hereford, earl of 13
Hermann of Carinthia 76
Hermannus Contractus 76
Hermes Trismegistes 70
Heroides (Ovid) 48
Hexameron 96
Higden, Ranulph 121

Historia animalium (Aristotle) 69
Historia scholastica (Peter Comestor) 36
Hodierna, AN's mother 1, 2 n., 79
Holcot, Robert OP 121, 123
Homer 82
Homilies on Ecclesiastes (Hugh of St Victor) 81 n.
Honorius III, pope 28
Horace 35, 39, 48
Hubert Walter, archbishop of Canterbury 12
Hugh of St Victor 81 n.
Hugh Primas 57

Immaculate Conception, doctrine of 117
    feast of 7–8
In Canticum Canticorum (Origen) 81 n.
Institutiones (Priscian) 37, 45
Interdict 13
Isaac de Stella O.Cist. 82 n.
Isaac Israeli, medical writer 72
Isagoge (Johannitius) 72
Isidore of Seville 33, 34, 74, 81
Italy, AN's discussion of 52, 67

Jacobus Hose 2
Jerome, St 45, 81, 101, 108, 115
Jocelin of Furness O.Cist. 10 n.
Johannitius, medical writer 72
John, King of England 2, 14, 28
John of Abbeville, preacher 153
John of Garland 20, 28, 32, 33
John of Hastings, clerk to archbishop of Canterbury 13
John of Liège, preacher 22, 150
John of Salisbury 6, 32 n., 35, 37 n., 44, 53 n.
Julius Caesar 52
Juvenal 35, 48

Kempsey (Worcs.), AN dies at 14
Kenilworth (Warwicks.) 13
Kilwardby, Robert OP, archbishop of Canterbury 40
Knoyle Hodierne (Wilts.) 2

Lanthony (Secunda: Glouc.) 13, 57
Latin language 92–3
Leland, John 18, 60, 63, 123 n., 125, 136, 137

Liber de causis 70
Liber de eligendis (*Liber eligendorum*) 70
Liber de expositionibus uocabulorum biblie (Rogerus Compotista) 120
Liber XXIV philosophorum 70
Libya 78
Lincolnshire 57
Lindau, Marquart von 124
Lottin, O. 116
Lucan 35, 47, 48, 53
Lucretius 45
Lundy Island 121
Lyons 119

Mabillon, J. 94
Macrobius 66, 82 n.
Madox, T. 17
Malmesbury, prior of 12, 119
Man in the Moon, AN's reference to 57
Mandonnet, P. 102
Manitius, M. 30 n., 123
Marchall, Roger 28
Martial 46, 47
Martianus Capella 60
Mary Magdalen, St 55–6, 105–6
Mary the Virgin, St 24, 55–6, 104, 106, 107 n.
Matthew, prior of St Albans 3
Matthew Paris 2, 3, 4, 18
Matthew of Vendôme 61, 62 n.
Maurice of St Victor, preacher 22
Maurus of Salerno, medical writer 71–2
Maximian 47
Medusa 78
Metamorphoses (Ovid) 44, 46, 48
Metaphysics (Aristotle) 68
Meyer, P. 36
Michael de Meaux, archbishop of Sens 101–2 n.
Michael Scot, translator of Aristotle 69
Midas 90
Mirabilia Angliae 51
Moralia in Job (Gregory the Great) 95
Moralitates super Ysaiam (school of Holcot) 121
Moretum (attrib. Virgil) 33, 44–5, 49, 50
Mythographus tertius (Alberic of London) 21, 148

Naples 53
Narcissus 91
Natural History (Pliny) 74
Nicholas of Tournai, preacher 153

Octavian 51
Odes (Horace) 48
Odo of Châteauroux, preacher 20
Ogier the Dane 51
Oliver 51
Organon (Aristotle) 68
Origen 81
Osbern of Gloucester 34
Otto von Passau OFM, 124
Ovid 44, 46, 47, 48, 60 n., 80
Owl and the Nightingale 75
Oxford 1, 4, 7, 8, 21, 24, 54, 56, 84, 87–8, 91, 93, 122

Paetow, L. J. 28–9
Pamphilus 47
Pannonia 78
Panormia (Osbern of Gloucester) 34
Pantegni (Constantinus Africanus) 72
Pantheologus (Peter of Cornwall) 73–4
Paradise, four rivers of 96
Paris 3, 4, 5, 7, 19–20, 41, 123
Pauline Epistles, in scholastic curriculum 98
Persius 49
Peter (AN's nephew?) 12
Peter Abailard 25
Peter Comestor 10, 22, 36, 96 n., 98, 153
Peter Lombard 98, 100, 101, 103, 108 n., 109, 110, 111, 112, 114
Peter of Blois 9, 10, 11, 12, 19, 41 n., 44
Peter of Cornwall 74
Peter of Poitiers 101, 111
Peterborough Abbey (Northants.) 18
Petit Pont, school of 5, 19, 33, 35
Petronius 50
Petrus Cantor 100–1, 102
Petrus Helias 37, 40
Petrus Riga 61
Phale tolum (Adam de Parvo Ponte) 20, 33, 34–5
Pharsalia (Lucan) 48
Philippe de Grèves, hymnographer 55
Philosophia mundi (William of Conches) 45

Physiologus (*see Bestiary*)
Pitra, J. B. 50, 57
Pliny 74
Policraticus (John of Salisbury) 44, 53
Polychronicon (Higden) 121, 123
Postilla on Proverbs (Ringstead) 60, 123
Priscian 35, 37, 38, 45
Prometheus 36, 58
Promisimus (gloss on Priscian) 38–9
Prudentius 45, 50
Psalter, in scholastic curriculum 98
Ptolemy 76

Questiones Naturales (Adelard of Bath) 73

Raimund de Beziers 124
Ralph, school-master 12–13, 54
Reginald of Walsingham, monk of Bury St Edmunds 120
Registrum Anglie 21, 125
Reichenau 76
Remains concerning Britain (Camden) 63
Remedium amoris (Ovid) 48
Remigius of Auxerre 69
Richard, abbot of Cirencester 14
Richard I, King of England 1, 2, 104
Ringstead, Thomas OP 60, 123, 146
rivers (in Europe, AN's description of) 78
Robertus de Salerno, monk at St Albans 3
Roger Bacon OFM 76, 119
Roger of Wendover 18
Rogerus Compotista, monk of Bury St Edmunds 120
Roland 51
Rome 11, 50, 53, 78
Romulus (fables) 42
Rouen 26
Russell, J. C. 14, 25
Rutherford, W. G. 41, 42

S., prior of Malmesbury 12, 119
St Albans (Herts) 1, 2, 3, 4, 5, 11, 17, 18, 21
St Frideswide's, Oxford 7, 24, 93
St Peter's, Gloucester 12, 24
Salerno, school of 71
Saluatio Romae 53

Satires (Horace) 48
Sedulius Scotus 50
Selden, J. 121
Seneca 50, 53
Sentences (Peter Lombard) 111, 114 n.
Serlo of Wilton 62 n.
Simon, abbot of St Albans 3
Simon of Hinton OP 119-20
Simon of Tournai, theologian 111
Solinus 50, 74
Sophistici Elenchi (Aristotle) 5
Spain 67
Spicilegium Solesmense (Pitra) 57
Statius 48
Stephen Langton, archbishop of Canterbury 96 n., 98, 102, 113 n., 116, 153
stars, AN's enumeration of 78
Stephen of Salley O.Cist. 107 n.
Stoneleigh O.Cist. (Warwicks.) 11
Summa super Priscianum (Petrus Helias) 37, 40
Super Isagogen Iohannitii (Maurus of Salerno) 72 n.
synderesis, doctrine of 115-16

Tabula septem custodiarum 122
Talmud 89, 90 n., 109-10
Tegni (Galen) 72
Terence 49
Thebaid (Statius) 48
Theodolus 35, 41
Thierry of Chartres 5, 6 n.
Third Crusade 26-7
Thomas de Bredone, abbot of St Peter's, Gloucester 24, 54, 141, 146
Thomas Docking OFM 121
Thurot, C. 40
Tobias (Matthew of Vendôme) 61
Topographia hibernica (Giraldus Cambrensis) 73
Trinity, doctrine of 111
Tristia (Ovid) 48

Trivet, Nicholas OP 1
Troades (Seneca) 49 n.

Urso of Salerno, medical writer 71, 74

Valerius Maximus 50
Variae (Cassiodorus) 74
Vienne 51
Vierundzwanzig Alten (Otto von Passau) 124
Vincent of Beauvais OP 44
Vir bonus (attrib. Virgil) 50
Virgil 41, 46, 49, 51-2, 53
Vitae patrum 89, 90 n.
Vitalis of Blois 58-9
Vocabularium (William Brito) 26

Walsingham, Thomas, monk of St Albans 18
Walter, abbot of Tavistock (Devon) 15
Walter, AN's clerk 13
Walter the cellarer, succeeded AN as abbot of Cirencester 15
Walter Melidie, canon of Cirencester 12
Whethamstede, John, abbot of St Albans 120
Willelmus Mercator 2
Willelmus de Montibus 27, 84, 101
William Brito 26, 119
William d'Eyncourt OP 121
William of Conches 45, 73
William of Malmesbury 51
William of Nottingham OFM 117
William of Ware OFM 117
William Rufus, King of England 104
Wiltshire 2
Windsor (Berks.) 1
Worcester 14
Wright T. 65, 77, 138

Zazenhausen, Johannes von OFM 124
Zodiac 80